GUIDE TO COMMERCIAL REAL ESTATE LOAN DOCUMENTATION

Guide to Commercial Real Estate Loan Documentation

Donald E. Rapp, Jr.

PRENTICE HALL
Englewood Cliffs, New Jersey 07632

Prentice-Hall International (UK) Limited, *London*
Prentice-Hall of Australia Pty. Limited, *Sydney*
Prentice-Hall Canada, Inc., *Toronto*
Prentice-Hall Hispanoamericana, S.A., *Mexico*
Prentice-Hall of India Private Limited, *New Delhi*
Prentice-Hall of Japan, Inc., *Tokyo*
Simon & Schuster Asia Pte, Ltd., *Singapore*
Editora Prentice-Hall do Brasil, Ltda., *Rio de Janeiro*

10 9 8 7 6 5 4 3 2 1

Library of Congress Cataloging-in-Publication Data

Rapp, Donald E.
    Guide to commercial real estate loan documentation / Donald
E.Rapp, Jr.
    p. cm.
    ISBN 0-13-370842-X
    1. Mortgage loans--United States.   2. Commercial loans--United
States.   3. Commercial loans--Law and legislation--United States--
Forms. I. Title.
    HG2040.5.U5R37   1990
    332.7'2'068--dc20
                                                       90-32742
                                                      CIP

ISBN 0-13-370842-X

PRENTICE HALL
BUSINESS & PROFESSIONAL DIVISION
A division of Simon & Schuster
Englewood Cliffs, New Jersey 07632

Printed in the United States of America

DEDICATION

This book is dedicated to a person who inspired the author in me, who never failed to offer encouragement and support, who withstood the creative turmoil, and who gave unselfishly of her time and energy to keep our world together while I chased my dream. To my wife, Sharon, forever and beyond.

ABOUT THE AUTHOR

Donald Rapp is well-qualified to write on the subject of commercial real estate documentation. He has spent 20 years in the lending business, 15 of those years involved with lending on commercial properties. Mr. Rapp headed the Southern California commercial mortgage office for one of the state's major banks, where he oversaw the documentation of loans on all manner of income-producing real estate. His experience includes working with a major nationwide commercial real estate builder. There he was intimately involved in construction documentation. At present Mr. Rapp is Senior Vice-President and Senior Commercial Real Estate Lender for a Beverly Hills, California bank. He is involved with commercial real estate loan documentation on a daily basis.

Mr. Rapp holds a Bachelor of Arts degree in Economics from the University of California, Santa Barbara, and a Masters, Business Administration degree in real estate finance from the University of Southern California. He is the co-author of two articles on the relationship between interest rates and budget deficits, published by A.B. Laffer & Associates and the Federal Reserve Bank of Atlanta.

In addition to lending and writing, Mr. Rapp currently teaches real estate appraisal at the Extension Program of the University of California, Los Angeles.

What This Book
Will Do for You

Documenting real estate loans is an art separate from generating loan requests. During the lending process you justify loan approval and satisfy bank auditors that all necessary documentation about the loan decision exists. Then you document the indebtedness and the security for the loan.

Excellence in new business production is important to real estate lenders. It is the first step towards high quality portfolios. Equally important is the use of documentation to translate the intent of commitments into the reality of secure earning assets. Documentation is the tool that reflects the intent of the lender when the loan was granted. Proper use of this tool helps avoid the creation of loans different from those intended.

This book clears away mists shrouding the documentation process. With this guide you have available documentation covering every part of commercial real estate lending, from initial request to loan closing. We will discuss specific forms to use, and will tell why a form is used, how to use it, and when its use may be safely avoided.

Use this book to sharpen existing skills, or look for documentation needed to solve difficult problems. It will be invaluable as a training guide for junior loan officers or documentation specialists. Use it to teach the basics of sound documentation, saving senior people hours of instruction time.

Aspects of documentation covered include:

• Documenting loan applications. How are applications taken? How is additional information requested? Should you take application fees, and how?

• Documenting loan analysis. What documentation justifies loan requests, both to internal loan committees and to auditors who review lending decisions? How can you demonstrate why the loan was made, while minimizing questions?

• Documenting construction loans. What documentation insures consideration of all aspects of this important lending?

• Documenting loan approval. How should lending terms be conveyed to borrowers? How do you commit them to your deal?

• Documenting indebtedness, security interests, property rights, property ownership, and borrowing entities. Proper documentation saves time and money later, especially if problems arise with a loan.

• Documenting loan servicing, including defaults and foreclosures. What documentation helps if delinquencies occur?

• Controlling the construction process. Construction loans are unique, requiring special controls. What documentation insures a smooth construction process, delivering the building on time and meeting the permanent lender's conditions? How do you exercise control without interference?

This book shows the path through the pitfalls and dangers, and leads you through to a secure, quality loan portfolio. Documentation is the tool that reflects the intent when the loan was granted. Proper use of this tool helps avoid the creation of loans different from those intended.

This book contains a comprehensive collection of documents, covering all aspects of commercial real estate lending. Pick and choose ones appropriate to the loan you are funding. There are checklists for each part of the lending process. Use these to insure that all bases are covered.

Care exercised in documenting real estate loans saves time later. This book was written to save you time and money, and through its use to lead to high quality loans.

A Note
from the Author

At first glance a book of this size about commercial real estate loan documentation would seem to indicate that such lending is fairly complex. Commercial real estate lending can be complex, as well as difficult. This is especially true when working with an area such as construction lending, where documentation is more intensive. But commercial lending is also rewarding, both in higher yields and service to customers.

You can make use of the forms and checklists this book provides to help guide you through the commercial real estate lending process. Seek legal help whenever uncertainties exist. Laws vary from state to state, and the documents in this book can easily be tailored to reflect the laws in your state.

Commercial real estate lending is a tool that you should have available to be competitive in your marketplace.

Donald E. Rapp, Jr.

Numerical
Listing of Exhibits

Alphabetical
Listing of Exhibits

Table of Contents

1

How to Document the Loan Application Process

Real estate lending begins with the application process. The usual starting point is a phone call or letter inquiry questioning the lender's willingness to consider a loan against the property type in question. Sometimes, however, that starting point is bypassed and a formal application and loan package are submitted. Regardless of the approach a response by the lender is required. If that response is a decline, the process ends. But if there is interest on the part of the lender in the loan requested, the process will begin.

Expressions of Preliminary Interest

An expression of interest from the lender means that he has conducted a preliminary review of the material submitted and, based on that review, he's interested in further pursuing the deal. This interest is preliminary in nature. A thorough analysis is still needed, as well as verification of statements made and data provided by the borrower. Usually it is based on the borrower's presentation taken as fact.

Use a letter such as the one in Exhibit 1-1 to express preliminary interest. This letter states that a loan on certain terms can be considered subject to complete underwriting by the lender. Care must be exercised in issuing such a letter. Borrowers sometimes attempt to construe any expression of interest as a firm commitment. The lender must be clear that no commitment is being issued, only a statement of the lender's willingness to take the next step on a road that might eventually lead to a formal commitment.

Complete the letter as follows:

1. Fill in a reference that identifies the property under consideration, a street address or a lot and tract number.

2. The name of your bank.

3. The dollar amount of the loan being requested or the amount which you are willing to lend, if less than the borrower's figure.

4. The interest rate you are proposing. Alternatively, committing to a specific rate may not be desirable. A better statement may be "To be determined based on the lender's rates in effect 30 days prior to loan funding."

5. The loan term in years.

6. The total loan fee required for such a loan.

7. The dollar amount of fee required to be submitted with the application. Usually this is an amount sufficient to cover costs if for some reason the loan does not materialize, but not so high as to discourage applications.

Loan Application Form

The loan application form asks that the borrower provide certain basic information about the loan request and the use to which loan proceeds will be put. This is a key element in the application process. An application should be taken early on, before extensive work has been performed. Exhibit 1-2 is an application form to use with commercial real estate loan requests. It should be completed as follows:

1. Applicant. The name of the borrower exactly as it appears on the title to the property.

2. Co-Applicant. Other parties applying for the loan, if any.

3. Name of Principals. Name the key parties if the borrower is an entity other than an individual. Indicate the nature of the borrowing entity; e.g., partnership, corporation, trust.

4. Address of Security Property. The address of the property that will be the security for the loan requested.

5. City. The city in which the property in question is located.

6. County. The county in which the property in question is located.

7. State. The state in which the property in question is located.

8. Present Address of Applicant. The street address at which the applicant does business, or to which notices are to be sent. Also include city, state, zip code, and phone number.

9. Amount. The loan amount requested.

10. Rate. The interest rate requested.

11. Fee. The fee the borrower is willing to pay for the loan requested.

12. Term. The term requested.

13. Sq.Ft.Bldg. The square footage of the building to be financed.

14. Year Built. The year in which the building was built.

15. Sq.Ft.Land. The square footage of the land area on which the building sits.

16. No. Stories. The height in stories of the building.

17. Zoning. The zoning of the land.

18. No. Units/Suites. If the property is broken down by units or suites, identify the number.

EXHIBIT 1-1

PRELIMINARY EXPRESSION OF INTEREST LETTER

April 23, 19—

Mr. Frederick James
1433 South Grand Avenue
Los Angeles, California

Re: (1)

Dear Sir:

_____ (2)_____ Bank is willing in concept to provide permanent mortgage financing for the above-referenced project. This letter is not a commitment to lend and should not in any way be construed as binding on _____ (2)_____ Bank. It is merely an expression of interest based on representations made by the borrower and is subject to satisfactory appraisal, complete underwriting, and appropriate approvals within the bank. In concept we are prepared to consider a loan on the following parameters:

    Amount: $_____ (3)_____ , subject to a maximum advance of 75% of appraised value as defined by an appraisal acceptable to the bank.

    Rate: _____(4)_____ %

    Term: _____(5)_____ years.

    Fee: _____(6)_____ %, plus all costs.

Should these terms be acceptable, we will ask you to complete the enclosed Loan Application Form and return it along with your check for $_____(7)_____ as an application fee. The fee will be applied to appraisal and other underwriting costs and any unused portion will be refunded to you or credited against loan fees. Naturally costs may eventually exceed this figure. Appraisal work will begin upon receipt of the application and fee.

The terms outlined in this letter will be held for 30 days. If the application and fee have not been received within that time, the bank reserves the right to change any and/or all of them.

Sincerely,

Theodore Jones
Vice-President

19. Parking Spaces. The number of on-site parking spaces available.

20. Amenities. Identify any amenities the property has. For example, if an apartment, amenities might be pool, rec room, and elevator.

21. Additional Data. Check the additional items that are being submitted with the application.

EXHIBIT 1-2

APPLICATION FOR REAL ESTATE LOAN

Application Number _____

Office _____

Date _____

. BORROWER

ANY MARRIED APPLICANT MAY APPLY FOR SEPARATE ACCOUNT

Applicant (Please print or type name(s) as they will be used in vesting) (1)	Co-Applicant (Give relationship - or describe entity) (2)			

Name of Principals if (3) ☐ Partnership ☐ Corporation ☐ Trust ☐ Other entity please specify _____ (see financials)

Address of security Property (4)	City (5)	County (6)	State (7)	Zip Code
Present address of applicant (for Notices) (8)	City	State	Zip Code	Telephone No.

II. PROJECT

I/WE HEREBY APPLY FOR A LOAN IN THIS AMOUNT OF $ ____(9)____ AT (10) % INTEREST, FOR A FEE OF ____(11)____ POINTS FOR A TERM OF (12) YEARS IN ACCORDANCE WITH THE FOLLOWING CONDITIONS:

ACCEPTANCE OF APPLICATION

1. Acceptance of this application does not bind _____ BANK (hereinafter referred to as the Bank) to make any loan or to approve the assumption of any existing Bank loan. (In the following, the singular shall include the plural.)

ACCEPTANCE OF LOAN

2. If I accept a loan which you may offer, or receive your approval to assume an existing Bank loan, I agree to execute such documents, pay such fees and provide and pay for such Title and Hazard Insurance and other items which you may require.

NON RELIANCE

3. If this loan is requested for the purpose of buying the above described property, I hereby acknowledge that the Bank has made no representation to me as to condition of said property and that I have relied, and will rely, upon my own opinion of the value and condition of said property.

EXISTING LIENS

4. I understand that if this loan is requested for the purpose of refinancing an existing loan, the Bank will require payment in full, through escrow, of all existing bonds, assessments and property taxes that are due and payable.

PROPERTY DESCRIPTION

____(13)____ SQ. FT. BLDG. ____(14)____ YEAR BUILT ____(15)____ SQ. FT . LAND ____(16)____ NO. STORIES

____(17)____ ZONING ____(18)____ NO. UNITS/SUITES ____(19)____ PARKING SPACES _____

Please specify amenities _____ (20) _____

Additional Data to be submitted with application, if available (21)

☐ TITLE POLICY ☐ 3 YRS. ANNUM OPERATING STATEMENTS (19 _____ , 19 _____ , 19 _____)

☐ CURRENT RENT SCHEDULE ☐ GROUND LEASE

III. PURPOSE

PURPOSE OF LOAN (22) ☐ PURCHASE Complete Section A. ☐ REFINANCE Complete Section B. ☐ CONSTRUCTION Complete Section C.
(Please "X" appropriate box)

A . PURCHASE			LOAN AMOUNT REQUESTED	$ (23)
Second Loan (Give holder's name and address) (24)	Mo. payment $	Int. Rate %	Term (Yrs.)	$
Other consideration (Please describe) (25)				$
Source of cash being provided for down payment (26)		CASH PAID THROUGH ESCROW		$ (27)
Escrow company (28)	Escrow No. (29)	Telephone No. (30)	PURCHASE PRICE OF PROPERTY	$ (31)
Settlement date ____(32)____ per sales agreement (attach copy)				

B. REFINANCE					LOAN AMOUNT REQUESTED	$ (33)
Items to be paid off: FIRST LOAN HOLDER	Maturity or	Name (34)	Address	Account No.	Balance owed $	
SECOND LOAN HOLDER		(35)			$	
OTHERS		(36)			$	
					$	
Remaining Funds to be Used to		Please specify (37)			$	

C. CONSTRUCTION		LOAN AMOUNT REQUESTED	$ (38)
Contractor's name (39)	Address	CONSTRUCTION TO COST	$ (40)
For ☐ OWNER OCCUPANCY (41) ☐ SPECULATION	Is Land Owned Free and Clear? ☐ YES ☐ NO (42)	If no. What is owed on land? $ (43)	LAND COST $ (44)
		TOTAL COST	$ (45)

EXHIBIT 1-2 (cont'd.)

☐ Owner/Builder (46)   ☐ General Contactor _____   (Total Amount of Contracts) _____ (47)

Estimated Construction Period _____ (48) _____ Mos.   Construction Start Date _____ (49) (please specify) 19_____

STATUS OF DETAILED PLANS   (50)

☐ Scheduled For Completion _____ (please specify)
☐ Completed And Submitted For Plan Check _____ (please specify)
☐ Approved For Plan Check

STATUS OF PERMANENT FINANCING   (51)

☐ Application Submitted _____ (please specify)
☐ Commitment Approved (Please Attach)
☐ Amount Requested _____

ADDITIONAL DATA TO BE SUBMITTED WITH APPLICATION, IF AVAILABLE   (52)

☐ Detailed Cost Breakdown
☐ General Construction Contract
☐ Contractor/Supervisor Resume
☐ Project Budget

☐ Pro Forma Oper. Status
☐ Projected Sales Schedule
☐ Permanent Loan Committee
☐ Detailed Plans

IV. PRINCIPAL OWNERS OF BORROWING ENTITY:

(53)

If a corporation, list all stockholders owning 10% or more of the outstanding shares. If a partnership, list all general partners; if a trust or unincorporated association, list all holders of 10% or greater beneficial interest.

1. Name: _____
   Address: _____
   Percent Ownership _____
   Position/Title _____

   Tax I.D. or Social Security No. _____ Age: _____
   Active in Mgt? _____
   How Long With Borrowing Entity? _____

2. Name: _____
   Address: _____
   _____
   Percent Ownership _____
   Position/Title _____

   Tax I.D. or Social Security No. _____ Age: _____
   Active in Mgt? _____
   How Long With Borrowing Entity? _____

3. Name: _____
   Address: _____
   _____
   Percent Ownership _____
   Position/Title _____

   Tax I.D. or Social Security No. _____ Age: _____
   Active in Mgt? _____
   How Long With Borrowing Entity? _____

4. Name: _____
   Address: _____
   _____
   Percent Ownership _____
   Position/Title _____

   Tax I.D. or Social Security No. _____ Age: _____
   Active in Mgt? _____
   How Long With Borrowing Entity _____

LOAN GUARANTORS: (54)

1. Name: _____ Soc. Sec. No. _____
   Address: _____
   Position or Employment _____

2. Name: _____ Soc. Sec. No. _____
   Address: _____
   Position or Employment _____

KEY MANAGEMENT PERSONNEL OF BORROWING ENTITY: (Omit, if Listed Above).   (55)

Name	Age	Position/Title	How Long With Firm
1. _____	_____	_____	_____
2. _____	_____	_____	_____
3. _____	_____	_____	_____

PLEASE SUBMIT   FINANCIAL STATEMENT FORM ATTACHED FOR ALL BORROWERS AND GUARANTORS.

_____

_____ (56)

_____

_____

_____

_____

EXHIBIT 1-2 (cont'd.)

V. CERTIFICATIONS BY APPLICANTS

Statement of loans held by

I/We hereby certify that the total of all loans made by this Bank to Applicant(s) and to all other persons and entities as defined below are:

1. This Loan _____ *(Estimated amount applied for)* $ _____(57)_____

2. Other Loans applied for or made: *(If none, state "None")*

NAME OF APPLICANT OR ENTITY	LOAN NO.	AMOUNT
(58)		

NOTE: If more loans are held than space is provided for, please describe each additional loan on a separate schedule.

I/We understand that "persons and entities" are defined to include:

1. Any person or entity that is, or that upon the making of a loan will become, obligor on a loan on the security of real estate;

2. Nominees of such obligor;

3. All persons, trusts, partnerships, syndicates and corporations of which such obligor is a nominee or a beneficiary, partner, member of record or beneficial stockholder owning 10 percent or more of capital stock, or a nominee for any of these persons.

4. If such obligor is a trust, partnership, syndicate, or corporation, all trust, partnerships, syndicates, and corporations of which any beneficiary, partner, member of record or beneficial stockholder owning 10 percent or more of the capital stock of such obligor; and

5. Members of the immediate family of any applicant.

I/WE CERTIFY: *(Please "X" appropriate box)*   **(59)**

A. FOR INDIVIDUAL APPLICANT(S)
That I/we am/are the Applicant(s); and

FOR CORPORATIONS, PARTNERSHIPS, ETC.

We, _____ and _____
                    NAME   Name

are _____ and _____
                    Title   Title

respectively of _____ , the applicant for the loan
                    Name of applicant (corporation, partnership, etc.)

or loans herein applied for; and

B. that all statements, including but not limited to Certifications and the Financial Statement, contained in the Application and upon all attachments hereto are true; and

C. that my/our tax returns, financial statements or other financial attachments furnished by me/us to the Bank are true and complete statements of the financial condition of the undersigned applicant(s) as of the date they bear; and

D. that the statements made herein are for the purpose of inducing the Bank to grant or permit assumption of a loan and may be relied upon by the Bank for that purpose; and

E. that the Bank is authorized to communicate with any employer, former employer, bank or other credit reference listed herein or any attachment hereto for verification.

I/WE DECLARE UNDER PENALTY OF PERJURY THAT THE FOREGOING IS TRUE AND CORRECT

If this loan is not consummated for any reason, after approval of this application, I/we agree to pay all expenses, charges, and fees incurred by the Bank in connection therewith in addition to a non-refundable application fee of $ **(60)** submitted herewith.

Executed on _____(61)_____ At _____(62)_____ ,

_____(63)_____   _____
Applicant's Signature   Applicant's Signature

_____   _____
Applicant's Signature   Applicant's Signature

22. Purpose of Loan. Check the appropriate purpose for the loan.

If the property is being purchased:

23. Loan Amount Requested. Fill in the amount of the loan being requested.

24. Second Loan. Fill in the details of any other financing applicable to the purchase transaction.

25. Other Consideration. Detail any other items of value that are a part of the purchase transaction, other than cash.

26. Source of Cash. Show from what source the cash used for down payment will come.

27. Cash Paid Through Escrow. Show the dollar amount of cash currently in escrow or to be paid through escrow later.

28. Escrow Company. The name of the company handling the escrow.

29. Escrow Number. The number assigned to the escrow.

30. Telephone Number. The phone number of the escrow company.

31. Purchase Price of Property. The total purchase price of the property.

32. Settlement Date. The date on which escrow will close and all funds be transferred.

If the property is to be refinanced:

33. Loan Amount Requested. The amount of the loan being requested.

34. First Loan Holder. The lender who has the current 1st Trust Deed on the property, his address, the maturity date, and the amount currently owing.

35. Second Loan Holder. If applicable, the lender who has the current 2nd Trust Deed on the property, his address, the maturity date, and the amount currently owing.

36. Others. Any other lenders who have liens against the property.

37. Remaining Funds to Be Used. Detail the use of funds left over after indebtedness is handled.

If the property is to be built:

38. Loan Amount Requested. The amount of the loan being sought.

39. Contractor's Name, Address. The name and address of the general contractor who will be responsible for construction.

40. Construction to Cost. The total cost of construction.

41. For. Check the box to indicate whether the property is being built to be owner-occupied; that is, occupied by the borrower, or being built for speculation to be occupied by others.

42. Check the box to indicate whether or not the land is owned free and clear.

43. Fill in any amount owing on the land.

44. Land Cost. Total cost to acquire the land.

45. Total Cost. Total cost to build.

46. Check the box to indicate whether the owner/borrower is also the builder or whether there is a general contractor involved. If a general contractor is involved, fill in the name.

47. Total Amount of Contracts. The dollar amount of the contract or contracts to build.

48. Estimated Construction Period. The time in months from start to finish of the project.

49. Construction Start Date. The date when construction is anticipated to begin.

50. Status of Detailed Plans. Check the appropriate box to indicate current status.

51. Status of Permanent Financing. Check the appropriate box to indicate status.

52. Additional Data to be Submitted with Application. Check the box if any additional items are being submitted with the application.

53. Principal Owners of Borrowing Entity. For corporate borrowers, fill in name, address, and other information, including:

     a. Percent Ownership. The percent of the company owned by the individual in question.

     b. Position/Title. The position and/or title held by the individual in question.

     c. Tax I.D. or Social Security Number. Appropriate identification number, usually a social security number.

     d. Age. The age of the individual in question.

     e. Active in Mgt. Is the individual active in the managment of the company, yes or no.

     f. How Long with Borrowing Entity. The length of time the individual has spent working for the borrowing entity.

54. Loan Guarantors. For each individual who will guarantee the loan, fill in the name, address, social security number, and position with the firm (or outside employment, if applicable).

55. Key Management Personnel of Borrowing Entity. For any key individuals not already identified, list name, age, position/title with the firm, and how long they have been employed by the firm.

56. Use this space to name any borrowers or guarantors who should submit a bank financial statement form with the application.

57. Estimated Amount Applied For. Fill in the amount of the current loan request.

58. Other Loans Applied for or Made. For each additional loan within your institution, list the name of the borrowing entity, the loan number (if already granted), and the amount of the loan.

59. Certification. For corporate borrowers, whether corporations or partnerships, the certification should spell out the principals attesting to the information included in the application. For partnerships, these should be the main partners, or enough partners to constitute the required percentage (as spelled out in the partnership documents). For corporations, these should be the officers authorized to commit the company.

60. Application Fee. The fee to be submitted along with the application.

61. The date the application was signed.

62. The city in which the application was signed.

63. The signature of the applicant, or applicants, or parties authorized to sign on behalf of the applicant.

Take the application when you are getting serious about your interest in the loan. Be careful, however, about the implication taking it can give, that the loan in its basic parameters is acceptable to you. If any terms or conditions set forth in the application are unacceptable to you or are not consistent with your current policies and guidelines, tell the prospective borrower right away. Problems can arise later if terms requested, which are clearly spelled out in the application, turn out to have been unacceptable to you, the lender, all along.

EXHIBIT 1-3

LETTER REQUESTING ADDITIONAL INFORMATION

March 1, 19—

Mr. Albert Ansen
President
Ansen Development Company
14556 West Oak Lane
Parker, Illinois

Re: _____ (1) _____

Dear Sir:

As we discussed we would be pleased to consider your formal application for a construction loan on the above-referenced property. A loan of $ ____ (2) ____ should be possible, subject, of course, to our complete underwriting and appraisal. The following items will be needed for us to pursue this request further:

1. Loan Application (form enclosed).
2. Plans.
3. Letter of Intent from _____ (3) _____ .
4. Copy of lease from _____ (4) _____ .
5. Your current financial statement on our form with attached supplemental real estate schedule (forms enclosed).
6. Appraisal report acceptable to our bank.

Please feel free to call us with any questions you may have. Thank you for considering a loan with First National Bank.

Sincerely,

John Johnson
Assistant Vice-President

Letters Requesting Additional Information

Exhibit 1-3 is a letter requesting the submission of additional items to further the analysis of the loan request. Such a letter should be used after a preliminary review of the initial loan package submitted by the borrower. Before additional information is requested, the lender should be satisfied on the basic parameters of the deal and be interested in moving forward with the request. The letter asks the borrower to submit other items needed in order to better understand the request, or to verify and analyze the facts presented or assumptions made.

The lender should be specific about the items needed. Borrowers generally do not like repeated requests for information. They would much prefer to get one request that is comprehensive in scope and covers everything the lender wants.

Include in your letter:

1. A reference to the property under consideration, either a street address, or some other identifying description.

2. The amount of the loan you are willing to consider. Alternatively you might want to say "A loan not to exceed 75% of our appraisal value."

3. If there are letters of intent regarding space in the building, you should request copies.

4. If there are signed leases, you should get copies.

List in this letter all other information that you consider important to the loan decision, or that should be a part of the loan file. This is the best time to go on record as to what items are needed in order to reach a final decision on the loan request.

Agreements Regarding the Refunding of Application Fees

While lenders are clear on the desirability of collecting fees for services, many are not clear on when, and whether, to return any unused portion to their customers. Processing the commercial real estate loan application can be costly, especially given the escalating fees for appraisals and the valuable time of loan officers involved. Collecting a fee with the application seems reasonable.

Most customers or prospective customers want to know what happens if a portion of that fee is not used to cover processing costs, and the loan is not granted. Do they get a portion back? Probably it depends on the relationship between the individual and the lender, or the image the lender is trying to create in the community.

Exhibit 1-4 shows an agreement to use when such a fee is to be taken. The form can be attached as an addendum to the loan application and should be completed as follows:

1. The percent of the loan to be taken as an origination or application fee.

2. The dollar amount to which this percentage equates.

3. The percent of the loan to be taken as a loan fee if the loan is closed. This amount is in addition to the fee submitted with the application.

4. The dollar amount to which this percentage equates.

5. Fill in the type of loan, construction or permanent.

6. The address of the applicant or applicants.

7. The signature of the applicant or applicants.

Request for Appraisal

The last step in the application process occurs when the lender orders the appraisal report. Usually this step isn't taken until all the necessary items are in hand, including the loan application and fee.

EXHIBIT 1-4

AGREEMENT REGARDING APPLICATION FEE

To be considered, the Application to which this form is attached must be submitted to the Bank with a Loan Origination Fee equal to ____ (1) ____% ($ ____ (2) ____) of the mortgage loan amount. Said fee is nonrefundable and is consideration for the substantial services which the Bank will render and the costs which it will incur in preparation of the issuance of the Bank's Commitment to make the mortgage loan. However, should the Commitment to make the mortgage loan not be issued, the Bank will refund said fee provided that the Bank shall first be entitled to deduct from such fee all of its actual costs incurred in considering this Application, which costs shall include but not be limited to appraisal fees and legal fees.

The undersigned further agrees to pay an additional loan fee equal to ____ (3) ____ % ($ _____ (4) _____) of the mortgage loan amount payable at the time the _____ (5) _____ loan is funded.

_____ (6) _____	_____ (6) _____
Address	Address
_____ (7) _____	_____ (7) _____
Signature	Signature

Exhibit 1-5 is a form to use when requesting an appraisal report. It can be used either with in-house or outside appraisers. The more information that is given to the appraiser, and the more complete the information, the more likely the job will be performed in a timely manner with the correct valuation being derived.

This form should be completed with the following:

1. Date. The date of the request for appraisal work.
2. Applicant's Name. The name of the entity requesting the loan.
3. Address. The applicant's address.
4. Telephone No. The applicant's phone number.
5. Location of Property. The street address of the property to be appraised. Include the legal description if possible to make identification more certain.
6. Purchase Price. If a sale is involved, the price the applicant is paying to purchase the property.
7. Owner's Valuation. The value estimate used by the applicant. What does he think the property is worth?
8. Lot Size. The square foot size of the land.
9. Improvements. Check the box to indicate whether the improvements are existing or to be built.
10. Amount of Loan Requested. The loan amount requested by the applicant.
11. Terms. The proposed loan term and amortization period. Also include the proposed interest rate for the loan.

EXHIBIT 1-5

REQUEST FOR INCOME PROPERTY LOAN APPRAISAL

	DATE
	-(1)

APPLICANT'S NAME	ADDRESS	TELEPHONE NO.
(2)	(3)	(4)

LOCATION OF PROPERTY—INCLUDE LEGAL DESCRIPTION, IF POSSIBLE

(5)

PURCHASE PRICE	OWNER'S VALUATION	LOT SIZE	IMPROVEMENTS
$ (6)	$ (7)	(8)	☐ EXISTING ☐ PROPOSED (9)

AMOUNT OF LOAN REQUESTED	TERMS	PURPOSE OF LOAN
$ (10)	(11) YEARS AT	(12)

OWNER OF RECORD	PROPERTY TAXES	ASSESSMENT BONDS
(13)	(14)	(15)

TYPE OF IMPROVEMENTS—DESCRIBE BRIEFLY

(16)

PRESENT LOAN BALANCE	ORIGINAL LOAN—AMOUNT & DATE MADE	HELD BY
(17)	(18)	(19)

ARRANGE INSPECTION THROUGH	TELEPHONE NO.
(20)	(21)

INCOME/LEASE INFORMATION

TENANT	SQ. FT.	MONTHLY RENT	TERM
	(22)		

REMARKS

(23)

ENCLOSURES AS APPLICABLE: (24)

☐ Copy of Leases
☐ Income & Expense Statements
☐ Current Preliminary Title Report
☐ Purchase Agreement
☐ Plans and Specifications
☐ Other

APPRAISAL REQUESTED BY—NAME AND TITLE	OFFICE NAME AND NUMBER
(25)	(26)

12. Purpose of Loan. This should be a brief statement of the purpose of the loan; for example, refinance or new construction.

13. Owner of Record. The name of the party who currently owns the property.

14. Property Taxes. The amount of taxes currently charged to the property.

15. Assessment Bonds. The amount of any assessment bonds that may be charged against the property.

16. Type of improvements. Briefly describe the nature of the improvements to be appraised; for example, a 10-story, 80,000-sq ft., steel-and-glass office building.

17. Present Loan Balance. The current loan balance for any financing against the property.

18. Original Loan—Amount and Date Made. The original loan amount and the date the loan was made.

19. Held By. The lender who made the loan.

20. Arrange Inspection Through. The party the appraiser should contact to gain access to the property.

21. Telephone No. The phone number of the party the appraiser should contact to gain access.

22. Income/Lease Information.

    a. Tenant. The name of all the tenants occupying or to be occupying space in the building.

    b. Sq Ft. The square footage of space occupied by each tenant.

    c. Monthly Rent. The rent paid by each tenant.

    d. Term. The term of the lease, or, if appropriate, the remaining term.

23. Remarks. Use this section to expand on the information included above, or to inform the appraiser of any facts that might affect the value determination.

24. Enclosures. Check boxes to indicate attachments provided for the appraiser's review.

25. Appraisal Requested By. Put in the name and title of the loan officer requesting the appraisal.

26. Office Name and Number. The name and number of the office within the lender's system making the appraisal request.

End Note

Exhibit 1-6 is a checklist to use to guide you through the loan application process. Fill in the checklist as follows:

1. Property Type. The type of property under consideration.

2. Acceptable. Is this an acceptable property type to you—yes or no? If no, stop the process right away and issue a declination.

3. Net Income from Property. Estimate the net income the property will generate, or use the actual figure if that is available. This is net income before debt service, and excluding depreciation.

4. Capitalization Rate Likely. Fill in the capitalization rate prevalent in the marketplace for the property type in question.

5. Estimated Value. Using the net income and the capitalization rate, estimate the value the appraiser is likely to derive.

EXHIBIT 1-6

CHECKLIST FOR LOAN APPLICATION PROCESS

Loan Qualification

    Property Type: _____ (1) _____ Acceptable ____ (2) ____

    Net Income from Property: _____ (3) _____

    Capitalization Rate Likely: _____ (4) _____

    Estimated Value: _____ (5) _____

    Loan Requested: _____ (6) _____

    Indicated Loan-to-Value: _____ (7) _____ %

    Debt Service on Loan: _____ (8) _____

    Indicated Debt Service Coverage: ____ (9) ____

Given Ratios, Is Loan Acceptable: _____ (10) _____

If No, Date of Declination: _____ (11) _____

Borrower's Response: _____

_____ (12) _____

_____

	Needed	Date Sent	Date Rec'd
If Yes:			
Preliminary Expression of Interest Letter	_____	_____ (13)	_____
Loan Application	_____	_____	_____
Additional Information Requested	_____	_____	_____
Application Fee Received/ Form Signed	_____	_____	_____
Appraisal Requested	_____	_____	_____

6. Loan Requested. Fill in the amount of loan being requested by the applicant.

7. Indicated Loan-to-Value. Given the loan amount requested and the estimated property value, estimate the loan-to-value ratio.

8. Debt Service on Loan. Given your loan terms for such loans, and the loan requested, estimate the debt service.

9. Indicated Debt Service Coverage. With the debt service and the net income from the property, you can estimate the debt service coverage ratio.

10. Is Loan Acceptable? Given the loan-to-value ratio and the debt service coverage ratio, is the loan acceptable to you? Does it fit within your current criteria for such loans?

11. Date of Declination. If the answer to the above question is no, then the loan should be declined immediately. Fill in the date the declination was conveyed to the borrower.

12. Borrower's Response. Fill in the response given by the borrower. This will leave a trail for the future in case the subject of the declination and the reasons for it

come up again. A senior officer reviewing the borrower's response may find reason to make an exception to policy and consider the loan anyway.

13. Use the columns in this section to indicate which items are needed, when they were requested or sent out by the lender, and when the response was received.

Use this time to do some initial qualifying of the loan requests. Weed out the ones that obviously do not conform to your current underwriting guidelines. A lot of time can be saved at this point if nonqualifying loans are not allowed to go any further than the point where it is obvious that they don't fit.

This time can also be used to save frustration on both sides by not getting into the process of requesting additional information if the loan clearly can't be granted. As the next chapters will show, a lot of additional information is needed to get from an initial review to a loan commitment. Most lenders see far too many requests to spend time on those that just don't work.

2

How to Document the Loan Analysis-Real Estate Information

For most lenders commerical real estate lending is a two-part process, analyzing real estate and analyzing the financial strength of the entities behind the loan. In this chapter and the next we will consider the documentation necessary to a proper analysis of the two parts of the lending puzzle.

There are many tools used in the analysis of real estate, but none more useful or important than the real estate appraisal. It is hard to imagine making a proper loan without some form of appraisal in hand. Even an in-house analysis that produces a "fast and dirty" approximation of value is none-the-less an appraisal of market value.

Using the Three Types of Appraisal Reports

Let's consider the types of appraisal report used by lenders and some of the documentation for which you should look. This is not a consideration of how to appraise—that's a subject for other books. Rather, it's a look at documentation that supports the lending decision.

Letter Appraisal

A letter appraisal is a brief estimate of value in letter form. It is nothing more than an educated guess as to value. The appraiser will have done no independent analysis, and may have done no more than drive by the property to get a feel for its outward appearance. The appraiser will then translate this into an approximation of value based on his knowledge of the marketplace in general and the nature of the property in question relative to other comparable real estate.

A letter appraisal should not be used to document a lending decision unless your

EXHIBIT 2-1

LETTER APPRAISAL

September 23, 19___

Mr. Joseph Smith
Vice-President
1st National Bank
123 Main Street
Madison, Wisconsin

Dear Sir,

At your request we conducted a drive-by inspection of the property located at _____ (1) _____ . Our assignment was limited to a cursory review of the exterior of the building, as well as the surrounding neighborhood.

Based on our review we can report that the exterior of the building is in good condition, with no observable deferred maintenance. The surrounding neighborhood is well-maintained and has good appeal. We noted no adverse conditions that could have a negative impact on value. Therefore, as of _____ (2) _____ it is our opinion that the market value of the subject property is _____ (3) _____.

Sincerely,

knowledge of the market is so comprehensive that you need an outside appraiser only to confirm the value decision you've already reached. Mostly such a report is useful for checking upon the status of properties after the loan has been granted. Then, a regular program of having a staff appraiser drive-by and give a brief letter report is a useful check to insure that the security for your loan is maintaining its value.

Exhibit 2-1 is a sample letter appraisal. The following blanks should be filled in with:

1. The address of the property appraised. Make sure this address matches that on the loan documents.

2. The date of valuation. This could be important if subsequent intervening events occur that have a major impact on a neighborhood, say the approval of a new interstate route or the ban of truck traffic on certain roads.

3. The value estimate. This can be a precise dollar amount. More often, for letter appraisals, this will be a range, say $400-500,000, or be expressed as "value is not less than $400,000." How the appraiser expresses this should be consistent with your needs as the lender.

Form Appraisals

As the name implies this type of appraisal makes use of a "fill in the blank" type of form. It is perfectly adequate for lending purposes as long as the information included is thorough enough to facilitate the lending decision. Therefore, the form used is not what's important, but the information included in the form.

The scope of this book does not include a detailed review of an appraisal form and what to put there. That is more properly found in many appraisal texts available. But we do want to comment on a summary page to use and a review certificate. The latter will be useful if an outside appraiser prepares the report, but in-house people review it for acceptability.

Exhibit 2-2 is a recommended summary page to use with form appraisals. It contains on one page the key facts that have a bearing on value and therefore on the loan decision. The blanks should be filled in with:

1. Applicant's Name. The name of your borrower or the borrowing entity.

2. Project Name. The name of the project being appraised; for example, Mapleton Apartments or Axelrod Industrial Park.

3. Property Type. What kind of property was appraised; for example, industrial, or warehouse, or apartment.

4. Street Address. The street address of the property appraised.

5. City, County, State. The rest of the property address.

6. Ownership Interest. How is title held? Fee? Leasehold Estate? What was the interest that was valued during the appraisal process?

7. HUD Flood Hazard Area. Is the property located in a flood hazard area, yes or no?

8. Map Grid. If your institution makes regular use of a map book, put the grid location of the subject property here. For example, Thomas Bros. Guide 42A6.

9. Land Area. The square footage of the land area appraised.

10. Land Value. The appraised value of the underlying land, exclusive of the improvements on the land.

11. Gross Building Area. The gross square footage of the building or buildings.

12. Net Building Area. The net square footage of the building; that is, net of areas generally considered not to produce rent. This is also called net rentable area, net leaseable area, and net usable area.

13. Remaining Economic Life. The time measured in years during which the building will have economic use, will be able to generate reasonable income.

14. Gross Income. The gross income from rent and other occupancy sources that will be generated from the building.

15. Net Income. This is income available to support debt—gross income less occupancy expenses.

16. Conditions of Value. This is where any limiting conditions should be presented; that is, conditions that impact or limit value. For example, if the appraiser assumed that a leaky roof would be repaired, or deteriorating parking lot paving fixed, and his value was based on these assumptions, then here is where he would set those conditions out.

EXHIBIT 2-2

1ST BANK AND TRUST APPRAISAL REPORT

SUMMARY:

Applicant's Name: _____ (1) _____

Project Name: _____ (2) _____

Property Type: _____ (3) _____

Street Address: _____ (4) _____

City, County, State: _____ (5) _____

Ownership Interest: _____ (6) _____

HUD Flood Hazard Area: _____ (7) _____ Map Grid:_____ (8) _____

Land Area: _____ (9) _____ Land Value: _____ (10) _____

Gross Building Area: _____ (11) _____ Net Building Area: _____ (12) _____

Remaining Economic Life: _____ (13) _____

Gross Income: _____ (14) _____

Net Income: _____ (15) _____

Conditions of Value:

The appraised value is based on the statements and conditions listed in FHLMC Form 439, Rev. 10/78 and the conditions listed below:

_____

_____

_____ (16) _____

_____

Value Conclusion:

As a result of our investigation and analysis, as outlined in the report on the following pages, the estimated market value of the subject property is:

Value: _____ (17) _____

Date of Value: _____ (18) _____

Appraiser: _____ (19) _____

Signature/Date: _____ (20) _____

Appraiser: _____ (19) _____

Signature/Date: _____ (20) _____

17. Value. The conclusion of market value; for example, $400,000.

18. Date of Value. The date as of which value is assumed to be the figure set forth.

19. Appraiser. The name of the person or persons who performed the appraisal and their designation, if any.

20. Signature/Date. The signature and date of signing by the people who did the report.

Exhibit 2-3 shows a review certificate usable by in-house staff when they review appraisals prepared by outside appraisers. This can be used in addition to or in place of the summary page. The blanks of this form are completed as follows:

1. Applicant. The name of your borrower or borrowing entity.

2. Property Location. The street address, city, county, and state for the property being appraised.

3. Property Type. The type of property being appraised; for example, industrial, apartments, warehouse.

4. Value Estimate. This is the estimate of value established by the outside appraiser.

5. Date of Value. The date of the outside appraiser's value estimate.

6. Special Limiting Conditions and Assumptions. Here your appraiser should outline those conditions that serve to limit the value estimate and the key assumptions that were made in arriving at the valuation. If any of these conditions or assumptions are altered, the value would change.

7. Source of Income. How does the property generate income? Through leases? Rental to tenants on a month-to-month basis? Operation of a business, such as a congregate care facility, or car wash, or gas station?

8. Income Available for Debt Service. This is an estimate by your review appraiser of the net income generated over a period of four or five years, the income that will be available to make loan payments. This will also reflect his estimate of the trend in the marketplace. Will rents be growing? Stable? Declining?

9. Absorption. How fast will the rental space available in the subject property be absorbed by the marketplace? Three months? Six months? One year? Whatever this crucial estimate, you will then know the negative cash flow the property will generate, given the loan you are making, and will be able to estimate the borrower's capacity to deal with that shortfall.

10. Reviewer's Comments. This is where your review appraiser should outline his thinking on the appraisal under review. He should comment on the quality of the report, its strengths and weaknesses, bring out any points to which the lenders should be particularly sensitive, and indicate any difference of opinion he has over the value conclusion.

11. Reviewed By. The name of your in-house appraiser making this review.

12. Signature/Date. The review appraiser should sign the review sheet and date it to reflect the date of his comments.

Narrative Appraisals

Narrative appraisals are usually the most comprehensive and detailed of appraisal reports. They are written out in narrative style, although they also include tables and exhibits that can look a lot like those found in form appraisal reports. They differ from a form report in that they provide insight into the appraiser's thought processes, why he weighted the report the way he did, why he chose one particular figure from another. Narrative reports are particularly useful for more complex pieces of real estate, where elaboration is needed to properly analyze the situation and where condensation on a form would cut out too much important intervening material. Narrative appraisals are also useful when lending out of your normal market area, in places where you are not familiar with the neighborhood.

Narrative reports have certain key elements for which the lender should look.

EXHIBIT 2-3

APPRAISAL SUMMARY AND REVIEW

Applicant: _____ (1) _____

Property Location: _____ (2) _____

Property Type: _____ (3) _____

_____

Value Estimate _____ (4) _____ Date of Value: _____ (5)_____

Special Limiting Conditions and Assumptions:

_____

_____

_____ (6) _____

_____

Source of Income:_____ (7) _____

	Year 1	Year 2	Year 3	Year 4
Income Available (8) For Debt Service:	_____	_____	_____	_____

Absorption: _____ (9) _____

_____

Reviewer's Comments:

_____

_____

_____ (10)_____

_____ Reviewer's Value:_____

Reviewed By: _____ (11) _____

Signature: _____ (12) _____ Date: _____

First is the summary page or narrative letter. Exhibit 2-4 shows a sample of one. The key elements to look for are:

1. The address of the property being appraised. Make sure it's the same as the property on which you're making your loan.

2. The type of value estimate being made. Is it fee interest? Leased fee? Leasehold estate? What is being valued?

3. The date of the value estimate.

4. The estimated value of the interest in question.

5. The name and designation, if any, of the appraiser or appraisers certifying as to the value estimate.

The next element that should be present is the certification. A sample is presented in Exhibit 2-5. It is important to know that the appraiser was independent in his judgment, that he has no vested interest in the amount of the value estimate, and that his work covered the steps necessary to a proper determination of fair market value.

EXHIBIT 2-4

NARRATIVE LETTER

March 30, 19___

Manhattan Bank
1436 Wall Street
New York, New York

Gentlemen:

At your request, Robert C. Jones Appraisal Company is submitting its appraisal report for the property located at _____ (1) _____. The parcel is further identified as Lot 4, Block 64, Book 12 of Maps, Pages 2 and 3, recorded in the County of Orange, State of California.

It is the opinion of the undersigned that the estimated market value of the ___ (2) _____ interest of the subject property as of ___ (3) _____ is:

(4)

Twelve Million Dollars
($12,000,000)

We are pleased to have had this opportunity to be of service. Please feel free to contact us with any questions you may have.

Sincerely,
Robert C. Jones Appraisal Company
By: _____ (5) _____

Key parts of the certification include:

1. Statements of fact in the appraisal report are correct, or, if estimates, are identified as such.

2. Value estimated is impacted only by the limiting conditions and assumptions which are detailed in the report.

3. The appraiser has no interest in the property at present and is not contemplating any future involvement as an owner or investor.

4. The appraiser's compensation for the preparation of the report was not contingent on the value estimate.

5. The certification should also state that the appraiser inspected the property. If more than one person was involved in the preparation of the report, comment should be made as to which of the parties saw the property.

The next element, the limiting conditions, is one of the most important of any appraisal report, yet is frequently overlooked or ignored by lenders. With limiting conditions the appraiser is outlining what facts influenced the market value decision.

EXHIBIT 2-5

CERTIFICATION

I certify that, to the best of my knowledge and belief,
1. The statements of fact contained in this report are true and correct.
2. The reported analyses, opinions, and conclusions are limited only by the reported assumptions and limiting conditions, and are my personal, unbiased professional analyses, opinions, and conclusions.
3. I have no present or prospective interest in the property that is the subject of this report, and have no personal interest or bias with respect to the parties involved.
4. My compensation is not contingent on any action or event resulting from the analyses, opinion, or conclusions in, or the use of, this report.
5. The analyses, opinions, and conclusions were developed, and this report has been prepared in conformity with the requirements of the Code of Professional Ethics and the Standards of Professional Practice of the American Institute of Real Estate Appraisers.
6. The use of this report is subject to the requirements of the American Institute of Real Estate Appraisers relating to review by its duly authorized representatives.
7. I have made a personal inspection of the property that is the subject of this report.
8. I am currently certified under the voluntary continuing education program of the American Institute of Real Estate Appraisers.
9. No one other than the undersigned provided significant professional assistance in the preparation of this report.

By: _____

Date: _____

He is also commenting on assumptions he made. As a lender it's crucial that these match the ones you use in making your decisions on lending and loan amount.

Exhibit 2-6 shows a sample of the limiting conditions attached to a typical narrative appraisal report. Some are quite innocent—a definition of what market value is, assumptions as to the continued physical condition of the property, the condition of title that was assumed by the appraiser. Some conditions can be trickier, though. Note the comment about ". . . subsurface or hazardous waste conditions." Suppose a hazardous leak of some kind is found on site. Maybe the site used to be a gas station, with a fuel tank. The whole value determined by the appraiser could be drastically altered.

Most appraisers are good about outlining truly crucial conditions in the body of their report. But a failure to look at the limiting conditions could mean that the loan you are making is not as secure as you think it is.

The statement of purpose is the last element of a narrative appraisal report we will consider. As the name implies, it is a statement that says why the report is being

EXHIBIT 2-6

CONTINGENT AND LIMITING CONDITIONS

This report is subject to the following conditions and to such other limitations as may be set forth in this report by the appraiser:

1. That no opinion as to title is rendered. Data related to ownership and legal description was obtained from documents deemed reliable. Title is assumed to be marketable and free and clear of all liens and encumbrances, easements, and restrictions, except those specifically discussed in this report. The property is appraised assuming that it is under competent management.

2. All information has been checked where possible and is believed to be correct, but is not guaranteed as such.

3. Any plot plans, sketches, drawings, or other exhibits in this report are included only to assist the reader in visualizing the property. We have made no survey for this report and assume no responsibility for such an undertaking.

4. The appraiser assumes no liability for structural conditions not visible through ordinary, careful inspection or a review of the plans and specifications, if the property is proposed, nor is there any responsibility for subsurface or hazardous waste conditions. The appraiser is not qualified to detect such substances. An expert in this field should be retained if desired.

5. Except as noted this analysis assumes the land to be free of adverse soil conditions which would prohibit development of the property to its highest and best use.

6. Maps, plats, and exhibits included in the report are for illustration only, and as an aid in visualizing the matters discussed within the report. They should not be considered as surveys, nor relied upon for any other purpose, nor should they be removed from or used apart from this report.

7. The appraiser is not required to give testimony or appear in court in connection with this appraisal unless arrangements have been previously made.

8. Neither all nor any part of the contents of this report shall be disseminated to the public through advertising, public relations, news sales, or other media without the written consent and approval of the appraiser, particularly as to the valuation conclusions, the identity of the appraiser, or any reference to the American Institute of Real Estate Appraisers or the M.A.I. designation.

prepared. For example, "The purpose of the appraisal is to express an opinion of the fair market value of the subject property more fully described elsewhere in this report."

The statement might go on to define fair market value and to set forth the conditions that are implicit in a definition of what is "fair." The lender needs to know why the report was being prepared. A value is not objective, rather it is subjective. It is dependent to some extent on the use to which the report will be put. Value to a lender is different than value to a buyer or seller. Be sure to know what you're getting.

Beyond the appraisal report there are other tools that the lender uses to evaluate the real estate.

Certified Rent Roll

The rent roll can be used in two ways. First, for properties that do not have formal leases, it can be used to summarize rental arrangements. The property type that would most usually fall into this category is the apartment building. The second use would be as a summary of lease agreements, say for an office building. That way the borrower can certify on a page or two as to the accuracy of all of the leases delivered to the lender during the underwriting process. Exhibit 2-7 is a sample rent roll, certified, that is signed and dated, by the borrower. A rent roll should include certain basic elements to be useful to the lender. These are:

1. Name. The name of the occupant of the space. This could also be the trade name; for example, Smith's Family Deli. Also included here could be a functional description, like restaurant, or cleaners. This is especially helpful when the property is outside your normal geographic area of operations, and no one from your organization will visit the site.

2. Space. The space occupied by the tenant, or the unit number if the property is an apartment building.

3. Size. The square foot size of the unit occupied.

4. Rent. The rent paid and whether the figure is monthly or annual.

EXHIBIT 2-7

CERTIFIED RENT ROLL

Name (1)	Space (2)	Size (3)	Rent (4)	Term (5)	Comments (6)
Smith	101A	1,400 sf	$1,425/mo.	5 yrs	Triple net
Jones	102A	1,000 sf	$1,000/mo.	5 yrs	Triple net
Allen	103A	500 sf	$600/mo.	3 yrs	Triple net
Park	104A	1,200 sf	$1,500/mo.	10 yrs	Triple net, COL 5 yrs
Clark	105A	2,000 sf	$2,500/mo.	20 yrs	Triple net, COL every 5 yrs
Total Retail		6,100 sf	$7,025/mo.		
Cole	201A	1,000 sf	$2,000/mo.	5 yrs	Gross
Wilson	202A	1,000 sf	$2,000/mo.	5 yrs	Gross
Chou	203A	700 sf	$1,400/mo.	6 yrs	Gross
Vacant	204A	1,200 sf	$2,400/mo.		Gross
Carson	205A/ 206A	3,400 sf	$6,500/mo.	10 yrs	Gross
Total Office		7,300 sf	$14,300/mo. (7)		

I hereby certify this to be a true and correct rent roll as of April 1, 19__.

Signed _____

5. Term. The term of the rental arrangement; for example, monthly, or one year, or five years.

6. Comments. Any other facts about the rental arrangement that are important to note. In the exhibit these are the nature of the rent payments, whether gross or triple net. Another feature mentioned is the Cost of Living Adjustment included in several of the leases and the frequency of the adjustment. The rent roll should also comment on rent concessions made in order to attract the particular tenant to the property.

7. Certification. This statement and the borrower's signature attest to the accuracy of the information and give the lender some assurance, and documentation, as to the borrower's representations about the status of the property.

Note also that the rent roll identifies the vacant spaces and sets forth the rent that is lost as a result of the vacancy.

How to Use Letters of Intent

Exhibit 2-8 sets forth a sample letter of intent. Such a letter indicates interest on the part of a prospective tenant in taking occupancy in a particular project. They are especially useful when a loan is being made on new construction, a building that will not be ready for a substantial period of time. In such a case tenants are not likely to commit themselves to a lease until the point of occupancy is much closer. People are suspicious until they see building construction underway; and most prospective lessees have a hard time visualizing their space off a set of plans.

A letter of intent is not binding. It is merely an expression of interest. The lender should not place great reliance on such an instrument as a device for justifying the loan. But viewed as an indication of market interest in a given project, and in the intensity of such interest, it can be a useful tool in the evaluation of real estate.

Note that the letter identifies the building to be occupied and elaborates on the proposed lease terms. This letter is contingent on the owner being able to put the building in place and get it ready for occupancy by a certain time. Many other letters are far more vague. They may say no more than "assuming you build a building we're interested in talking to you about a lease."

How and When to Use Feasibility Studies

A feasibility study is a comprehensive analysis of a market situation in anticipation of developing a particular type of property in the area studied. One of the types of properties for which such a study should be performed is the hotel. In a feasibility study the market is dissected and inspected in its component parts to determine if the property proposed is really needed, and to assess the likelihood for a successful development.

Some of the aspects such a study would cover include:

1. Site analysis. An analysis of the proposed site—where is it and what is it? What are the characteristics of the surrounding area? How is the accessibility and visibility? Will the site support the structure planned?

EXHIBIT 2-8

LETTER OF INTENT

May 1, 19___

Mr. William J. Boston
123 Main Street
Wilmington, Delaware

Dear Sir,

This will confirm our recent discussions concerning your proposed office building to be built at 14 Front Street, Wilmington, Delaware. National Paint Company would be interested in relocating our headquarters to your building assuming suitable lease arrangements can be negotiated.

We propose to take approximately 4,000 square feet of space on the second floor of the building, at a rent not to exceed $5,000 per month. You agree to provide all service to the space, including janitorial and utilities. This expression of interest is contingent on and assumes completion of the building by June 1, 19___.

Sincerely,
Robert James
President
National Paint Company

2. Analysis of the market area. What are the characteristics of the market for the property type planned? This part of the study would assess economic factors prevalent in the market, especially those that might impact the property in question. Population demographics would be analyzed, especially the segment of the population that is viewed as the target market, or likely user, for the subject property.

3. Analysis of the supply of the property type under consideration. For example, if it's an hotel, how many competing projects are there in the market area? How many rooms? What type of vacancy is the market experiencing? How's the major competition doing? What are the room rates that are available? What new projects are on the drawing boards, and when will they likely be ready and on the market?

4. What is the demand for the kind of space the subject offers? Now that the supply is known, how strong has the demand been? Is there an abundance of similar projects available, so that everyone is experiencing economic troubles? Are people waiting in lines to get in? Naturally these questions must be dealt with in a quantitative way, by measuring traffic, flow of visitors, business users, vacancy factors and timing of vacancy, convention business potential, and tourist traffic.

5. Growth in demand. Has demand been growing, stable, or declining? What do the statistics show?

6. Projected income and expense for the subject property. Based on all the

EXHIBIT 2-9

CHECKLIST

Type of Appraisal Needed:
    Letter   _____
    Form   _____
    Narrative   _____

Date Appraisal Ordered: _____
Appraiser:
    Name   _____
    Address   _____
    Phone   _____

Date Appraisal Received _____
Fair Market Value _____

Other Exhibits:	Needed	Date Requested	Date Received
Certified Rent Roll	_____	_____	_____
Letters of Intent	_____	_____	_____
Feasibility Study	_____	_____	_____

economic factors and an analysis of competing projects, what is the operating experience of the subject property likely to be? What does the growth trend appear to be?

7. Conclusion. Will this be a successful project? Is this the right project at the right time? Is it feasible?

A feasibility study is more comprehensive than an appraisal report, although the two have similarities to some extent in the information considered and presented. A feasibility study is usually more detailed in its consideration of economic trends and factors, and demographic factors. Use such reports for more complex situations, or ones where market characteristics are crucial to the success of the real estate.

End Note

Exhibit 2-9 is a checklist to use to make sure that your real estate underwriting documentation is in order. We've considered documentation that applies to an evaluation of the real estate aspect of the loan decision. These tools help define the property and the value to be used in determining the amount of loan to make available.

Equally important is the financial side of the equation. That is the topic of the next chapter.

3

How to Document the Loan Analysis-Financial Information

In the prior chapter we discussed the information important to the analysis of real estate. Lenders use that data to define the property and its characteristics. In this chapter we will discuss the second part of the equation, the financial information. These documents define the capacity of the borrower or borrowers to service the debt, over and beyond any cash flow that may be generated from the property.

Most lenders are very familiar with the concept of financial statement analysis. In most cases such analyses are easier for them than dealing with aspects of real property when considering the commercial real estate loan. We won't attempt to cover how to analyze statements and what they mean, but will rather focus on the forms that can be used to gather and present the information necessary to an analysis.

Forms to Use for Financial Statement Analysis

Financial statements can be grouped in two categories, personal and corporate. Corporate statements can be prepared for partnerships or corporations. First let's consider the personal statement.

Personal Financial Statements

A personal financial statement primarily reports assets and liabilities. Schedules should be included for expansion of certain asset categories to provide more detail. Exhibit 3-1 is a personal financial statement form, a two-page summary that gives the lender a good idea as to the substance of the individual borrower. The form should be filled out as follows.

EXHIBIT 3-1
PERSONAL FINANCIAL STATEMENT

INSTRUCTIONS — MARRIED PERSONS:

If married you may apply for separate or joint credit.

SEPARATE CREDIT — Please provide information about your spouse if you are relying upon community property to repay the credit requested.
(Community property includes among other things, wages and salaries of both you and your spouse earned during marriage.)
Other Income — You do not have to list alimony, child support or separate maintenance unless you want such to be considered as a basis for repaying this obligation.

JOINT CREDIT If this financial statement is provided in connection with an application for joint credit, include information about your spouse and have your spouse sign this form.

If you are married and not separated, and unless you indicate otherwise, all stated income and assets will be presumed to be community property and all stated debts and obligations will be presumed to be liabilities of the community property.

TO YOUR BANK		DRIVERS LICENSE		
		SPOUSE'S DRIVERS LICENSE		
NAME IN FULL		SOCIAL SECURITY NO.	AGE	PHONE NUMBER
SPOUSE'S NAME (1)		SOCIAL SECURITY NO.	AGE	DEPENDENTS No. Ages
RESIDENCE ADDRESS (NO., STREET, CITY, STATE, ZIP CODE)		HOW LONG?	MARITAL STATUS ☐ married date married	☐ unmarried ☐ separated

PREVIOUS ADDRESSES IF AT ABOVE ADDRESS LESS THAN 5 YEARS (NO. AND STREET, CITY, STATE, ZIP CODE)

1.
2.

EMPLOYER	ADDRESS (NO. AND STREET)	CITY	PHONE & EXTENSION
SPOUSE'S EMPLOYER	ADDRESS (NO. AND STREET)	CITY	PHONE & EXTENSION

FINANCIAL CONDITION AS OF _____(2)_____ , 19 _____

ASSETS (3)	AMOUNT		LIABILITIES (3)	AMOUNT	
CASH: This Bank			NOTES PAYABLE TO BANKS		
Other (Name)			Other (Itemize, Schedule 4)		
STOCKS AND BONDS			OTHER NOTES AND ACCOUNTS PAYABLE		
Listed (Schedule 1)			Real Estate Loans (Schedule 2)		
Unlisted (Schedule 1)			Sales Contracts & Sec. Agreements (Schedule 4)		
REAL ESTATE			Loans on Life Insurance Policies (Schedule 4) ...		
Improved (Schedule 2)			TAXES PAYABLE		
Unimproved (Schedule 2)			Current Year's Income Taxes Unpaid		
Trust Deeds and Mortgages (Schedule 3).......			Prior Years' Income Taxes Unpaid		
LIFE INSURANCE			Real Estate Taxes Unpaid		
Cash Surrender Value			OTHER LIABILITIES		
ACCOUNTS AND NOTES RECEIVABLE			Unpaid Interest		
Relatives and Friends (Schedule 4)			Other (Itemize, Schedule 4)		
Collectible (Schedule 4)					
Doubtful (Schedule 4)			TOTAL LIABILITIES		
OTHER PERSONAL PROPERTY					
Automobile			NET WORTH		
Other (Itemize, Schedule 4)					
TOTAL			TOTAL		

ANNUAL INCOME (4)	(Refer to Federal Income Tax Returns for Previous Year)		ANNUAL EXPENDITURES (4)	(Refer to Federal Income Tax Returns for Previous Year)	
SALARY OR WAGES			PROPERTY TAXES AND ASSESSMENTS		
DIVIDENDS AND INTEREST			FEDERAL AND STATE INCOME TAXES		
RENTALS (GROSS)			REAL ESTATE LOAN PAYMENTS		
BUSINESS OR PROFESSIONAL INCOME (NET).			PAYMENTS ON CONTRACTS & OTHER NOTES		
OTHER INCOME (DESCRIBE)...........			INSURANCE PREMIUMS.............		
			ESTIMATED LIVING EXPENSES..........		
TOTAL INCOME			OTHER _____ TOTAL EXPENDITURES		

LIFE INSURANCE	FACE AMOUNT	BENEFICIARY (5)	COMPANY

1832 10:77

EXHIBIT 3-1 (Cont'd.)

Give details of any contingent liability as endorser or guarantor, or on suits or judgments pending. (If necessary, use separate sheet.) **(6)**

___

Do you do business with any other bank? ___ If so, give details ___

Have you ever gone through bankruptcy? ___ If you are married, are any of the assets described in this statement your wife's (husband's) separate property? ___

If so, state which ___

Have your Income Tax Returns ever been questioned by the Internal Revenue Service? ___ If so, most recent year ___

Have you made a will? ___ Who is the executor/executrix? ___ Are you a U.S. citizen? ___

Name of Attorney ___ Name of Accountant ___

SCHEDULE 1: LISTED AND UNLISTED STOCKS AND BONDS OWNED

Stocks (no. of shares) Bonds (par value)	Description	Issued in Name of	Joint Tenancy Ten. in Common Comm. Property	Market Value
LISTED:	**(7)**			
			TOTAL LISTED	
UNLISTED:				
			TOTAL UNLISTED	

SCHEDULE 2: REAL ESTATE OWNED   (DESIGNATE: I=IMPROVED, U=UNIMPROVED)

Location or Description	Title in Name of	Joint Tenancy Ten. in Common Comm. Property	Cost	Present Value	Trust Deeds, Mortgages or other Liens			
					Unpaid Bal.	Rate %	monthly paymnt.	Held By
	(8)							
	TOTAL				X X X	X X X X	X X X X X X X	

SCHEDULE 3: TRUST DEEDS AND MORTGAGES OWNED

Name of Payer	Legal Desc., Street Address, & Type of Improvements	Unpaid Bal.	Joint Tenancy Ten. in Common Comm. Property	Terms	1st or 2nd lien	Value of Property
	(9)					
	TOTAL			X X X	X X X X	

SCHEDULE 4: DETAILS RELATIVE TO OTHER IMPORTANT ASSETS AND LIABILITIES

(10)

___

This financial statement is furnished in connection with an application for credit and is to be regarded as continuous until another shall be substituted for it. If the undersigned, or any endorser or guarantor of the obligations of the undersigned, at any time becomes insolvent, or commits an act of bankruptcy, or dies, or if any writ of attachment, garnishment, execution or other legal process be issued against property of the undersigned, or if any assessment for taxes against the undersigned, other than on real property, is made by the Federal or State government, or any department thereof, or if any of the representations made above prove to be untrue, or if the undersigned fails to notify _____ Bank _____ of any material change in financial condition as given above, then and in either such case, all of the obligations of the undersigned to or held by _____, either as borrower or guarantor, shall immediately become due and payable, without demand or notice. In consideration of the granting or renewing of any credit to the undersigned hereafter, the undersigned hereby waives the pleading of the statute of limitations as a defense to any obligation of the undersigned to

I hereby certify that I have carefully read the above personal financial statement, including the reverse side, and it is a complete, true and correct financial statement to the best of my knowledge and belief.

(11)

Applicant's Signature	Date	Co-Applicant/Spouse's Signature Date

Spouse sign Above if this is to be a joint account.

Spouse sign Below to authorize verification of income or credit history ONLY.

Spouse's Signature	Date

1. Section 1 should be completed with basic historical information about the borrower, such as name, address, social security number, and employment information. Care should be exercised not to violate laws concerning the information that can properly be requested when contemplating an extension of credit.

2. Date of the financial data. This is important and is often excluded. A lender should know how current the information is. For commercial loan requests the statement should be no more than one year old, but preferably be within 90 days old.

3. Assets and liabilities should be itemized in the section provided. New categories can be added if applicable. The borrower should reflect good value estimates for all assets of consequence.

4. Summarize income and expenditures based on financial records or tax returns. At least two years of federal tax returns should be provided with the application. Such a requirement sometimes meets with resistance on the part of borrowers, many of whom seem to feel that tax returns should not be given to the lender. Given the dollar amount usually associated with commercial property loans, however, the importance of a thorough knowledge of the borrower cannot be overemphasized.

5. Section 5 calls for information concerning active life insurance policies. This information is rarely important to the commercial real estate loan decision.

6. Section 6 calls for information about past judgments, suits, and contingent liabilities. It also asks other, general questions important to the lender. Any answers that raise questions in the lender's mind should be investigated further.

7. Section 7 provides space for a listing of stocks, both those that are listed on exchanges, and therefore are marketable, and those that are unlisted and would be difficult to sell. Such information helps define a borrower's liquidity.

8. Section 8 provides a schedule for listing real estate owned. In addition to the information called for in the schedule, the borrower should provide details on income and expenses from any real estate owned. This helps substantiate other sources of cash flow as well as assets that might be a drain on financial resources and therefore imperil the property under consideration.

9. Section 9 calls for a listing of trust deeds and mortages owned. Such instruments are a source of cash flow to the borrower.

10. Section 10 provides space to give details on any assets and liabilities for which elaboration may be warranted.

11. The borrower should sign and date the financial statement, attesting to its accuracy and acknowledging that the lender will place reliance on it for lending purposes. Most lenders generally concede that a signature from the spouse is no longer required for credit extensions. Any spouse can pledge the community assets. One should obtain the signature of the non-borrowing spouse if their credit history is to be checked or their income verified.

Corporate Financial Statements

Corporate financial statements can be provided on a form or in an acceptable format prepared by the company's accountant. Exhibit 3-2 is a form which can be used. Like the personal statement, there is room for an itemization of assets and liabilities, shown on the form in Section 1. The categories are a little different, though, reflective of the kinds of assets and liabilities commonly held by a corporate entity.

EXHIBIT 3-2

NAME _____

TAXPAYER
IDENTIFICATION NO. _____

ADDRESS _____

BUSINESS _____ ACCOUNT AT _____ OFFICE OF BANK _____

STATEMENT AS OF _____ , 19 ____ .

This statement is furnished for the purpose of procuring credit, and is to be regarded as continuous until another shall be substituted for it. If the undersigned, or any endorser or guarantor of the obligations of the undersigned, at any time becomes insolvent, or commits an act of bankruptcy, or dies, or if any writ of attachment, garnishment, execution or other legal process be issued against property of the undersigned, or if any assessment for taxes against the undersigned, other than on real property, is made by the Federal or State government, or any department thereof, or if any of the representations made below prove to be untrue, or if the undersigned fails to notify   Bank   of any material change in financial condition as given below, then and in either such case, all of the obligations of the undersigned to or held by   either as borrower or guarantor, shall immediately become due and payable, without demand or notice. In consideration of the granting or renewing of any credit to the undersigned hereafter, the undersigned hereby waives the pleading of the statute of limitations as a defense to any obligation of the undersigned to

ASSETS (1)	AMOUNT		LIABILITIES (1)	AMOUNT	
CASH:			NOTES PAYABLE (Schedule E)		
. . . .			. . . .		
Other (Name)			Other (Banks)		
			For Merchandise		
TRADE ACCOUNTS RECEIVABLE:			To Others (Schedule E).		
Current . . . . $ _____					
Past Due, 90 days or more . $ _____			TRADE ACCOUNTS PAYABLE (Schedule F) . . .		
TOTAL ACCOUNTS . . $ _____			TRADE ACCEPTANCES PAYABLE		
Less Res. for bad debts . $ _____			OTHER ACCOUNTS PAYABLE		
TRADE ACCEPTANCES			ACCRUED ITEMS (Except Income Taxes-see below)		
TRADE NOTES RECEIVABLE			TAX LIABILITIES (Schedule H):		
			Income Taxes Accrued for Current Year		
MERCHANDISE (Schedule A)			Income Taxes for Prior Years		
Prepaid Expenses			Employees Income Tax Withholds		
			Fed. Ins. Contrib. Act. (Include Emp. Withholds) .		
TOTAL CURRENT ASSETS			State and Federal Unemployment Insurance		
			Other Taxes (Schedule H)		
Land & Bldgs. (Schedule B). . $ _____					
Depreciation . . . . $ _____			TOTAL CURRENT LIABILITIES		
Furniture and Fixtures . . . $ _____			SEC. AGREEMENTS — LEASE CONTRACTS . . .		
Machinery and Equipment . . $ _____			TRUST DEEDS OR LIENS ON REAL ESTATE . .		
Automobiles and Trucks . . $ _____			(Schedule B)		
TOTAL . . . . $ _____					
Depreciation . . . . $ _____			Due to Officers, Stockholders, Employees,		
Stocks, Bonds and Investments (Schedule C)			Affiliated Companies, or Relatives (Schedule G)		
Investment in Subsidiary or Allied Concerns					
Due from Subsidiary or Allied Concerns			OTHER LIABILITIES (Itemize)		
Due from Officers, Directors, Stockholders, . . .			Subordinated Debts		
Employees, or Relatives (Schedule D)			TOTAL LIABILITIES		
Goodwill, Trade Marks, etc.					
Other Assets (Itemize).			CAPITAL STOCK:		
_____			Preferred — Outstanding		
_____			Common — Outstanding		
_____					
_____			SURPLUS AND UNDIVIDED PROFITS:		
_____					
_____			NET WORTH (if unincorporated)		
TOTAL			TOTAL		

1831 10:77

EXHIBIT 3-2 (Cont'd.)

CONDENSED PROFIT AND LOSS STATEMENT FOR FISCAL YEAR OR _____ MONTHS ENDING _____ 19____

COSTS AND EXPENSES (2)			INCOME (2)		
Cost of Goods Sold.			SALES		
Actual Expense of Conducting Business, including			Less Returns and Allowances		
Rent, General Taxes, Insurance, etc.			Net Sales.		
Commissions, Advertising and Sales Expense			Discounts Earned on Purchases		
Salaries to Officers or Partners			Income from Investments		
Interest.			Other Income (Describe).		
Social Security Taxes.					
Bad Debts Charged Off.					
Depreciation Provision					
Other Expenses (Describe large items)			Gross Income		
			LESS: Costs and Expenses.		
			NET PROFIT — BEFORE INCOME TAXES		
			LESS: Federal and State Income Taxes		
Total Costs and Expenses			NET PROFIT — AFTER INCOME TAXES		

(3)   RECONCILEMENT OF SURPLUS (OR NET WORTH)

Surplus and Undivided Profits (or Net Worth) Close of Previous Fiscal Year . . . .19____ $_____

Less Charges Not Applicable to Current Year . . . .$_____ $_____

Add Net Profits as Above . . . . $_____ $_____

Less Dividends, Preferred _____ Per Cent . . . . $_____

Less Dividends, Common _____ Per Cent (if unincorporated - withdrawals by owner or partners) . . . . $_____

Other Charges to Surplus (Explain) _____ $_____ $_____

Surplus and Undivided Profits (or Net Worth) as at Date of this Statement . . . . $_____

DO YOU HAVE PENSION AND/OR PROFIT SHARING PLAN?   WHO IS THE TRUSTEE? _____

DETAILS — ASSETS

SCHEDULE A — MERCHANDISE (4)

Raw Materials	$_____	How Much of Merchandise Is Over One Year Old?	$_____
In Process	$_____	Are Figures Actual Inventory or Estimated? _____	
Finished	$_____	Amount Pledged Under W/R or Otherwise	$_____
TOTAL	$_____	Regular Date for Taking Inventory _____	
Held on Consignment	$_____	By Whom Taken?_____	
Commitments to Purchase Within 90 Days	$_____	Valued at Cost or Market _____	
Commitments to Purchase After 90 Days	$_____	Terms of Sale _____	

SCHEDULE B — LAND/BUILDINGS AND EQUIPMENT (5)

TITLE STANDS IN NAME OF _____

LEGAL DESCRIPTION, LOCATION AND CLASS OF IMPROVEMENT	COST OF LAND	VALUE OF IMPROVEMNTS. & LAND	TRUST DEEDS OR LIENS	HOLDER OF LIEN	REPAYMENT TERMS
TOTALS					

EXHIBIT 3-2 (Cont'd.)

SCHEDULE C — STOCKS, BONDS AND INVESTMENTS (6)

ISSUED TO OR STANDING IN NAME OF _____

Stocks (no. of shares) Bonds (par value)	DESCRIPTION	COST OR FACE VALUE			MARKET VALUE			AMT. PLEDGED		
	TOTAL									

SCHEDULE D — DUE FROM OFFICERS, DIRECTORS, STOCKHOLDERS, EMPLOYEES OR RELATIVES (7)

NAME	TITLE	PURPOSE	AMOUNT		TERMS

DETAILS — LIABILITIES

SCHEDULE E — NOTES PAYABLE (8)

Amount of your notes payable secured by collateral $ _____ To whom? _____ Collateral _____

SCHEDULE F — TRADE ACCOUNTS PAYABLE (9)

What are your usual terms of purchase? _____

Names and Addresses of Concerns from which you make your principal purchases:

1. _____
2. _____
3. _____

SCHEDULE G — DUE TO OFFICERS, STOCKHOLDERS, EMPLOYEES, AFFILIATED COMPANIES OR RELATIVES (10)

To Whom? _____ For what? _____

SCHEDULE H — TAX INFORMATION (11)

Describe "Other Taxes" shown on Page 1:

Is any of your tax liability payable on a deferred basis? Describe:

THROUGH WHAT YEAR HAVE YOUR FEDERAL AND STATE TAX RETURNS BEEN CLEARED? _____

OTHER BANK ACCOUNTS — Give names of other banks where you carry accounts and account numbers:

Do you borrow? _____ Secured or unsecured? _____

(12) CONTINGENT LIABILITY (If no liability, mark "none")

NOTES AND ACCOUNTS RECEIVABLE OR TRADE ACCEPTANCES DISCOUNTED OR PLEDGED $ _____

ACCOMMODATION ENDORSEMENTS, SURETY ON BONDS OR OTHER CONTINGENT LIABILITIES (Describe) $ _____

ARE THERE ANY TAX LIENS, JUDGMENTS UNSATISFIED OR SUITS PENDING AGAINST YOUR CONCERN? _____

LEASE LIABILITY — Give monthly rental rate and date of maturity of lease.

(Tumble)

EXHIBIT 3-2 (Cont'd.)

MISCELLANEOUS INFORMATION

INSURANCE

Fire & ECE — Buildings		Comprehensive Public Liab. Inc. Auto	
Fire & ECE — Mach., Equip., & Fixtures.		(a) Bodily Injury (Limits)	
Fire & ECE — Merchandise . . . . (13)		(b) Property Damage (Limits).	
Fire & ECE — Use and Occupancy		Life — Payable to this Business	
Earthquake — Bldgs., Equip. &/or Mdse..		Life — Payable Otherwise	
Fidelity Bonds Amt. any one Employee		Annual Premiums Life Insurance	
Name(s) and Address(es) of your Insurance Broker(s)			

CAPITAL ADDITIONS DURING PAST FISCAL YEAR (Before depreciation or write-offs) (14)

Land	$ _____	Furniture and Fixtures	$ _____
Buildings	_____	Autos and Trucks	_____
Machinery and Equipment	_____	Total . . . . $	_____

(15) FIRM OR CORPORATE DATA

Date Incorporated		Under the Laws of What State?
Preferred Stock Authorized _____		Common Stock Authorized _____
Issued _____		Issued _____
Par Value _____		Par Value _____
Dividend Rate _____		Date of Last Dividend _____
Dividend Cumulative or Non-Cumulative? _____		Amount of Last Dividend _____
Date to Which Paid _____		
Nature of Preference		

OFFICERS, DIRECTORS AND PRINCIPAL STOCKHOLDERS AND NUMBER OF SHARES OWNED BY EACH			PARTNERSHIP ☐ GENERAL ☐ LIMITED LIST ALL PARTNERS & PERCENTAGE OF INTEREST		
OFFICERS AND DIRECTORS	PREFERRED	COMMON	PARTNERS	LIMITED %	GENERAL %
President					
Vice President					
Secretary					
Treasurer					

By Whom Were Your Books Last Audited? _____   On What Date? _____

What Is Your Regular Fiscal Period? _____   Name of Attorney _____

Comments _____

CERTIFICATION

I hereby certify that I have carefully read the above statement, including all pages hereof, and it is a complete, true and correct statement of the undersigned to the best of my knowledge and belief.

(If a Firm or Corporation, Sign Below)   *(If an Individual, Sign Here)* _____

(16)

_____
PRESIDENT/GENERAL PARTNER

_____
FIRM OR CORPORATE NAME

_____
SECRETARY/GENERAL PARTNER

_____
FIRM OR CORPORATE NAME

Date Signed _____ 19 ____

The undersigned, Secretary of the Corporation making the within statement, hereby certifies this ____ day of _____ , 19 ____ , that the officers who signed the same were duly authorized to do so by a proper resolution, which has not been revoked.

_____
(CORPORATE SEAL)   Secretary

The other sections should be completed as follows:

1. Section 2 is a condensed statement of profit and loss, also called an income statement. This will serve if the company's operations are not complex, but in most instances a more detailed statement is in order, especially as to selling, general, and administrative expenses.

2. Section 3 reconciles net worth, reflecting any changes that result from non-operating factors. These might include dividends paid, or withdrawals of capital by the partners.

3. Section 4 is a more detailed analysis of merchandise on hand. This is useful if the company is in a line of business that requires substantial inventory.

4. Land, buildings, and equipment owned by the company can be detailed in Section 5. As with an individual these assets can be a drain on cash flow to the extent that resources are needed to support them. A schedule will help the lender understand the impact of such assets on the company.

5. If the company owns stocks or bonds they should be listed in Section 6.

6. Section 7 provides space for listing amounts due from related parties. The lender is always concerned whether sums due are too large relative to the size of the company, and whether there is intent to ever repay the loans. Such assets have questionable value when considering the strength of a company in a real estate transaction.

7. Notes payable should be listed in Section 8. Details as to amount, to whom payable, and what collateral, if any, has been given are important in assessing impact on the company and the ability to service the proposed real estate debt.

8. Section 9 calls for a schedule of trade accounts payable. A real estate lender is looking more at long-term factors in assessing the company, factors like cash flow, rather than current accounts. Nonetheless, large amounts of payables that are delinquent would be cause for concern about the company's health.

9. Section 10 should be completed with loans due to officers and related parties. Again, the question to ask is are these debts ever intended to be repaid. Further, could the company repay them if the need arose?

10. Tax information called for in Section 11 impacts the real estate lender only if the taxes are unusual in amount or the timing of required payments. If taxes might adversely impact the real estate loan, then they are cause for concern.

11. Contingent liabilities should not be overlooked. These could become real liabilities of the company, and they should be listed in Section 12. A company that has too large a total in this category may be heading for trouble. Lease liabilities, for example, reflect contracts that will have to be serviced, along with the new real estate debt.

12. Section 13 provides space for listing insurance carried by the company. The only insurance important to the real estate lender is the insurance that must be carried to cover the building or buildings against which he is lending.

13. Section 14 allows a reconciliation of capital expenditures made during the year. Capital additions affect cash flow, and cash flow repays real estate debt.

14. Firm or corporate historical information can be listed in Section 15. Since knowing the borrower is important to all lending, this section should be given attention.

15. In Section 16 company officers should sign and date the financial statement certifying as to the accuracy of the data. If the company is a corporation, the corporate seal can be affixed under the signatures.

When and How to Use the Supplemental Schedule of Real Estate

Other financial information can be useful in the analysis of financial strength. The Supplemental Schedule of Real Estate Investments should be used for any borrower who invests in and owns a lot of real estate. Real estate has value, but that value is most often a reflection of the income and expenses that are attributable to the property. Some properties, however, generate real losses that must be serviced with the borrower's overall cash flow. A knowledge of the position of the borrower and the cash flow available helps in the credit decision.

Exhibit 3-3 shows a sample Supplemental Schedule. It should be completed with the following information:

1. Address of Property. Show the complete street address, city, and state for each piece of real estate owned. If there is no street address, the borrower can use lot and tract, or approximate location.

2. Type of Property and Ownership %. The property type, such as single family, industrial, or office should be shown. Underneath, in the same box, show the percent of ownership held by the borrower.

3. Original Cost and Acquisition Date. The cost of the property when purchased by the borrower, and the date ownership was acquired.

4. Present Market Value. The borrower should reflect his estimate of value for the property. The lender will make his own determination based on the other information included in the schedule.

5. Current Balance of Mortgages and Interest Rate. Show the balance outstanding for all mortgages against the property. Detail the interest rate being paid on each mortgage.

6. Annual Rent and Occupancy Percentage. The gross income that the property generates yearly should be shown here. The percent of the property that is occupied in order to generate that annual income should also be shown.

7. Annual Mortgage Payments. The annual mortgage payments for each loan against the property should be listed.

8. Annual Taxes, Insurance, Maintenance. List all the expenses of operating the property.

9. Annual Net Cash Flow. The net annual cash flow to the property should be derived by subtracting the mortgage payments and operating expenses from the gross income shown in the earlier boxes. If the net figure is not correct, something has been omitted.

10. Name and Address of Lender, Loan Account Number. The complete name and address of the lender for each mortgage loan against the property should be given. The borrower should fill in the account number. This information will be helpful should any separate verification be desired.

11. Totals. The columns can be totaled, and the totals should conform to those on the financial statement.

EXHIBIT 3-3

SUPPLEMENTAL SCHEDULE OF REAL ESTATE INVESTMENTS

APPLICANT'S NAME: _____   DATE: _____

LIST APPLICANT'S SHARE OF COST, PRESENT VALUE, MORTGAGES AND CASH FLOW ITEMS

ADDRESS OF PROPERTY (1)	TYPE OF PROPERTY & OWNERSHIP % (2)	ORIGINAL COST AND ACQUISITION DATE (3)	PRESENT MARKET VALUE (4)	CURRENT BALANCE OF MORTGATES & INT. RATE (5)	ANNUAL RENT & OCCUPANCY PERCENTAGE (6)	ANNUAL MORTGAGE PAYMENTS (7)	ANNUAL TAXES, INS. MAIN-TENANCE (8)	ANNUAL NET CASH FLOW (9)	NAME AND ADDRESS OF LENDER LOAN ACCOUNT NUMBER (10)
					(11)				

TOTAL FOR APPLICANT: _____

When to Obtain a Certification of Financial Statement

A Certification of Financial Statement should be obtained whenever a personal financial statement is provided on a form other than that used by your bank. Your bank form should already have such a certification typed at the bottom where the borrower signs. By signing the certification, the borrower attests to the accuracy and correctness of information provided. A sample certification is shown in Exhibit 3-4 and should be completed with:

1. Date. The date of the certification.
2. To: The bank to which the certification is addressed, your bank.

EXHIBIT 3-4

CERTIFICATION OF FINANCIAL STATEMENT

_____ (1) _____ , 19 ___

TO: _____ (2) _____
The attached is the financial statement of the undersigned as of _____ (3) _____ , 19 ___ , which is the most recent financial statement prepared by or for the undersigned. It is furnished for the purpose of procuring and establishing credit from you and to induce you to permit the undersigned to become indebted to you on notes, endorsements, guarantees, overdrafts, or otherwise. The undersigned agrees to notify you immediately of the extent and character of any material change in said financial statement, and also agrees that if the undersigned, or any endorser or guarantor of any of the obligations of the undersigned, at any time fails in business or becomes insolvent, or commits an act of bankruptcy, or dies, or if a writ of attachment, garnishment, execution, or other legal process be issued against property of the undersigned or if any assessment for taxes against the undersigned, other than taxes on real property, is made by the federal or state government or any department thereof, or if any of the representations made in said statement prove to be untrue, or if the undersigned fails to notify you of any material change as above required, or if such change occurs, or if the business, or any interest therein, of the undersigned is sold, then and in such case all of the obligations of the undersigned to you or held by you shall immediately become due and payable, without demand or notice. Said statement shall be construed by you to be a continuing statement of the condition of the undersigned, and a new and original statement of all assets and liabilities upon each and every transaction in and by which the undersigned hereafter becomes indebted to you, until the undersigned advises in writing to the contrary. The undersigned declares and certifies that the attached statement and supporting schedules, both printed and written, gives a full, true and correct statement of the financial condition of the undersigned as of the date indicated above.

Signature _____ (4) _____

3. As Of. The date of the financial statement to which the certification is to be attached. This should be the same date as the statement on which you are relying in the analysis of your loan.

4. Signature. The certification should be signed by the party whose financial statement is being taken and to which it will be attached.

Securing an Authorization to Check Credit

An Authorization to Check Credit Form authorizes the lender to collect credit information from agencies and from other lenders who have had dealings with the borrower. A sample form is shown in Exhibit 3-5. The borrower should sign and date the form where indicated.

Uses and Limitations of Credit Reports

Credit reports are used by lenders in the analysis of the financial position of the borrower. When dealing with a corporate borrower, a report from an agency such as Dun & Bradstreet, Inc. can provide useful information about the company, its history, its principals, and its credit paying habits.

If the borrower is an individual, reports from agencies such as TRW or Equifax provide the same kind of information. These are tools that can provide some warning about problems a borrower may be having. They do not substitute for the lender's own, independent analysis. The lending decision finally rests with the party who is putting the money out the door.

EXHIBIT 3-5

AUTHORIZATION TO CHECK CREDIT

I promise that all of the information I've given you in my application for a real estate loan is true and correct. I understand that you will retain this information whether or not the application is approved. You have my permission to verify this information and to solicit any additional information you may require from the references I have provided. I understand that periodically you may receive information about me from other sources, and you may answer questions and requests from others, like credit reporting agencies, about me or my transactions with you.

If two of us have signed, this statement applies to each of us.

_____   _____

Name   Date

_____   _____

Name   Date

EXHIBIT 3-6

CHECKLIST OF FINANCIAL INFORMATION

	Needed (Y/N?)	Date Rqst'd	Date Rec'd
1. Financial Statements	————	————	————
a. Personal Statement	————	————	————
1) Certification of Financial Statement	————	————	————
b. Company Financial Statement	————	————	————
2. Supplemental Schedule of Real Estate	————	————	————
3. Credit Reports			
a. On Individuals	————	————	————
b. On Company	————	————	————
4. Information Waived (Explain):			

_____

_____

_____

_____

_____

End Note

Exhibit 3-6 is a checklist to use to make sure financial information needed for the real estate loan request is received. Information that is waived should be detailed and an explanation for the waiver given. This will leave a trail for anyone who picks up the file in the future, for auditors, and for the loan officer who may later be unsure why things were done the way they were. Real estate lenders tend to focus on the real estate when considering loan requests. Such a focus is natural, of course, but an analysis of the financial strength of the borrower should not be ignored. Other obligations or ventures can create a cash flow drain that will eventually impact the property under current consideration. The real estate is not operated in a vacuum, but as part of the total portfolio of assets owned and managed by the borrower.

4

How to Document the Analysis of Construction Loan Requests

Construction loans present a more difficult challenge to the commercial real estate lender. Underwriting considerations can be more complex than with the permanent loan, and the documentation needed to support construction lending is more intensive. This chapter is the first of three in this book that will cover the topic of construction lending. Consideration will be given first to handling construction loans during the underwriting process. Later chapters will cover putting the loan on the books and controlling it once funding begins.

The basic analysis of the real estate and the borrower should be handled in the same manner whether the loan will be for construction or permanent financing. These topics have been covered in earlier chapters. Construction adds other dimensions, such as considering the costs to build, assessing whether the people involved can actually build the project, and how the lender will control the whole process. Our discussion will begin with the cost breakdown.

How to Assemble a Cost Breakdown

A cost breakdown is an itemized listing of all of the costs that are attributable to the project. There are three basic categories of costs: hard costs, soft costs, and land cost. If the lender is involved in the project at an early stage, the costs may not be firm. Any loan that is granted should be subject to receipt and approval of final costs.

Exhibit 4-1 is a cost breakdown form that can be used by the borrower or contractor to detail hard costs, the costs of materials and labor that will be used for the construction of the building. The form has room for a line-item by line-item estimate of cost. There is also space to indicate which contractor will be doing the work. Most

EXHIBIT 4-1

CONSTRUCTION COST BREAKDOWN

Property Address:_____ (1) _____

General Contractor:_____ (2) _____
Address:_____ (3) _____
Phone: _____ (4) _____

Line Item (5)	Estimate (6)	Contractor (7)
1. Building Permit		
2. Water Meter		
3. Survey		
4. Temporary Facilities		
5. Demolition & Site Preparation		
6. Earthwork		
7. Sewer/Cesspool		
8. Concrete Forms		
9. Structural Concrete Including Floors		
10. Lumber-Rough		
11. Lumber-Finish		
12. Carpenter Labor-Rough		
13. Carpenter Labor-Finish		
14. Doors & Frames		

EXHIBIT 4-1 (Cont'd.)

15. Window Frames,
      Sash & Screen

_____

16. Cabinets &
      Millwork

_____

17. Hardware-Rough

_____

18. Hardware-Finish

_____

19. Piling in Place

_____

20. Reinforcing Steel

_____

21. Structural Steel

_____

22. Plumbing-Ground

_____

23. Plumbing-Rough

_____

24. Plumbing-Finish

_____

25. Electrical-Rough

_____

26. Electrical-Finish

_____

27. Lighting Fixtures

_____

28. Roof Trusses

_____

29. Roof Cover

_____

30. Structural Masonry

_____

31. Masonry Veneer

_____

32. Stucco-Exterior

_____

33. Other Exterior Wall
      Construction

_____

34. HVAC-Rough

_____

EXHIBIT 4-1 (Cont'd.)

35. HVAC-Finish

36. Sheetmetal &
    Flashing

37. Glass-Glazing-
    Curtain Wall

38. Lath & Plaster

39. Insulation &
    Soundproofing

40. Fireproofing

41. Formica

42. Tilework

43. Carpet

44. Finish Flooring

45. Painting &
    Decorating

46. Fire Sprinklers

47. Elevators

48. Toilet Accessories

49. Built-In Equipment

50. Weatherstripping,
    Shades, Blinds

51. Miscellaneous Metal

52. Fences & Retaining
    Walls

53. Fireplace

EXHIBIT 4-1 (Cont'd.)

54. Garage Door &
    Hardware

_____

55. Cleanup

_____

56. Drain Tile

_____

57. Landscaping

_____

58. Concrete or
    Asphalt Paving

_____

59. Walks & Exterior
    Stairs

_____

60. Insurance

_____

61. Supervision

_____

62. Contingency

_____

63.

_____

64.

_____

65.

_____

66.

_____

67.

_____

68.

_____

69. Architectural &
    Engineering Fees

_____

70. Contractor's Overhead
    & Fee

_____

Total Cost

_____

I certify that the above is to the best of my knowledge a true and correct estimate of the costs of this job.

Signed_____ (8) _____ Date _____ (9) _____

general contractors will subcontract a majority of the work to other contractors who have expertise in a given field. These others become the subcontractor of the general contractor. Some general contractors may perform certain work themselves, especially if they have an area of expertise—for example, concrete work or plumbing.

The form may initially be completed by the borrower. Before the loan funds, however, the general contractor should provide his own cost breakdown, on this or a similar form. The cost breakdown should be completed with the following information:

1. The address of the subject property, the property on which construction will take place. The street address may not be available at the time the loan is processed. Use the legal address in that case. The address used should be the same one used with the rest of your loan documents.

2. The name of the general contractor. If a contractor has not been chosen when loan application is made, a new cost breakdown on this form should be prepared at a later date by the contractor.

3. The address of the general contractor.

4. The phone number of the general contractor.

5. In this column are the various line items relating to hard costs. They can be changed to reflect the individual job. They can also be numbered to correspond to computer programs you may have for controlling the disbursement process as draw requests are made.

6. For each line item the contractor should estimate the cost of the work.

7. The name of the subcontractor who will perform that particular piece of the work. If a subcontractor has not yet been selected, the name can be filled in later.

8. The contractor should sign the estimate certifying that it is correct to the best of his knowledge.

9. The date of the certification.

Exhibit 4-2 shows the rest of the cost breakdown, which includes soft costs and land cost. Soft costs are those items that relate to construction, that support it, but that are not specifically materials or labor applied to the physical structure. These costs should be provided by the borrower, but should be checked for accuracy by the lender.

1. Total cost is the complete cost for the individual line item.

2. The amount prepaid, which is referred to as a "prepaid item," is money already spent by the borrower/owner. The total of these prepaid items can count as additional equity or can be reimbursed to the owner from the proceeds of the construction loan, if sufficient funds are available.

3. Net cost, cost after deducting for prepaid items, is the amount needed to carry construction through to completion. The sum of net cost for individual line items should be fairly close to the amount of loan needed.

4. In this row fill in the total land cost, any funds already prepaid for land acquisition, and compute the net land cost.

5. Direct costs are synonymous with hard costs and should correspond to the itemized construction cost breakdown presented in a form similar to the one in Exhibit 4-1.

6. The indirect costs should be itemized by type of cost for ease in controlling

EXHIBIT 4-2

OWNER'S COST BREAKDOWN

	Total Cost (1)	Amount Prepaid (2)	Net Cost (3)
Land Cost	(4)		
Direct Costs	(5)		
Indirect Costs:	(6)		
Interest Reserve			
Loan Fees:			
Construction			
Permanent			
Insurance			
Taxes			
Permits/Fees			
Architecture & Engineering			
Legal			
Accounting			
Other			
Contingency			
Total Indirect Costs			
Total Costs	(7)		
Proposed Loan Amount	(8)		
Equity Required	(9)		

disbursements during the course of construction. Some of these costs, like Architecture or Permits, may be included in hard costs if the general contractor is going to handle these items. More often they are found as a part of indirect cost.

7. Total cost is the total of land cost, direct cost, and indirect cost.

8. Proposed loan amount is your best estimate, or actual amount, of the loan to be granted.

9. Equity required is the cash the owner has to put up, or the prepaid items approved in lieu of cash. Prepaid items must be verified with paid bills and cancelled checks.

What to Look for in Architectural Contracts

Early in the building process the owner will consult with an architect. The architect will develop concepts for a building or buildings to be constructed on the owner's land. Initially the architect will probably require that the owner sign a letter of agreement covering the development of concepts or preliminary schemes.

Later in the process the owner and architect will enter into an architectural contract, which will spell out in more precise detail the obligations of each party. Usually architectural drawings are underway by the time a lender gets involved with the project. Many times the plans have already been submitted to the appropriate governmental agency controlling approval of working drawings.

Therefore, much that is in the architectural contract is beyond the control of the lender. Nevertheless, it should be read to determine if there are clauses that are inconsistent with the lender's planned loan structure. At a minimum the lender should determine the extent of the architect's responsibilities during the construction process. For example, is the architect required to make regular inspections of the work and sign the draw requests signifying agreement with the progress of the job? If so, the lender should make this requirement part of his loan documents, thereby providing additional support for his own inspections.

A clause that should be present in the architectural contract is a requirement that the architect approve any changes made to his plans. Failure to obtain that approval may negate any responsibility the architect has for errors.

What You Should Know About Construction Contracts

The construction contract is one of the most important documents that a lender will evaluate during the course of construction loan analysis. This document contains the legal agreement between the contractor and the owner/borrower for the construction of the building. The lender must be sure that the terms of the loan and the terms of the construction contract are compatible. Otherwise there is a risk that problems will arise during the construction process when conflicting terms in the contract and the loan documents collide.

Contracts are widely divergent and often contain special language unique to a particular transaction. The industry has developed certain standard forms that can be used, however, to document the basic agreement. Exhibit 4-3 is a Standard Form of Agreement Between Owner and Contractor as published by the American Institute of Architects. This particular contract is known as a "cost plus" contract, where the contractor is paid the costs of the job plus a fee for his work. Other contracts can be used to cover other situations.

It isn't necessary for the lender to be legally conversant with all the terms of the contract. He must be aware, however, of the basic agreement between the owner and contractor, which responsibilities each will handle, and whether or not these agreements are consistent with the proposed structure of the loan.

You are urged to seek advice from legal counsel if questions arise as to the meaning of specific clauses in a contract. You should review:

1. The date of the contract.
2. The name and address of the owner of the property.
3. The name and address of the contractor.
4. A description of the project to be built; for example, "Construct a single-story

EXHIBIT 4-3

Courtesy of the American Institute of Architects

T H E   A M E R I C A N   I N S T I T U T E   O F   A R C H I T E C T S

AIA Document A111

Standard Form of Agreement Between Owner and Contractor

where the basis of payment is the

COST OF THE WORK PLUS A FEE

with or without a Guaranteed Maximum Price

1987 EDITION

THIS DOCUMENT HAS IMPORTANT LEGAL CONSEQUENCES; CONSULTATION WITH AN ATTORNEY IS ENCOURAGED WITH RESPECT TO ITS COMPLETION OR MODIFICATION.

The 1987 Edition of AIA Document A201, General Conditions of the Contract for Construction, is adopted in this document by reference. Do not use with other general conditions unless this document is modified.

This document has been approved and endorsed by The Associated General Contractors of America.

AGREEMENT

made as of the (1)   day of   in the year of
Nineteen Hundred and

BETWEEN the Owner: (2)
(Name and address)

and the Contractor: (3)
(Name and address)

the Project is: (4)
(Name and address)

the Architect is: (5)
(Name and address)

The Owner and Contractor agree as set forth below.

EXHIBIT 4-3 (Cont'd.)

ARTICLE 1 (6)
THE CONTRACT DOCUMENTS

1.1   The Contract Documents consist of this Agreement, Conditions of the Contract (General, Supplementary and other Conditions), Drawings, Specifications, Addenda issued prior to execution of this Agreement, other documents listed in this Agreement and Modifications issued after execution of this Agreement; these form the Contract, and are as fully a part of the Contract as if attached to this Agreement or repeated herein. The Contract represents the entire and integrated agreement between the parties hereto and supersedes prior negotiations, representations or agreements, either written or oral. An enumeration of the Contract Documents, other than Modifications, appears in Article 16. If anything in the other Contract Documents is inconsistent with this Agreement, this Agreement shall govern.

ARTICLE 2 (7)
THE WORK OF THIS CONTRACT

2.1   The Contractor shall execute the entire Work described in the Contract Documents, except to the extent specifically indicated in the Contract Documents to be the responsibility of others, or as follows:

ARTICLE 3 (8)
RELATIONSHIP OF THE PARTIES

3.1   The Contractor accepts the relationship of trust and confidence established by this Agreement and covenants with the Owner to cooperate with the Architect and utilize the Contractor's best skill, efforts and judgment in furthering the interests of the Owner; to furnish efficient business administration and supervision; to make best efforts to furnish at all times an adequate supply of workers and materials; and to perform the Work in the best way and most expeditious and economical manner consistent with the interests of the Owner. The Owner agrees to exercise best efforts to enable the Contractor to perform the Work in the best way and most expeditious manner by furnishing and approving in a timely way information required by the Contractor and making payments to the Contractor in accordance with requirements of the Contract Documents.

ARTICLE 4 (9)
DATE OF COMMENCEMENT AND SUBSTANTIAL COMPLETION

4.1   The date of commencement is the date from which the Contract Time of Subparagraph 4.2 is measured; it shall be the date of this Agreement, as first written above, unless a different date is stated below or provision is made for the date to be fixed in a notice to proceed issued by the Owner.
(Insert the date of commencement, if it differs from the date of this Agreement or, if applicable, state that the date will be fixed in a notice to proceed.)

Unless the date of commencement is established by a notice to proceed issued by the Owner, the Contractor shall notify the Owner in writing not less than five days before commencing the Work to permit the timely filing of mortgages, mechanic's liens and other security interests.

AIA DOCUMENT A111 • OWNER-CONTRACTOR AGREEMENT • TENTH EDITION • AIA® • ©1987 • THE
AMERICAN INSTITUTE OF ARCHITECTS, 1735 NEW YORK AVENUE, N.W., WASHINGTON, D.C. 20006   **A111-1987   2**

EXHIBIT 4-3 (Cont'd.)

4.2   The Contractor shall achieve Substantial Completion of the entire Work not later than

(Insert the calendar date or number of calendar days after the date of commencement. Also insert any requirements for earlier Substantial Completion of certain portions of the Work, if not stated elsewhere in the Contract Documents.)

, subject to adjustments of this Contract Time as provided in the Contract Documents.

(Insert provisions, if any, for liquidated damages relating to failure to complete on time.)

ARTICLE 5   (10)
CONTRACT SUM

5.1   The Owner shall pay the Contractor in current funds for the Contractor's performance of the Contract the Contract Sum consisting of the Cost of the Work as defined in Article 7 and the Contractor's Fee determined as follows:

(State a lump sum, percentage of Cost of the Work or other provision for determining the Contractor's Fee, and explain how the Contractor's Fee is to be adjusted for changes in the Work.)

5.2   GUARANTEED MAXIMUM PRICE (IF APPLICABLE)

5.2.1   The sum of the Cost of the Work and the Contractor's Fee is guaranteed by the Contractor not to exceed

Dollars ($), subject to additions and deductions by Change Order as provided in the Contract Documents. Such maximum sum is referred to in the Contract Documents as the Guaranteed Maximum Price. Costs which would cause the Guaranteed Maximum Price to be exceeded shall be paid by the Contractor without reimbursement by the Owner.

(Insert specific provisions if the Contractor is to participate in any savings.)

EXHIBIT 4-3 (Cont'd.)

5.2.2 The Guaranteed Maximum Price is based upon the following alternates, if any, which are described in the Contract Documents and are hereby accepted by the Owner:

(State the numbers or other identification of accepted alternates, but only if a Guaranteed Maximum Price is inserted in Subparagraph 5.2.1. If decisions on other alternates are to be made by the Owner subsequent to the execution of this Agreement, attach a schedule of such other alternates showing the amount for each and the date until which that amount is valid.)

5.2.3 The amounts agreed to for unit prices, if any, are as follows:

(State unit prices only if a Guaranteed Maximum Price is inserted in Subparagraph 5.2.1.)

ARTICLE 6 (11)
CHANGES IN THE WORK

6.1 CONTRACTS WITH A GUARANTEED MAXIMUM PRICE

6.1.1 Adjustments to the Guaranteed Maximum Price on account of changes in the Work may be determined by any of the methods listed in Subparagraph 7.3.3 of the General Conditions.

6.1.2 In calculating adjustments to subcontracts (except those awarded with the Owner's prior consent on the basis of cost plus a fee), the terms "cost" and "fee" as used in Clause 7.3.3.3 of the General Conditions and the terms "costs" and "a reasonable allowance for overhead and profit" as used in Subparagraph 7.3.6 of the General Conditions shall have the meanings assigned to them in the General Conditions and shall not be modified by Articles 5, 7 and 8 of this Agreement. Adjustments to subcontracts awarded with the Owner's prior consent on the basis of cost plus a fee shall be calculated in accordance with the terms of those subcontracts.

6.1.3 In calculating adjustments to this Contract, the terms "cost" and "costs" as used in the above-referenced provisions of the General Conditions shall mean the Cost of the Work as defined in Article 7 of this Agreement and the terms "fee" and "a reasonable allowance for overhead and profit" shall mean the Contractor's Fee as defined in Paragraph 5.1 of this Agreement.

EXHIBIT 4-3 (Cont'd.)

6.2 CONTRACTS WITHOUT A GUARANTEED MAXIMUM PRICE

6.2.1 Increased costs for the items set forth in Article 7 which result from changes in the Work shall become part of the Cost of the Work, and the Contractor's Fee shall be adjusted as provided in Paragraph 5.1.

6.3 ALL CONTRACTS

6.3.1 If no specific provision is made in Paragraph 5.1 for adjustment of the Contractor's Fee in the case of changes in the Work, or if the extent of such changes is such, in the aggregate, that application of the adjustment provisions of Paragraph 5.1 will cause substantial inequity to the Owner or Contractor, the Contractor's Fee shall be equitably adjusted on the basis of the Fee established for the original Work.

ARTICLE 7 (12)
COSTS TO BE REIMBURSED

7.1 The term Cost of the Work shall mean costs necessarily incurred by the Contractor in the proper performance of the Work. Such costs shall be at rates not higher than the standard paid at the place of the Project except with prior consent of the Owner. The Cost of the Work shall include only the items set forth in this Article 7.

7.1.1 LABOR COSTS

7.1.1.1 Wages of construction workers directly employed by the Contractor to perform the construction of the Work at the site or, with the Owner's agreement, at off-site workshops.

7.1.1.2 Wages or salaries of the Contractor's supervisory and administrative personnel when stationed at the site with the Owner's agreement.
(If it is intended that the wages or salaries of certain personnel stationed at the Contractor's principal or other offices shall be included in the Cost of the Work, identify in Article 14 the personnel to be included and whether for all or only part of their time.)

7.1.1.3 Wages and salaries of the Contractor's supervisory or administrative personnel engaged, at factories, workshops or on the road, in expediting the production or transportation of materials or equipment required for the Work, but only for that portion of their time required for the Work.

7.1.1.4 Costs paid or incurred by the Contractor for taxes, insurance, contributions, assessments and benefits required by law or collective bargaining agreements and, for personnel not covered by such agreements, customary benefits such as sick leave, medical and health benefits, holidays, vacations and pensions, provided such costs are based on wages and salaries included in the Cost of the Work under Clauses 7.1.1.1 through 7.1.1.3.

7.1.2 SUBCONTRACT COSTS

Payments made by the Contractor to Subcontractors in accordance with the requirements of the subcontracts.

7.1.3 COSTS OF MATERIALS AND EQUIPMENT INCORPORATED IN THE COMPLETED CONSTRUCTION

7.1.3.1 Costs, including transportation, of materials and equipment incorporated or to be incorporated in the completed construction.

7.1.3.2 Costs of materials described in the preceding Clause 7.1.3.1 in excess of those actually installed but required to provide reasonable allowance for waste and for spoilage. Unused excess materials, if any, shall be handed over to the Owner at the completion of the Work or, at the Owner's option, shall be sold by the Contractor; amounts realized, if any, from such sales shall be credited to the Owner as a deduction from the Cost of the Work.

7.1.4 COSTS OF OTHER MATERIALS AND EQUIPMENT, TEMPORARY FACILITIES AND RELATED ITEMS

7.1.4.1 Costs, including transportation, installation, maintenance, dismantling and removal of materials, supplies, temporary facilities, machinery, equipment, and hand tools not customarily owned by the construction workers, which are provided by the Contractor at the site and fully consumed in the performance of the Work; and cost less salvage value on such items if not fully consumed, whether sold to others or retained by the Contractor. Cost for items previously used by the Contractor shall mean fair market value.

7.1.4.2 Rental charges for temporary facilities, machinery, equipment, and hand tools not customarily owned by the construction workers, which are provided by the Contractor at the site, whether rented from the Contractor or others, and costs of transportation, installation, minor repairs and replacements, dismantling and removal thereof. Rates and quantities of equipment rented shall be subject to the Owner's prior approval.

7.1.4.3 Costs of removal of debris from the site.

7.1.4.4 Costs of telegrams and long-distance telephone calls, postage and parcel delivery charges, telephone service at the site and reasonable petty cash expenses of the site office.

7.1.4.5 That portion of the reasonable travel and subsistence expenses of the Contractor's personnel incurred while traveling in discharge of duties connected with the Work.

EXHIBIT 4-3 (Cont'd.)

7.1.5 MISCELLANEOUS COSTS

7.1.5.1 That portion directly attributable to this Contract of premiums for insurance and bonds.

7.1.5.2 Sales, use or similar taxes imposed by a governmental authority which are related to the Work and for which the Contractor is liable.

7.1.5.3 Fees and assessments for the building permit and for other permits, licenses and inspections for which the Contractor is required by the Contract Documents to pay.

7.1.5.4 Fees of testing laboratories for tests required by the Contract Documents, except those related to defective or nonconforming Work for which reimbursement is excluded by Subparagraph 13.5.3 of the General Conditions or other provisions of the Contract Documents and which do not fall within the scope of Subparagraphs 7.2.2 through 7.2.4 below.

7.1.5.5 Royalties and license fees paid for the use of a particular design, process or product required by the Contract Documents; the cost of defending suits or claims for infringement of patent rights arising from such requirement by the Contract Documents; payments made in accordance with legal judgments against the Contractor resulting from such suits or claims and payments of settlements made with the Owner's consent; provided, however, that such costs of legal defenses, judgment and settlements shall not be included in the calculation of the Contractor's Fee or of a Guaranteed Maximum Price, if any, and provided that such royalties, fees and costs are not excluded by the last sentence of Subparagraph 3.17.1 of the General Conditions or other provisions of the Contract Documents.

7.1.5.6 Deposits lost for causes other than the Contractor's fault or negligence.

7.1.6 OTHER COSTS

7.1.6.1 Other costs incurred in the performance of the Work if and to the extent approved in advance in writing by the Owner.

7.2 EMERGENCIES: REPAIRS TO DAMAGED, DEFECTIVE OR NONCONFORMING WORK

The Cost of the Work shall also include costs described in Paragraph 7.1 which are incurred by the Contractor:

7.2.1 In taking action to prevent threatened damage, injury or loss in case of an emergency affecting the safety of persons and property, as provided in Paragraph 10.3 of the General Conditions.

7.2.2 In repairing or correcting Work damaged or improperly executed by construction workers in the employ of the Contractor, provided such damage or improper execution did not result from the fault or negligence of the Contractor or the Contractor's foremen, engineers or superintendents, or other supervisory, administrative or managerial personnel of the Contractor.

7.2.3 In repairing damaged Work other than that described in Subparagraph 7.2.2, provided such damage did not result from the fault or negligence of the Contractor or the Contractor's personnel, and only to the extent that the cost of such repairs is not recoverable by the Contractor from others and the Contractor is not compensated therefor by insurance or otherwise.

7.2.4 In correcting defective or nonconforming Work performed or supplied by a Subcontractor or material supplier and not corrected by them, provided such defective or nonconforming Work did not result from the fault or neglect of the Contractor or the Contractor's personnel adequately to supervise and direct the Work of the Subcontractor or material supplier, and only to the extent that the cost of correcting the defective or nonconforming Work is not recoverable by the Contractor from the Subcontractor or material supplier.

ARTICLE 8 (13)

COSTS NOT TO BE REIMBURSED

8.1 The Cost of the Work shall not include:

8.1.1 Salaries and other compensation of the Contractor's personnel stationed at the Contractor's principal office or offices other than the site office, except as specifically provided in Clauses 7.1.1.2 and 7.1.1.3 or as may be provided in Article 14.

8.1.2 Expenses of the Contractor's principal office and offices other than the site office.

8.1.3 Overhead and general expenses, except as may be expressly included in Article 7.

8.1.4 The Contractor's capital expenses, including interest on the Contractor's capital employed for the Work.

8.1.5 Rental costs of machinery and equipment, except as specifically provided in Clause 7.1.4.2.

8.1.6 Except as provided in Subparagraphs 7.2.2 through 7.2.4 and Paragraph 13.5 of this Agreement, costs due to the fault or negligence of the Contractor, Subcontractors, anyone directly or indirectly employed by any of them, or for whose acts any of them may be liable, including but not limited to costs for the correction of damaged, defective or nonconforming Work, disposal and replacement of materials and equipment incorrectly ordered or supplied, and making good damage to property not forming part of the Work.

8.1.7 Any cost not specifically and expressly described in Article 7.

8.1.8 Costs which would cause the Guaranteed Maximum Price, if any, to be exceeded.

EXHIBIT 4-3 (Cont'd.)
ARTICLE 9 (14)
DISCOUNTS, REBATES AND REFUNDS

9.1   Cash discounts obtained on payments made by the Contractor shall accrue to the Owner if (1) before making the payment, the Contractor included them in an Application for Payment and received payment therefor from the Owner, or (2) the Owner has deposited funds with the Contractor with which to make payments; otherwise, cash discounts shall accrue to the Contractor. Trade discounts, rebates, refunds and amounts received from sales of surplus materials and equipment shall accrue to the Owner, and the Contractor shall make provisions so that they can be secured.

9.2   Amounts which accrue to the Owner in accordance with the provisions of Paragraph 9.1 shall be credited to the Owner as a deduction from the Cost of the Work.

ARTICLE 10 (15)
SUBCONTRACTS AND OTHER AGREEMENTS

10.1   Those portions of the Work that the Contractor does not customarily perform with the Contractor's own personnel shall be performed under subcontracts or by other appropriate agreements with the Contractor. The Contractor shall obtain bids from Subcontractors and from suppliers of materials or equipment fabricated especially for the Work and shall deliver such bids to the Architect. The Owner will then determine, with the advice of the Contractor and subject to the reasonable objection of the Architect, which bids will be accepted. The Owner may designate specific persons or entities from whom the Contractor shall obtain bids; however, if a Guaranteed Maximum Price has been established, the Owner may not prohibit the Contractor from obtaining bids from others. The Contractor shall not be required to contract with anyone to whom the Contractor has reasonable objection.

10.2   If a Guaranteed Maximum Price has been established and a specific bidder among those whose bids are delivered by the Contractor to the Architect (1) is recommended to the Owner by the Contractor; (2) is qualified to perform that portion of the Work; and (3) has submitted a bid which conforms to the requirements of the Contract Documents without reservations or exceptions, but the Owner requires that another bid be accepted, then the Contractor may require that a Change Order be issued to adjust the Guaranteed Maximum Price by the difference between the bid of the person or entity recommended to the Owner by the Contractor and the amount of the subcontract or other agreement actually signed with the person or entity designated by the Owner.

10.3   Subcontracts or other agreements shall conform to the payment provisions of Paragraphs 12.7 and 12.8, and shall not be awarded on the basis of cost plus a fee without the prior consent of the Owner.

ARTICLE 11 (16)
ACCOUNTING RECORDS

11.1   The Contractor shall keep full and detailed accounts and exercise such controls as may be necessary for proper financial management under this Contract; the accounting and control systems shall be satisfactory to the Owner. The Owner and the Owner's accountants shall be afforded access to the Contractor's records, books, correspondence, instructions, drawings, receipts, subcontracts, purchase orders, vouchers, memoranda and other data relating to this Contract, and the Contractor shall preserve these for a period of three years after final payment, or for such longer period as may be required by law.

ARTICLE 12 (17)
PROGRESS PAYMENTS

12.1   Based upon Applications for Payment submitted to the Architect by the Contractor and Certificates for Payment issued by the Architect, the Owner shall make progress payments on account of the Contract Sum to the Contractor as provided below and elsewhere in the Contract Documents.

12.2   The period covered by each Application for Payment shall be one calendar month ending on the last day of the month, or as follows:

12.3   Provided an Application for Payment is received by the Architect not later than the
day of a month, the Owner shall make payment to the Contractor not later than the   day of the
month. If an Application for Payment is received by the Architect after the application date fixed above, payment shall be made by the Owner not later than   days after the Architect receives the Application for Payment.

12.4   With each Application for Payment the Contractor shall submit payrolls, petty cash accounts, receipted invoices or invoices with check vouchers attached, and any other evidence required by the Owner or Architect to demonstrate that cash disbursements already made by the Contractor on account of the Cost of the Work equal or exceed (1) progress payments already received by the Contractor; less (2) that portion of those payments attributable to the Contractor's Fee; plus (3) payrolls for the period covered by the present Application for Payment; plus (4) retainage provided in Subparagraph 12.5.4, if any, applicable to prior progress payments.

EXHIBIT 4-3 (Cont'd.)

12.5 CONTRACTS WITH A GUARANTEED MAXIMUM PRICE

12.5.1 Each Application for Payment shall be based upon the most recent schedule of values submitted by the Contractor in accordance with the Contract Documents. The schedule of values shall allocate the entire Guaranteed Maximum Price among the various portions of the Work, except that the Contractor's Fee shall be shown as a single separate item. The schedule of values shall be prepared in such form and supported by such data to substantiate its accuracy as the Architect may require. This schedule, unless objected to by the Architect, shall be used as a basis for reviewing the Contractor's Applications for Payment.

12.5.2 Applications for Payment shall show the percentage completion of each portion of the Work as of the end of the period covered by the Application for Payment. The percentage completion shall be the lesser of (1) the percentage of that portion of the Work which has actually been completed or (2) the percentage obtained by dividing (a) the expense which has actually been incurred by the Contractor on account of that portion of the Work for which the Contractor has made or intends to make actual payment prior to the next Application for Payment by (b) the share of the Guaranteed Maximum Price allocated to that portion of the Work in the schedule of values.

12.5.3 Subject to other provisions of the Contract Documents, the amount of each progress payment shall be computed as follows:

12.5.3.1 Take that portion of the Guaranteed Maximum Price properly allocable to completed Work as determined by multiplying the percentage completion of each portion of the Work by the share of the Guaranteed Maximum Price allocated to that portion of the Work in the schedule of values. Pending final determination of cost to the Owner of changes in the Work, amounts not in dispute may be included as provided in Subparagraph 7.3.7 of the General Conditions, even though the Guaranteed Maximum Price has not yet been adjusted by Change Order.

12.5.3.2 Add that portion of the Guaranteed Maximum Price properly allocable to materials and equipment delivered and suitably stored at the site for subsequent incorporation in the Work or, if approved in advance by the Owner, suitably stored off the site at a location agreed upon in writing.

12.5.3.3 Add the Contractor's Fee, less retainage of _____ percent (_____ %). The Contractor's Fee shall be computed upon the Cost of the Work described in the two preceding Clauses at the rate stated in Paragraph 5.1 or, if the Contractor's Fee is stated as a fixed sum in that Paragraph, shall be an amount which bears the same ratio to that fixed-sum Fee as the Cost of the Work in the two preceding Clauses bears to a reasonable estimate of the probable Cost of the Work upon its completion.

12.5.3.4 Subtract the aggregate of previous payments made by the Owner.

12.5.3.5 Subtract the shortfall, if any, indicated by the Contractor in the documentation required by Paragraph 12.4 to substantiate prior Applications for Payment, or resulting from errors subsequently discovered by the Owner's accountants in such documentation.

12.5.3.6 Subtract amounts, if any, for which the Architect has withheld or nullified a Certificate for Payment as provided in Paragraph 9.5 of the General Conditions.

12.5.4 Additional retainage, if any, shall be as follows:

(If it is intended to retain additional amounts from progress payments to the Contractor beyond (1) the retainage from the Contractor's Fee provided in Clause 12.5.3.3, (2) the retainage from Subcontractors provided in Paragraph 12.7 below, and (3) the retainage, if any, provided by other provisions of the Contract, insert provision for such additional retainage here. Such provision, if made, should also describe any arrangement for limiting or reducing the amount retained after the Work reaches a certain state of completion.)

12.6 CONTRACTS WITHOUT A GUARANTEED MAXIMUM PRICE

12.6.1 Applications for Payment shall show the Cost of the Work actually incurred by the Contractor through the end of the period covered by the Application for Payment and for which the Contractor has made or intends to make actual payment prior to the next Application for Payment.

12.6.2 Subject to other provisions of the Contract Documents, the amount of each progress payment shall be computed as follows:

12.6.2.1 Take the Cost of the Work as described in Subparagraph 12.6.1.

12.6.2.2 Add the Contractor's Fee, less retainage of _____ percent (_____ %). The Contractor's Fee shall be computed upon the Cost of the Work described in the preceding Clause 12.6.2.1 at the rate stated in Paragraph 5.1 or, if the Contractor's Fee is stated as a fixed sum in that Paragraph, an amount which bears the same ratio to that fixed-sum Fee as the Cost of the Work in the preceding Clause bears to a reasonable estimate of the probable Cost of the Work upon its completion.

12.6.2.3 Subtract the aggregate of previous payments made by the Owner.

12.6.2.4 Subtract the shortfall, if any, indicated by the Contractor in the documentation required by Paragraph 12.4 or to substantiate prior Applications for Payment or resulting from errors subsequently discovered by the Owner's accountants in such documentation.

AIA DOCUMENT A111 • OWNER-CONTRACTOR AGREEMENT • TENTH EDITION • AIA® • ©1987 • THE AMERICAN INSTITUTE OF ARCHITECTS, 1735 NEW YORK AVENUE, N.W., WASHINGTON, D.C. 20006

A111-1987 8

EXHIBIT 4-3 (Cont'd.)

12.6.2.5 Subtract amounts, if any, for which the Architect has withheld or withdrawn a Certificate for Payment as provided in the Contract Documents.

12.6.3 Additional retainage, if any, shall be as follows:

12.7 Except with the Owner's prior approval, payments to Subcontractors included in the Contractor's Applications for Payment shall not exceed an amount for each Subcontractor calculated as follows:

12.7.1 Take that portion of the Subcontract Sum properly allocable to completed Work as determined by multiplying the percentage completion of each portion of the Subcontractor's Work by the share of the total Subcontract Sum allocated to that portion in the Subcontractor's schedule of values, less retainage of _____ percent (%).
Pending final determination of amounts to be paid to the Subcontractor for changes in the Work, amounts not in dispute may be included as provided in Subparagraph 7.3.7 of the General Conditions even though the Subcontract Sum has not yet been adjusted by Change Order.

12.7.2 Add that portion of the Subcontract Sum properly allocable to materials and equipment delivered and suitably stored at the site for subsequent incorporation in the Work or, if approved in advance by the Owner, suitably stored off the site at a location agreed upon in writing, less retainage of _____ percent (%).

12.7.3 Subtract the aggregate of previous payments made by the Contractor to the Subcontractor.

12.7.4 Subtract amounts, if any, for which the Architect has withheld or nullified a Certificate for Payment by the Owner to the Contractor for reasons which are the fault of the Subcontractor.

12.7.5 Add, upon Substantial Completion of the entire Work of the Contractor, a sum sufficient to increase the total payments to the Subcontractor to _____ percent (%) of the Subcontract Sum, less amounts, if any, for incomplete Work and unsettled claims; and, if final completion of the entire Work is thereafter materially delayed through no fault of the Subcontractor, add any additional amounts payable on account of Work of the Subcontractor in accordance with Subparagraph 9.10.3 of the General Conditions.
(If it is intended, prior to Substantial Completion of the entire Work of the Contractor, to reduce or limit the retainage from Subcontractors resulting from the percentages inserted in Subparagraphs 12.7.1 and 12.7.2 above, and this is not explained elsewhere in the Contract Documents, insert here provisions for such reduction or limitation.)

The Subcontract Sum is the total amount stipulated in the subcontract to be paid by the Contractor to the Subcontractor for the Subcontractor's performance of the subcontract.

12.8 Except with the Owner's prior approval, the Contractor shall not make advance payments to suppliers for materials or equipment which have not been delivered and stored at the site.

12.9 In taking action on the Contractor's Applications for Payment, the Architect shall be entitled to rely on the accuracy and completeness of the information furnished by the Contractor and shall not be deemed to represent that the Architect has made a detailed examination, audit or arithmetic verification of the documentation submitted in accordance with Paragraph 12.4 or other supporting data; that the Architect has made exhaustive or continuous on-site inspections or that the Architect has made examinations to ascertain how or for what purposes the Contractor has used amounts previously paid on account of the Contract. Such examinations, audits and verifications, if required by the Owner, will be performed by the Owner's accountants acting in the sole interest of the Owner.

ARTICLE 13 (18)

FINAL PAYMENT

13.1 Final payment shall be made by the Owner to the Contractor when (1) the Contract has been fully performed by the Contractor except for the Contractor's responsibility to correct defective or nonconforming Work, as provided in Subparagraph 12.2.2 of the General Conditions, and to satisfy other requirements, if any, which necessarily survive final payment; (2) a final Application for Pay-

EXHIBIT 4-3 (Cont'd.)

ment and a final accounting for the Cost of the Work have been submitted by the Contractor and reviewed by the Owner's accountants; and (3) a final Certificate for Payment has then been issued by the Architect; such final payment shall be made by the Owner not more than 30 days after the issuance of the Architect's final Certificate for Payment, or as follows:

13.2   The amount of the final payment shall be calculated as follows:

13.2.1   Take the sum of the Cost of the Work substantiated by the Contractor's final accounting and the Contractor's Fee; but not more than the Guaranteed Maximum Price, if any.

13.2.2   Subtract amounts, if any, for which the Architect withholds, in whole or in part, a final Certificate for Payment as provided in Subparagraph 9.5.1 of the General Conditions or other provisions of the Contract Documents.

13.2.3   Subtract the aggregate of previous payments made by the Owner.

If the aggregate of previous payments made by the Owner exceeds the amount due the Contractor, the Contractor shall reimburse the difference to the Owner.

13.3   The Owner's accountants will review and report in writing on the Contractor's final accounting within 30 days after delivery of the final accounting to the Architect by the Contractor. Based upon such Cost of the Work as the Owner's accountants report to be substantiated by the Contractor's final accounting, and provided the other conditions of Paragraph 13.1 have been met, the Architect will, within seven days after receipt of the written report of the Owner's accountants, either issue to the Owner a final Certificate for Payment with a copy to the Contractor, or notify the Contractor and Owner in writing of the Architect's reasons for withholding a certificate as provided in Subparagraph 9.5.1 of the General Conditions. The time periods stated in this Paragraph 13.3 supersede those stated in Subparagraph 9.4.1 of the General Conditions.

13.4   If the Owner's accountants report the Cost of the Work as substantiated by the Contractor's final accounting to be less than claimed by the Contractor, the Contractor shall be entitled to demand arbitration of the disputed amount without a further decision of the Architect. Such demand for arbitration shall be made by the Contractor within 30 days after the Contractor's receipt of a copy of the Architect's final Certificate for Payment; failure to demand arbitration within this 30-day period shall result in the substantiated amount reported by the Owner's accountants becoming binding on the Contractor. Pending a final resolution by arbitration, the Owner shall pay the Contractor the amount certified in the Architect's final Certificate for Payment.

13.5   If, subsequent to final payment and at the Owner's request, the Contractor incurs costs described in Article 7 and not excluded by Article 8 to correct defective or nonconforming Work, the Owner shall reimburse the Contractor such costs and the Contractor's Fee applicable thereto on the same basis as if such costs had been incurred prior to final payment, but not in excess of the Guaranteed Maximum Price, if any. If the Contractor has participated in savings as provided in Paragraph 5.2, the amount of such savings shall be recalculated and appropriate credit given to the Owner in determining the net amount to be paid by the Owner to the Contractor.

ARTICLE 14 (19)
MISCELLANEOUS PROVISIONS

14.1   Where reference is made in this Agreement to a provision of the General Conditions or another Contract Document, the reference refers to that provision as amended or supplemented by other provisions of the Contract Documents.

14.2   Payments due and unpaid under the Contract shall bear interest from the date payment is due at the rate stated below, or in the absence thereof, at the legal rate prevailing from time to time at the place where the Project is located.

(Insert rate of interest agreed upon, if any.)

(Usury laws and requirements under the Federal Truth in Lending Act, similar state and local consumer credit laws and other regulations at the Owner's and Contractor's principal places of business, the location of the Project and elsewhere may affect the validity of this provision. Legal advice should be obtained with respect to deletions or modifications, and also regarding requirements such as written disclosures or waivers.)

EXHIBIT 4-3 (Cont'd.)

14.3 Other provisions:

ARTICLE 15 (20)

TERMINATION OR SUSPENSION

15.1 The Contract may be terminated by the Contractor as provided in Article 14 of the General Conditions; however, the amount to be paid to the Contractor under Subparagraph 14.1.2 of the General Conditions shall not exceed the amount the Contractor would be entitled to receive under Paragraph 15.3 below, except that the Contractor's Fee shall be calculated as if the Work had been fully completed by the Contractor, including a reasonable estimate of the Cost of the Work for Work not actually completed.

15.2 If a Guaranteed Maximum Price is established in Article 5, the Contract may be terminated by the Owner for cause as provided in Article 14 of the General Conditions; however, the amount, if any, to be paid to the Contractor under Subparagraph 14.2.4 of the General Conditions shall not cause the Guaranteed Maximum Price to be exceeded, nor shall it exceed the amount the Contractor would be entitled to receive under Paragraph 15.3 below.

15.3 If no Guaranteed Maximum Price is established in Article 5, the Contract may be terminated by the Owner for cause as provided in Article 14 of the General Conditions; however, the Owner shall then pay the Contractor an amount calculated as follows:

15.3.1 Take the Cost of the Work incurred by the Contractor to the date of termination.

15.3.2 Add the Contractor's Fee computed upon the Cost of the Work to the date of termination at the rate stated in Paragraph 5.1 or, if the Contractor's Fee is stated as a fixed sum in that Paragraph, an amount which bears the same ratio to that fixed-sum Fee as the Cost of the Work at the time of termination bears to a reasonable estimate of the probable Cost of the Work upon its completion.

15.3.3 Subtract the aggregate of previous payments made by the Owner.

The Owner shall also pay the Contractor fair compensation, either by purchase or rental at the election of the Owner, for any equipment owned by the Contractor which the Owner elects to retain and which is not otherwise included in the Cost of the Work under Subparagraph 15.3.1. To the extent that the Owner elects to take legal assignment of subcontracts and purchase orders (including rental agreements), the Contractor shall, as a condition of receiving the payments referred to in this Article 15, execute and deliver all such papers and take all such steps, including the legal assignment of such subcontracts and other contractual rights of the Contractor, as the Owner may require for the purpose of fully vesting in the Owner the rights and benefits of the Contractor under such subcontracts or purchase orders.

15.4 The Work may be suspended by the Owner as provided in Article 14 of the General Conditions; in such case, the Guaranteed Maximum Price, if any, shall be increased as provided in Subparagraph 14.3.2 of the General Conditions except that the term "cost of performance of the Contract" in that Subparagraph shall be understood to mean the Cost of the Work and the term "profit" shall be understood to mean the Contractor's Fee as described in Paragraphs 5.1 and 6.3 of this Agreement.

ARTICLE 16 (21)

ENUMERATION OF CONTRACT DOCUMENTS

16.1 The Contract Documents, except for Modifications issued after execution of this Agreement, are enumerated as follows:

16.1.1 The Agreement is this executed Standard Form of Agreement Between Owner and Contractor, AIA Document A111, 1987 Edition.

16.1.2 The General Conditions are the General Conditions of the Contract for Construction, AIA Document A201, 1987 Edition.

EXHIBIT 4-3 (Cont'd.)

16.1.3 The Supplementary and other Conditions of the Contract are those contained in the Project Manual dated and are as follows:

Document   **Title**   **Pages**

16.1.4 The Specifications are those contained in the Project Manual dated as in Paragraph 16.1.3, and are as follows:

(Either list the Specifications here or refer to an exhibit attached to this Agreement.)

Section   **Title**   **Pages**

EXHIBIT 4-3 (Cont'd.)

16.1.5 The Drawings are as follows, and are dated   unless a different date is shown below:

(Either list the Drawings here or refer to an exhibit attached to this Agreement.)

Number   **Title**   **Date**

16.1.6 The Addenda, if any, are as follows:

Number   **Date**   **Pages**

Portions of Addenda relating to bidding requirements are not part of the Contract Documents unless the bidding requirements are also enumerated in this Article 16.

EXHIBIT 4-3 (Cont'd.)

16.1.7 Other Documents, if any, forming part of the Contract Documents are as follows:

(List here any additional documents which are intended to form part of the Contract Documents. The General Conditions provide that bidding requirements such as advertisement or invitation to bid, Instructions to Bidders, sample forms and the Contractor's bid are not part of the Contract Documents unless enumerated in this Agreement. They should be listed here only if intended to be part of the Contract Documents.)

This Agreement is entered into as of the day and year first written above and is executed in at least three original copies of which one is to be delivered to the Contractor, one to the Architect for use in the administration of the Contract, and the remainder to the Owner.

OWNER   CONTRACTOR

(22)

_____   _____
(Signature)   *(Signature)*

_____   _____
(Printed name and title)   *(Printed name and title)*

commercial building with on-site parking for 100 cars, in addition to other improvements, on a site located at the southeast corner of Main and 5th Streets, Anaheim, California."

5. The name of the architect responsible for the plans that will be used for construction.

6. Article 1 is broad language describing the documents considered to be a part of the contract.

7. Article 2 describes in more detail the work to be performed. There should be specific reference to the plans to be used; for example, "Sheets A-1 through A-8, dated May 1, 1986." Check the dates against the plans used during loan analysis and by the appraiser. Any alterations should be reviewed to insure that there has been no material change that could affect appraised value or the viability of the project.

8. Article 3 broadly describes the contractor's duties and relationship to the owner. The article also describes the owner's relationship with the contractor.

9. Article 4 should contain language establishing the date on which construction will commence, and the date by which the project will be completed. Your loan should provide sufficient time to complete the work in accordance with the terms of the contract.

10. Article 5 gives the total price to be paid for the construction work. This price should be the total cost figure from the cost breakdown given to the lender by the contractor. Sufficient loan funds should be available to cover this cost. Other clauses can be added to the Article. For example, there might be language to describe which party benefits from savings on the job, if any, or one indicating the date by which the contractor must begin work in order for the owner to avoid an increase in the price of the contract. There are also provisions for a Guaranteed Maximum Price; that is, a price which represents the maximum the contractor will charge for the job.

11. Article 6 gives procedures for dealing with changes in the work, referred to as Change Orders. Make sure that the owner has the right to approve changes before any work is begun. You should reserve the right to approve changes also, or at least those changes over a certain dollar amount.

12. Article 7 describes the costs for the work which must be reimbursed by the owner. The lender should be satisfied that these costs are included in the cost breakdown, and that the provision is adequate for the job. If the provision is insufficient the owner will need to provide more funds later, something he may be unable to do.

13. Article 8 lists costs that the owner will not be asked to reimburse. These are usually costs of doing business that are separate from the construction contract.

14. Article 9 defines which party receives any discounts, rebates, or refunds realized during the course of construction.

15. Article 10 provides that work not performed by the general contractor will be covered by subcontracts.

16. Article 11 requires that the contractor maintain proper accounting records, and that the records be made available to the owner should he desire to review them. This clause should also give the lender the right to audit the records should the need arise.

17. Article 12 defines the form and method for handling payment requests, both for contracts with and without a guaranteed maximum price. It also details the terms under which payments are to be made to the contractor. Payment terms should be

consistent with the lender's procedures for disbursing a construction loan. You should pay special attention to the requirements for making the final contractor payment. Before final payment is made the project should be satisfactorily completed, and there should be no liens left against the property. Further, all necessary permits and approvals from governmental agencies should have been received.

18. Article 13 contains language outlining the handling of the final payment to the contractor. Final payment should be made only when both owner and lender are satisfied with the project.

19. Article 14 contains any Miscellaneous provisions of the contract. The lender should read and understand added clauses. This article is frequently used by contractors to identify work that is not included in the contract, work for which the contractor is not responsible. This work must be performed by someone, however. If the contractor doesn't do it, then the owner will need to contract with someone else later or perform the work himself. The lender should be satisified that the owner is qualified to handle the tasks required, and, further, that the funds needed are available in the loan.

20. Article 15 contains the terms under which the contract can be terminated. Be aware of any clauses that are added and make sure they are acceptable.

21. Article 16 provides space for a detailed and specific listing of all the contract documents. Make sure that you have all the ones that are appropriate and important to your loan.

22. The contract should be executed by the parties involved.

Building Plans and Their Uses

Plans are an important piece of documentation, and should be reviewed early in the loan analysis. Plans give the details on the building to be constructed, as well as the location of the building on the site. A good set of plans is a must for an accurate appraisal.

Building plans evolve over time. They start out as schematic drawings, concepts of various building designs that would fit on the subject site. Schemes are line drawings with a plot plan. They have no dimensions and may not even be drawn to scale.

Once a particular scheme has been selected by the owner, the architect will draw comprehensive preliminary plans. These include some dimensions and will be drawn to scale. Their purpose is to provide the owner with plans that can be presented to lenders, governmental agencies, and contractors.

The last stage in the architectural process is the development of working drawings. Working drawings are complete plans that show all dimensions and engineering detail. These are the plans that will be approved by the planning department of the local government. When the governmental body has approved these drawings, the plans will be used to build the building. The lender should receive approved working drawings before the loan is disbursed. They should be signed by the borrower and contractor. After funding, the working drawings can be given to the disbursement people for use in making periodic progress inspections during the course of the construction loan.

Using Project Specifications

Specifications are detailed lists of the materials to be used in the construction of the building. They are typically written by the architect and complement the building plans. Many times specification sheets are included as a part of the plans. Other times they may be a separate exhibit.

Exhibit 4-4 is a sample specification sheet that can be used by the lender. It should be given to the architect or the contractor to complete. You can review the completed form to satisfy yourself about project quality.

Have the form filled out as follows:

1. The name of the builder, usually the general contractor.
2. The address of the property on which the building will be built.
3. The name of the owner, your borrower.
4. The owner's phone number.
5. The description of the materials to be used for construction, including both type of materials and quantity. The quality of materials should correspond to any requirements the architect may have written into his plans. If the specifications are not provided by the architect, have him review and sign them.
6. The date that the specifications are signed.
7. The signatures of the owner, the contractor, and the lender should be affixed to the document. If appropriate, space can be added for the architect's signature.

Advantages of the CPM Schedule

A CPM schedule refers to a concept for planning called the "critical path method." Such a presentation provides a schedule for the various parts of construction, showing which work must be completed before other work can take place. For example, a CPM may show that plumbing under the building must be complete before the concrete slab can be poured. A CPM schedule also indicates completion dates that must be met for the various elements of the work in order to keep the job on a path that will result in completion by the desired date.

Preparation of a CPM does not have to be a requirement for granting a loan. Knowing the contractor is following one, however, should give the lender comfort that there is a better chance the project will stay on the proper time schedule that will result in completion in accordance with the loan agreement.

How to Find Out More About Unfamiliar Contractors

Exhibit 4-5 shows a Contractor's Qualification Statement. This form can be used to obtain information on the owner's contractor. The form is especially useful when the lender doesn't know the contractor and has not done business with him before. The depth of information required will serve as a good check on the qualifications of the contractor and will demonstrate his ability to properly complete the job.

EXHIBIT 4-4
OWNER CONSTRUCTION SPECIFICATIONS

BUILDER _____(1)_____ JOB ADDRESS _____(2)_____

OWNER _____(3)_____ PHONE _____(4)_____

INSTRUCTIONS

RESPONSIBILITY: The following information constitutes the owner's building specifica-tions. It is the responsibility of the owner and his contractor to comply with them fully. Any deviation from (1) these specifications, or (2) the _____ Bank's loan minimum specifications, by the owner, his contractor, or sub-contractors, will not relieve the owner of his responsibility to comply therewith.

DESCRIPTION: Describe all materials and equipment to be used in construction. Work, material, and equipment not specifically described below and shown on plans, will not be considered in the determination of reasonable value. Include no alternate "or equal" phases.

PLAN CHANGES: If it becomes necessary to make changes or variations from the original plans or specifications, such changes shall be submitted in writing to the _____ Bank, Real Estate Department for approval before proceeding with the work.

DESCRIPTION OF MATERIALS (5)

1. SOIL: Type _____ Fill: Yes ___ No ___ Compacted: Yes ___ No ___
   Reports Available: Soils __ Geological __ Grading Plan __ Excavation: Cubic Yards __

2. FOUNDATION: Type _____ Materials _____ Engineered? _____
   Reinforcing: Footages _____ Wall _____
   Slab Reinforcing _____ Base Course Material _____
   Damp Proofing Method _____ (Required in Living area slabs)

3. SUB FLOOR: First Floor _____ Second Floor _____

4. FRAMING: Girders: Species _____ Grade _____ Special _____
   Studs: Species _____ Grade _____ Special _____
   Joists/Rafters: Species _____ Grade _____
   Trusses _____ Beam Material _____ Other _____
   Roof Sheathing Material _____ Facia _____

5. ROOF: Material & Grade _____
   Underlayment weight _____ # of Plys _____ Special Nailing _____
   Aggregate _____ Size & Weight _____
   Pitch _____ Gutter & Downspout _____ Lineal Feet _____

6. EXTERIOR WALLS: Stucco _____ Siding Material _____ Other _____
   Eve Overhang Material _____ Soffits _____ Veneer _____

7. INSULATION: (Specify material and "R" rating or thickness)
   Exterior Walls _____ 1st Fl. Ceiling _____ 2nd Fl. Ceiling _____

8. SOUND CONTROL: Insulated Party Walls _____ Stagged Studs _____ Elastizell _____
   Other _____

9. INTERIOR WALLS: Lath & Plaster ____ Drywall ____ Thickness _____ Paneling _____

10. HEATING: Fuel _____ BTU/Watts _____
    Detail: FAU ___ Highboy ___ Wall Furn. ___ Radiant: Cable: _____ Wattage ___
    Heat-pump _____ Other _____ Engineered? _____

11. AIR CONDITIONING: Type _____ BTU Tons _____
    Detail: Nr. Units ____ Wall ____ Dual Pack _____ Central _____ Gas/Elec. _____

12. FIREPLACE: Masonry _____ Matel _____ Facing Material _____
    Woodburning _____ Log Lighter _____ Prefabricated _____ Free Standing _____

13. PLUMBING: Material: Drain & Waste _____ Vents _____ Nr. Gas Meter _____
    Water Service ____ Water Lines ____ Installation: Under Fl. ____ Overhead _____
    Water Heater: Type _____ Make _____ Size _____ Recirc. Pump _____
    Sink: Material _____ Color _____ Type _____ Make _____
    Lavatory: Nr. _____ Material _____ Color _____ Make _____
    Bath Tub: Nr. _____ Material _____ Color _____ Make _____
    Showers: Tub _____ Nr. _____ Wall _____ Stall _____ Nr. _____ Wall _____
    Enclosures: Nr. _____ Material _____ Mirrors: Plate _____ Crystal _____
    Fire Sprinklers: Size of Main _____ Nr. Heads _____ Alarm System _____

14. SEWAGE DISPOSAL: Public _____ Local _____ Individual _____

EXHIBIT 4-4 (Cont'd.)

15. ELECTRICAL: Flex _____ Romex _____ Number of 220 Volt Outlets ___ Color TV Lead in _____

16. CABINETS: Kit. Matl. _____ Finish _____ Pullmans: Matl. _____ Finish _____
    Cabinet Doors: Lip: ___ Flush ___ Overlay ___ Thickness _____ Raised Panel _____
    S.C.A.C.M. Grade: Standard _____ Medium _____ Premium _____

17. TILE-FORMICA: Drainboard _____ Splash Height _____ Bath Pullman _____
    Shower Pan _____ Shower Walls _____ Tub Walls _____ Height _____

18. DOORS: Interior Passage - type _____ Materials _____
    Interior: Closet: Type _____ Material _____ Mirrors ___ Nr. ___
    Exterior: Type _____ Material _____ Spec'l. _____
    S/Glasse Door: Brand _____ Plate _____ Crystal _____ Tempered _____

19. WINDOWS: Type _____ Material _____ Brand _____

20. PAINTING: Kit. & Bath: _____ Nr. Coats _____
    Other Interior Walls: Material _____ Nr. Coats _____
    Interior Trim _____ Coats _____ Exterior Trim _____ Coats _____
    Stucco Finish: Color Coat _____ Brush Coat _____ Special _____

21. FLOOR COVERING:
    Carpet Brand _____ Cost per Yard _____ Pad Type _____ Wt. _____
    Rooms _____
    Resilient Tile _____ Sheet _____
    Rooms _____
    Other _____ Rooms _____

22. DRAPES: Material _____ Nr. Openings _____

23. APPLIANCES: (State whether Gas or Electric - where applicable)

ITEM	AMOUNT	BRAND	MANUFACTURER NUMBER
Free Standing Range & Oven			
Drop-In Range & Oven			
Separate Built-In Range & Oven			
Garbage Disposal			
Dishwasher			
Hood & Fan			
Radio-Intercom			
Other			

24. BALCONIES: Floor Material _____ Ceiling Material _____ Rail Material _____

25. ELEVATOR: Manufacturer _____ Capacity _____ Number of Stops _____
    Electric _____ Hydraulic _____ Speed Per Minutes _____ Automatic Door Control _____

26. SPECIAL: Trash Chute _____ Garage Ventilation System _____

27. DRIVEWAY: Material _____ Thickness _____ Special Base _____

28. YARD IMPROVEMENTS: Front Landscaping _____ Front Sprinklers _____ Cost $ _____
    Rear Landscaping _____ Rear Sprinklers _____ Cost $ _____

29. WALLS AND FENCES:

    Block Wall _____ Lin. Ft. _____ Height _____ Width _____ Reinforced _____
    Eng'd Wall _____ Lin. Ft. _____ Height _____ Width _____
    Chain Link _____ Lin. Ft. _____ Height _____ Top Rail _____
    Wood Fence _____ Lin. Ft. _____ Height _____ Type _____

30. SWIMMING POOL: Dimensions _____ Maximum Depth _____ Minimum Depth _____
    Filter _____ Heater _____ Chlorinator _____ Diving Board _____ Decking - Sq. Feet _____

31. SPECIAL FEATURES: _____
    _____
    _____

32. SPECIAL INSTRUCTIONS: Please Sign and Date.

    DATE _____(6)_____

    OWNER _____

    CONTRACTOR _____(7)_____

    LOAN OFFICER _____

EXHIBIT 4-5

THE AMERICAN INSTITUTE OF ARCHITECTS

AIA Document A305

Contractor's Qualification Statement

1986 EDITION

This form is approved and recommended by The American Institute of Architects (AIA) and The Associated General Contractors of America (AGC) for use in evaluating the qualifications of contractors. No endorsement of the submitting party or verification of the information is made by the AIA or AGC.

The Undersigned certifies under oath that the information provided herein is true and sufficiently complete so as not to be misleading.

SUBMITTED TO: (1)

ADDRESS:

SUBMITTED BY:

NAME: (2)

ADDRESS:

PRINCIPAL OFFICE:

(3)

Corporation ☐
Partnership ☐
Individual ☐
Joint Venture ☐
Other ☐

NAME OF PROJECT (if applicable): (4)

TYPE OF WORK (file separate form for each Classification of Work): (5)

_____ General Construction   _____ HVAC

_____ Plumbing   _____ Electrical

_____ Other_____
            (please specify)

EXHIBIT 4-5 (Cont'd.)

1. ORGANIZATION

1.1   How many years has your organization been in business as a Contractor?

(6)

1.2   How many years has your organization been in business under its present business name?

(7)

1.2.1   Under what other or former names has your organization operated?

(8)

1.3   If your organization is a corporation, answer the following: (9)
1.3.1   Date of incorporation:
1.3.2   State of incorporation:
1.3.3   President's name:
1.3.4   Vice-president's name(s):

1.3.5   Secretary's name:
1.3.6   Treasurer's name:

1.4   If your organization is a partnership, answer the following: (10)
1.4.1   Date of organization:
1.4.2   Type of partnership (if applicable):
1.4.3   Name(s) of general partner(s):

1.5   If your organization is individually owned, answer the following: (11)
1.5.1   Date of organization:
1.5.2   Name of owner:

EXHIBIT 4-5 (Cont'd.)

1.6   If the form of your organization is other than those listed above, describe it and name the principals:

(12)

2.   LICENSING

2.1   List jurisdictions and trade categories in which your organization is legally qualified to do business, and indicate registration or license numbers, if applicable.

(13)

2.2   List jurisdictions in which your organization's partnership or trade name is filed.

(14)

3.   EXPERIENCE

3.1   List the categories of work that your organization normally performs with its own forces.

(15)

3.2   Claims and Suits. (If the answer to any of the questions below is yes, please attach details.)

     3.2.1   Has your organization ever failed to complete any work awarded to it?

(16)

     3.2.2   Are there any judgments, claims, arbitration proceedings or suits pending or outstanding against your organization or its officers?

(17)

     3.2.3   Has your organization filed any law suits or requested arbitration with regard to construction contracts within the last five years?

(18)

3.3   Within the last five years, has any officer or principal of your organization ever been an officer or principal of another organization when it failed to complete a construction contract? (If the answer is yes, please attach details.)

(19)

EXHIBIT 4-5 (Cont'd.)

3.4   On a separate sheet, list major construction projects your organization has in progress, giving the name of project, owner, architect, contract amount, percent complete and scheduled completion date.   **(20)**

    3.4.1   State total worth of work in progress and under contract:

        (21)

3.5   On a separate sheet, list the major projects your organization has completed in the past five years, giving the name of project, owner, architect, contract amount, date of completion and percentage of the cost of the work performed with your own forces.   **(22)**

    3.5.1   State average annual amount of construction work performed during the past five years:

        (23)

3.6   On a separate sheet, list the construction experience and present commitments of the key individuals of your organization.   **(24)**

4.   REFERENCES

4.1   Trade References:

        (25)

4.2   Bank References: **(26)**

4.3   Surety:

    4.3.1   Name of bonding company:

        (27)

    4.3.2   Name and address of agent:

        (28)

EXHIBIT 4-5 (Cont'd.)

5. FINANCING

5.1   Financial Statement.   (29)

         5.1.1   Attach a financial statement, preferably audited, including your organization's latest balance sheet and income statement showing the following items:

                 Current Assets (e.g., cash, joint venture accounts, accounts receivable, notes receivable, accrued income, deposits, materials inventory and prepaid expenses);

                 Net Fixed Assets;

                 Other Assets;

                 Current Liabilities (e.g., accounts payable, notes payable, accrued expenses, provision for income taxes, advances, accrued salaries and accrued payroll taxes);

                 Other Liabilities (e.g., capital, capital stock, authorized and outstanding shares par values, earned surplus and retained earnings).

         5.1.2   Name and address of firm preparing attached financial statement, and date thereof:
                                     (30)

         5.1.3   Is the attached financial statement for the identical organization named on page one?

                                             (31)

         5.1.4   If not, explain the relationship and financial responsibility of the organization whose financial statement is provided (e.g., parent-subsidiary).

                 (32)

5.2   Will the organization whose financial statement is attached act as guarantor of the contract for construction?

                               (33)

EXHIBIT 4-5 (Cont'd.)

6.   SIGNATURE

6.1   Dated at   this   day of
                                                    19

Name of Organization:

By: (34)

Title:

6.2

M   being
duly sworn deposes and says that the information provided herein is true and sufficiently complete so as not to be
misleading.

Subscribed and sworn before me this   day of
                                                    19

Notary Public:

My Commission Expires: (35)

The form should be filled out with the following information:

1. The name and address of the party to whom the report is addressed. Preferably the report should be addressed to the lender.

2. The name and address of the general contractor. If the contractor has a principal office different from the office with which you're dealing, that should be noted in the space provided.

3. The nature of the contractor entity, whether corporate, partnership, or individual.

4. The name of the project for which the contract is written.

5. The major type of work the general contractor performs.

6. The number of years the organization or individual has functioned as a general contractor.

7. The number of years the organization has had the same business name.

8. Other names under which the contractor entity has done business.

9. If the organization is a corporation, key corporate dates and officers can be filled in.

10. If the organization is a partnership, information should be provided concerning the date the organization was formed and the name and address of all the partners.

11. For organizations that are individually owned, the date of formation and the name of the owner should be given.

12. For organizations other than corporations or partnerships, describe the organization and name the various principals of the company.

13. List the states in which the organization can do business, and the classification of the licenses issued in those states. The license number should be provided to facilitate credit checks by the lender.

14. List the states in which the trade name of the organization is filed.

15. The contractor should detail the construction work performed with his own employees. For example, a contractor might subcontract all work except concrete, because he has expertise in this area and can perform the work better or more economically with his own employees.

16. This section should be completed in detail if the contractor has ever failed to finish a job. Such a failure would be cause for considerable concern on the part of the lender. The details and circumstances should be completely explained and thoroughly reviewed by your staff.

17. Details should be given regarding any judgments or pending lawsuits involving the contracting organization.

18. Information regarding suits filed by the contractor against owners should be given.

19. Failures in which key officers of the contractor have been involved while working for other entities should be explained in detail. Problems that may have been created or exacerbated by employees of the current contractor when they worked in other companies would be cause for concern. There should be assurances that the problem cannot be repeated.

20. In this section, or on an attached sheet, the contractor should give a complete listing of all work in progress as of the date the statement is prepared. Not only will this give the lender references to check regarding the contractor's current performance, but it will allow for an analysis of the contractor's workload.

21. The dollar value of work in progress or under contract should be outlined.

22. Information similar to that requested for work in progress should be provided for completed projects. You can check these references for comments concerning the quality of the contractor's work, and whether the job was brought in on time and within budget.

23. The dollar amount of work performed over the last five years gives an idea of how busy the contractor has been, and is also a measure of his success.

24. Construction experience of the contractor's key personnel should be given. The lender will want to pay special attention to the experience of the people who will be involved with the job he is planning to finance.

25. Trade references from key suppliers should be provided. The lender should check to see that bills are paid in a timely manner, and in keeping with subcontract terms.

26. Bank references should be given and checked by the lender.

27. & 28. Information about the bonding company and the surety agent should be given. Whether or not a contractor can obtain bonds is important information even if the lender does not plan to require one. If an insurance company is willing to provide bonds to the contractor, they have checked him out and are satisfied with his financial condition and performance record.

29. Financial statements in sufficient detail should be provided to the lender. You can make your own analysis of the contractor's ability to carry the job through to completion.

30. This section should be completed with the name and address of the accounting organization that prepared the contractor's financial statements, along with the name of a contact to consult with any questions that arise.

31. & 32. Many times the contractor may not have statements prepared for the contracting entity, but rather for a parent entity. If so the relationship between the entities should be explained. Indicate whether one entity will act as guarantor for the work performed by the other entity.

33. If financial statements are provided for an organization other than the contractor, then the issue of guarantees should be addressed.

34. The document should be dated and signed by the contractor.

35. This section provides space for a notary public to notarize the signature of the contractor.

The Contractor's Qualification Statement can provide a wealth of information that will help the lender determine whether the work will be properly performed.

Using the Contractor's Resume as an Alternative to the Contractor's Qualification Statement

A Contractor's Qualification Statement may require more information than is needed. The lender might have general knowledge about the contractor and may only need to be brought up to date about recently completed work and work in progress. A contractor resume can be used for this purpose. With the resume the lender can determine what work the contractor has been doing, and whether the workload is manageable. The list can also serve as a source of references concerning the contractor's performance.

The resume should include type of property (residential, industrial, office, etc.), dollar amount of contract, percent completed, name of owner, phone number of owner, scheduled completion date or date completed, name and phone number of lender financing the job, and explanation of any problem areas that delayed completion.

Credit Reports

A credit report on the contractor should be obtained. Credit reports are a good source of information regarding payment habits. Many of them list any items of a legal nature filed against the contractor. A BICA report, prepared by the Building Industry Credit Association, is one such report.

A credit report can list all Mechanic's Liens and suits that have been filed against a contractor. The contracting industry is litigious by nature, and all contractors have legal items pending from time to time. A lender should be concerned by an overly lengthy list, which may demonstrate financial problems.

Ask the contractor to respond with comments on major items. He should detail how the item arose, the nature of the dispute, and how he plans to resolve the matter.

EXHIBIT 4-6

CHECKLIST

	Needed	Date Requested	Date Received
1. Cost breakdown:			
From Contractor	_____	_____	_____
From Owner	_____	_____	_____
2. List of Prepaid Items	_____	_____	_____
3. Architectural Contract	_____	_____	_____
4. Construction Contract	_____	_____	_____
5. Preliminary Plans	_____	_____	_____
6. Final Working Drawings	_____	_____	_____
7. Specifications	_____	_____	_____
8. Critical Path Schedule	_____	_____	_____
9. Contractor's Qualification Statement	_____	_____	_____
10. Contractor's Resume	_____	_____	_____
11. Credit Report	_____	_____	_____

End Note

Use the checklist in Exhibit 4-6 to decide which documents should be obtained to assist in underwriting construction loans.

The loan officer can indicate "yes or no" in the "needed" column for those documents that are required. The date the document is requested and the date it is received should be noted in the respective column.

The construction lending process is a difficult one that requires extra documentation. It is important that the lender be satisfied that a project will be successfully carried through to completion. Care taken during the underwriting process, before commitment and funding, will help insure a successful loan.

5

How to Document
Loan Approval

Once the lender has analyzed the information provided and is satisfied that a loan should be granted, approval within the lending organization must take place. How approval is granted depends on the internal guidelines set by the organization. This chapter will deal with forms that can be used to document loan approval internally, and then communicate that approval to the borrower.

Using the Loan Approval Summary Sheet

Exhibit 5-1 is a form that can be used to summarize the important facts about the loan being approved. It can be used by loan officers within the real estate department to document approval. Other lending officers can use the form to communicate a loan approval request to the real estate department.

1. The name of the borrower.
2. The amount of the loan for which approval is being sought.
3. The proposed rate of interest to be charged.
4. The proposed term of the loan. If term and amortization differ, both should be indicated.
5. The proposed monthly payments of principal and interest.
6. The security instruments to be taken; for example, first Trust Deed.
7. The location of the subject property.
8. A description of the improvements that are located on the subject property. For example, this might read "A 3-story, garden office building with approximately 20,000 square feet net rentable area and on-site parking for 45 cars."
9. The appraised value of the property based on an acceptable appraisal report and reviewed by the appraisal department of your institution.
10. The loan-to-value ratio (loan amount divided by appraised value).
11. The loan fee to be charged; for example, "$20,000 (2%)."

EXHIBIT 5-1

INCOME PROPERTY LOAN APPROVAL FORM

Applicant: (1)

Loan Request	Amount: (2)	Rate: (3)	Term: (4)
	Monthly Payments: (5)		
Security In-struments	(6)		
Location of Property	(7)		
Type of Im-provements	(8)		
Appraised Value	(9)	Loan (10) % Ratio:	Loan $(11) Fee:
Purpose of the Loan	(12)		
Source of Repayment	(13)	Cash Payment or Equity:	(14)
Other Debts Due Bank (Excluding Subject Appli-cation)	Real Estate: (15)	Commercial (16)	Consumer: (17)

Deposit Accounts (Use Average Balances)	Carried: Savings: Checking: (18)	Influenced—Explain How: Savings Checking: (19)
Guarantor	(20)	
Guarantor's Other Debts Due Bank and Average Balances	(21)	
Remarks	(22)	
Attachments	(23)	

EXHIBIT 5-1 (Cont'd.)

Prepared by: Recommended by:
—————— (24) ——————   —————— (25) ——————

SIGNIFICANT RATIOS	APPROVAL SIGNATURES	
	Date	Signature
Loan to Value____ (26) ____	____ (27) ____	____ (28) ____
Loan per Sq. Ft.____ (29) ____	————————	————————
Rent per Sq. Ft.____ (30) ____	————————	————————
Debt Service____ (31) ____	————————	————————
Coverage		

12. The loan purpose should be clearly stated; for example, "New construction" or "Refinance."

13. Define the source of repayment for the subject loan.

14. List the sources of equity to be used as down payment.

15. List the other real estate debt owed to your institution by the borrower.

16. List the other commercial debt owed to your institution by the borrower.

17. List the other consumer or installment debt owed to your institution by the borrower.

18. List the average balances for savings and checking accounts carried with your institution by the borrower.

19. List the average balances for savings and checking accounts carried with your institution that are influenced in any way by the borrower. An explanation should be given as to the nature of the influence.

20. If the loan is to be guaranteed, the name of the guarantor should be shown.

21. Indicate and explain the guarantor's relationship with your institution, including both deposits and loans.

22. This section should be used for summary remarks about the credit request. A more detailed writeup and analysis should be attached to thoroughly explain the reasons why approval is warranted.

23. Any attachments to the approval sheet should be listed; for example, writeup, worksheet, location map, etc.

24. The party preparing the approval and writeup, if not signing as an approver, should sign here as preparer.

25. The head of the real estate department or team, as applicable, can sign here if not signing as an approver.

26. The loan-to-value ratio should be placed here.

27. The date that the particular signer approved the loan should be shown.

28. Spaces are provided for the signatures necessary for loan approval within the institution.

29. The loan per square foot of building improvements.

30. The rent per square foot of building improvements.

31. The debt service coverage ratio.

Any other key ratios deemed important by your institution can be put in the spaces at the end of the form. The form summarizes all of the key elements of the loan requested in two pages, making review easier. Any supporting data needed for loan approval within your organization should be attached to the form before it is circulated for approval.

Worksheets to Use to Summarize Key Elements

Use of worksheets is an excellent way to summarize the key elements of the real estate on which a loan is being contemplated. They can be attached to the loan writeup as an exhibit, if desired, or simply made a part of the file so that anyone who later looks into the loan can have a quick picture of the key elements of the transaction. They also serve to help more junior loan officers quickly decide whether the loan requested is appropriate, saving wasted time and effort analyzing deals that don't qualify.

Exhibit 5-2 is a worksheet for use with apartment projects. Fill it in as follows:

1. Check the appropriate box to indicate whether the project is existing or proposed.

2. If the project is existing, indicate the years for which fiscal year-end operating statements were obtained and reviewed.

3. If proposed indicate whether or not a pro-forma (estimated) operating statement was obtained from the owner.

4. Indicate the number of units by type in the project; for example, 24 1-bedroom units, 22 2-bedroom units, etc.

5. Indicate the square footage or square footage range for each type of unit.

6. Indicate the rent per month or range of rents for each type of unit.

7. Show the rent per square foot or the range of rents per square foot.

8. Use this space to indicate other types of units not already reflected on the worksheet.

9. Total the various columns to arrive at a project total.

10. Identify any amenities that the subject property has, especially those that will result in higher or lower rents when compared with the rest of the market.

11. Identify major competing projects.

12. Show the number of units for each competing project reviewed.

13. The type of units for competing projects reviewed.

14. The square footage size or range of sizes for competing unit types.

15. Give the rent or range of rents per month for units in competing projects.

16. Show the rent or range of rents per square foot for units in competing projects.

17. Discuss market occupancy levels for competing projects.

18. Indicate the number of each type of unit for the subject project. This figure can be obtained from the project details schedule in the first part of the worksheet.

19. Indicate the type of unit; for example, 1-bedroom.

20. Project the rent per month anticipated for each type of unit in the subject project. This should be consistent with the rents being obtained in competing projects, as reflected in the Major Competition section of the worksheet.

21. Reflect the Gross Monthly Rents for each type of unit, derived by multiplying the number of units times the rent per month.

EXHIBIT 5-2

APARTMENT WORKSHEET

Section 1 - Project Feasibility

A. Project is: (1)

( ) Existing

If existing, fiscal year-end financial statements reviewed:

_____ (2) _____

( ) Proposed

If proposed, did borrower provide a pro-forma statement of operations?

_____ (3) _____

B. Project Details

	Number of Units	Square Footage	Rent per Month	Rent per Sq Ft.
Efficiencies				
1 bedroom	___ (4) ___	___ (5) ___	___ (6) ___	___ (7) ___
2 bedrooms				
3 bedrooms				
___ (8) ___				
Total (9)				

Project Amenities: _____

_____ (10) _____

C. Major Competition:

Project	Units	Type	Size	Rent per Month	Rent per Sq Ft.
1. _____					
2. ___ (11) ___	___ (12) ___	(13) ___	(14) ___	(15) ___	(16)
3. _____					
4. _____					

D. Market occupancy level for competing units is: _____

_____ (17) _____

Section 2 - Income Analysis

Number of Units	Type of Units	Rent Per Mo.	Gross Monthly Rents	Gross Annual Rents
___ (18) ___	___ (19) ___	___ (20) ___	___ (21) ___	___ (22) ___

EXHIBIT 5-2 (Cont'd.)

Scheduled Gross Rent _____ (23) _____
Less: Vacancy and Collection Loss _____ (24) _____
Effective Gross Rent _____ (25) _____
Less: Operating Expenses (26)
    Real Estate Taxes _____
    Insurance _____
    Repairs/Maintenance _____
    Utilities _____
    On-Site Manager _____
    Professional Management _____
    Other:
    _____ _____
    _____ _____
    Reserves _____
    Total Operating Expenses _____ (27) _____
    Net Operating Income _____ (28) _____
    Capitalization Rate _____ (29) _____
    Market Value Estimate _____ (30) _____
Section 3 - Key Ratios
Debt Service Coverage _____ (31) _____
Breakeven Ratio _____ (32) _____
Operating Expense Ratio _____ (33) _____
Loan-to-Value _____ (34) _____
Loan per Square Foot _____ (35) _____
Loan per Unit _____ (36) _____
Discuss any ratios that are below the underwriting guidelines for apartment
loans: _____
_____ (37) _____
_____

Prepared by: _____ (38) _____ Date: _____ (39) _____
Approved by: _____ (40) _____ Date: _____ (41) _____

22. Show the Gross Annual Rents for each type of unit, derived by multiplying the Gross Monthly Rents by 12.

23. Scheduled Gross Rent is the sum of the various figures in the Gross Annual Rents column.

24. Vacancy and Collection Loss should be consistent with the level of market vacancy, as determined and discussed in Section 1, Part D of the worksheet.

25. Effective Gross Rent is the remainder derived by subtracting the Vacancy figure from Scheduled Gross Rent.

26. All of the anticipated annual operating expenses for the subject project should be estimated.

27. Total operating expenses can be shown in this space.

28. Net Operating Income is derived by subtracting Operating Expenses from Effective Gross Income.

EXHIBIT 5-3

INDUSTRIAL/WAREHOUSE WORKSHEET

( ) Industrial Building   ( ) Warehouse Building

Section 1—Project Feasibility

A. Project is: (1)
   ( ) Existing
       If existing, fiscal year-end financial statements
       reviewed:
       _____ (2) _____
   ( ) Proposed
       If proposed, did borrower provide a pro forma
       statement of operations? _____ (3) _____

B. Project Details
   Number of Buildings _____ (4) _____
   Total Square Footage _____ (5) _____
   Net Rentable Area _____ (6) _____
   Office Area _____ (7) _____
   Land Area _____ (8) _____
   Parking _____ (9) _____
   Number of Truck Docks_____ (10) _____
   Number of Truck Doors_____ (11) _____
     (Excl. Docks)
   Major Features: _____
   _____ (12) _____

C. Major Competition:

Project	Type	Size/ Percent Office	Rent per Month	Rent per Sq. Ft.
1._____	_____	_____	_____	_____
2.__ (13) __	__ (14) __	__ (15) __	__ (16) __	__ (17) __
3._____	_____	_____	_____	_____
4._____	_____	_____	_____	_____

D. Market Occupancy levels for similar properties are:_____
   _____ (18) _____

E. Lease Analysis (if subject property is or is to be leased)
   Date of Lease: _____ (19) _____
   Lessor: _____ (20) _____
   Lessee: _____ (21) _____
   Term of Lease: _____ (22) _____
   Rent: _____ (23) _____
   _____

EXHIBIT 5-3 (Cont'd.)

Expenses Paid by: _____ (24) _____
_____
_____

Section 2—Income Analysis
    Scheduled Gross Rent   _____ (25) _____
        (Estimated Rent Per SqFt.
        X Subject SqFt.)
    Less: Vacancy Allowance   _____ (26) _____
    Effective Gross Income   _____ (27) _____
    Less: Operating Expenses   _____ (28) _____
    Net Operating Expenses   _____ (29) _____
    Capitalization Rate   _____ (30) _____
    Market Value Estimate   = = = = (31) = = = =
Section 3—Key Ratios
  Debt Service Coverage   _____ (32) _____
  Breakeven Ratio   _____ (33) _____
  Operating Expense Ratio   _____ (34) _____
  Loan-to-Value   _____ (35) _____
  Loan per Square Foot   _____ (36) _____
  Land-to-Building Ratio   _____ (37) _____
Discuss any ratios that are below the underwriting guidelines for industrial/
warehouse property loans: _____
_____
_____ (38) _____
_____

Prepared by: _____ (39) _____   Date: _____ (40) _____
Approved by: _____ (41) _____   Date: _____ (42) _____

29. Show the capitalization rate indicated by your market research.

30. The value estimate derived from the previous analysis.

31 -36. Spaces are provided for key ratios important to the analysis of apartment projects.

37. Any ratio that deviates in a major way from the underwriting guidelines of your institution should be discussed. The reason for the deviation should be adequately explained and its impact on the overall risk of the anticipated loan should be assessed.

38 - 39. The person preparing the worksheet should sign and date in the spaces provided.

40 - 41. Space is provided for an approval signature by a more senior officer or department head.

Exhibit 5-3 is a worksheet that can be used for analyzing industrial or warehouse projects. Fill it out with the following information:

1. Check the appropriate box to indicate whether the subject is existing or proposed.

2. If the project is existing, indicate the years for which fiscal year-end operating statements were obtained and reviewed.

3. If proposed indicate whether or not a pro-forma, that is, estimated, operating statement was obtained from the owner.

4. Fill in the number of buildings in the subject project.

5. Fill in the total, or gross, square footage of the building(s).

6. Use this space to show the net rentable area of the building(s).

7. Give the square footage of office space in the buildings(s), and the percentage of office space to net rentable area.

8. Show the square footage of the land area on the site.

9. Give the number of on-site parking spaces, and indicate whether available parking meets the code requirements.

10. Truck-high docks allow trucks to back into a well, putting the truck bed level with the floor of the building. Note the number of such docks available in the subject building(s).

11. How many truck doors are there that are separate from the truck docks.

12. Identify and describe the major features of the building, especially those that will lead to higher or lower rents relative to the rest of the market.

13. Identify the major market competition for the subject project.

14. Note the type of building, warehouse or industrial.

15. Give the square foot size of the competing building and the percent of office space to total building size.

16. Show the rent per month paid by the lessee/user of the competing building.

17. Compute and show the rent per square foot for the competing building.

18. Discuss market occupancy levels in competing buildings.

19. The date of the lease or leases covering the subject property.

20. The name of the lessor(s), which should all be the owner/borrower.

21. The name(s) of the lessee(s) occupying space in the subject property.

22. The term of the lease or leases, both the original term and the number of years remaining.

23. The rent to be paid. Identify base rent and any increases, whether scheduled or tied to the movement of a specified index.

24. Identify which party is responsible for the payment of each of the operating expenses, the lessee or the lessor.

25. This space is for Scheduled Gross Rent, which is derived as indicated.

26. Vacancy should be consistent with the level of market vacancy, as derived and discussed in Section 1, Part D of the worksheet.

27. Effective Gross Rent is the remainder derived by subtracting the Vacancy figure from Scheduled Gross Rent.

28. The anticipated annual operating expenses for the subject project.

29. Net Operating Income is derived by subtracting Operating Expenses from Effective Gross Income.

30. Show the capitalization rate indicated by your market research.

31. A value estimate can be derived using the income figures developed in the worksheet.

32–37. Key ratios can be shown in the spaces provided.

38. Any ratio that deviates from the underwriting guidelines of your institution should be discussed. An adequate explanation should be given for the deviation, and the impact on the overall risk of the loan should be assessed.

39–40. The person preparing the worksheet should sign and date in the spaces provided.

41–42. Space is provided for approval of the analysis in the worksheet by a senior officer or department head.

Exhibit 5-4 is a worksheet to use in analyzing and presenting an office building. Complete it as follows:

1. Check the appropriate box to indicate whether the project is existing or proposed.

2. If the project is existing, indicate the years for which fiscal year-end operating statements were obtained and reviewed.

3. If proposed indicate whether or not a pro forma, that is, estimated, operating statement was obtained from the owner.

4. Identify the category into which the subject building falls.

5. Give the number of buildings in the project.

6. Give the total square footage for buildings in the project.

7. The net rentable area available in the subject building.

8. The number of elevators in the building.

9. The number of parking spots available under the building.

10. The number of outside parking spaces that will be available on-site.

11. Identify and describe the major features of the building, especially those that will lead to higher or lower rents relative to the rest of the market.

12. Identify the major market competition for the project.

13. Note the type of building (garden, low rise, etc).

14. Give the square foot size of the competing building.

15. Show the rent per month paid by the lessees/users of the building.

16. Compute the rent per square foot for the building.

17. Discuss market occupancy levels in competing buildings.

18. The range of dates of the subject property's leases.

19. The name of the lessor or lessors.

20. The major lessees occupying space in the building.

21. The average term of the leases, both original term and number of years remaining.

22. The range of rents to be paid. Identify base rent and any increases, whether scheduled or tied to the movement of a specified index. Also list any other rents to be paid, such as overages, expense pass-throughs, etc.

23. Identify which expenses are the lessor's responsibility.

24. Scheduled Gross Rent is computed as indicated.

25. Vacancy should be consistent with the level of market vacancy, as estimated and discussed in Section 1, Part D of the worksheet.

26. Effective Gross Rent is the remainder derived by subtracting the Vacancy figure from Scheduled Gross Rent.

27. The anticipated annual operating expenses for the project should be estimated.

28. Net Operating Income is derived by subtracting Operating Expenses from Effective Gross Income.

29. Show the capitalization rate indicated by your market research.

30. Value can be estimated using the income figures from the worksheet.

31–37. Key ratios can be computed.

EXHIBIT 5-4

OFFICE BUILDING WORKSHEET

Section 1—Project Feasibility

A. Project is: (1)
( ) Existing
If existing, fiscal year-end financial statements
reviewed:

_____ (2) _____
( ) Proposed
If proposed, did borrower provide a pro-forma
statement of operations? _____ (3) _____

B. Project Details
Type of Building (4)
( ) Garden (Up to 3 stories)
( ) Low Rise (Up to 6 stories)
( ) Mid Rise (Up to 10 stories)
( ) High Rise (Over 10 stories)

Number of Buildings _____ (5) _____
Total Square Footage _____ (6) _____
Net Rentable Area _____ (7) _____
Number of Elevators _____ (8) _____
Parking—Subterranean _____ (9) _____
Parking—Outside _____ (10) _____
Major Features: _____
_____ (11) _____

C. Major Competition:

Project	Type	Size	Rent per Month	Rent per Sq. Ft.
1._____	_____	_____	_____	_____
2.__ (12) __	__ (13) __	__ (14) __	__ (15) __	__ (16) __
3._____	_____	_____	_____	_____
4._____	_____	_____	_____	_____

D. Market occupancy levels for similar properties are:_____
_____ (17) _____

E. Lease Analysis (this analysis should be prepared for each lease in the building. For the worksheet, a summary of ranges for all leases would be most appropriate)
Dates of Leases: _____ (18) _____
Lessor: _____ (19) _____

EXHIBIT 5-4 (Cont'd.)

Major Lessees: _____ (20) _____
_____
_____

Average Term of Leases: _____ (21) _____
Range of Rent: _____ (22) _____
Expenses Paid by _____ (23) _____
Lessor: _____
_____

Section 2—Income Analysis

Scheduled Gross Rent _____ (24) _____
(Estimated Rent per
Sq. Ft. X Subject Sq. Ft.)
Less: Vacancy Allowance _____ (25) _____
Effective Gross Income _____ (26) _____
Less: Operating Expenses _____ (27) _____
Net Operating Expenses _____ (28) _____
Capitalization Rate _____ (29) _____
Market Value Estimate _____ (30) _____

Section 3—Key Ratios

Debt Service Coverage _____ (31) _____
Breakeven Ratio _____ (32) _____
Operating Expense Ratio _____ (33) _____
Operating Expenses per _____ (34) _____
Square Foot
Loan-to-Value _____ (35) _____
Loan per Square Foot _____ (36) _____
Building Efficiency Ratio _____ (37) _____

Discuss any ratios that are below the underwriting guidelines for office building loans:_____
_____ (38) _____
_____

Prepared by: _____ (39) _____   Date: _____ (40) _____
Approved by: _____ (41) _____   Date: _____ (42) _____

38. Any ratio that deviates from the underwriting guidelines of your institution should be discussed. An adequate explanation should be given for the deviation, and the impact on the overall risk of the loan should be assessed.

39–40. The person preparing the worksheet should sign and date in the spaces provided.

41–42. Space is provided for approval of the worksheet by a senior officer or department head.

Worksheets for other types of income property can be developed using the same format as for those presented in this chapter. You only need to make changes to reflect unique features of a particular property type.

EXHIBIT 5-5

FINANCIAL STATEMENT SPREAD SHEET

NAME (1)		SIC CODE NO. (2)	OFFICE (3)

		(4)				
	TYPE OF STATEMENT	(4)				
ASSETS (6)	STATEMENT DATE	(5)				
4	Cash					
5	Accounts Receivable (Net)					
6						
7						
8	Inventory					
9						
10						
11	CURRENT ASSETS					
12	Non-Current Receivables					
13						
14	Investments					
15						
16						
17						
18	Property, Plant & Equipment (Net)					
19						
20	Deferred and Prepaid					
21						
22	Reserve for Depreciation (Deducted above)					
23	TOTAL ASSETS					
24	LIABILITIES (7)					
25	Accounts Payable					
26	Accrued Liabilities					
27	Notes Payable to this Bank					
28						
29						
30						
31	Current Maturities of Long Term Debt					
32	Income Tax					
33	CURRENT LIABILITIES					
34						
35						
36						
37						
38	TOTAL LIABILITIES					
39						
40						
41	Common Stock					
42	Paid-in Capital					
43						
44	Retained Earnings (Net of Intangibles, Treasury Stock)					
45	TANGIBLE NET WORTH					
46	TOTAL LIABILITIES & NET WORTH					
47	Period of Operations					
48	Sales (8)					
49	Net Profit Before Taxes					
50	Net Profit After Taxes					
51						
52						
53	Dividends Paid or Withdrawlas					
54	CHANGE IN NET WORTH Plus or (Minus)					
55	Working Capital					
56	Current Ratio (9)					
57	Receivables DOH					
58	Inventory DOH (*COGS Includes Depreciation)					
59	Debt to Worth Ratio					
60						

Facilitate Year-by-Year Comparisons with a Financial Statement Spreadsheet

Exhibit 5-5 is a financial statement spreadsheet form. Spreadsheets are an excellent way to display financial statements to facilitate year-by-year comparisons. Any trends that develop can be spotted, and the analysis can focus on those areas where trends are adverse. The spreadsheet can be attached to the loan writeup to facilitate review by those who will approve the loan.

The spreadsheet should be completed with the following information:

1. The name of the entity whose statements are being spread on the form. Usually this will be the borrowing entity.

2. The Standard Industrial Classification (SIC) Code can be put on the spreadsheet.

3. The office within the organization which spread the financial statements.

4. The type of financial statement spread; for example, CPA-Audited, CPA-Review, Company-Prepared.

5. The date of the statement. Preferably, annual statements should be used. The major value of a spreadsheet is trend analysis, so consistency is important. If year-end statements are used, then only year-end statements should be reflected on the spreadsheet. If you want to spread six-month interim statements, use a separate spreadsheet form.

6. The assets from the financial statement should be detailed on the lines where indicated. Use the blank lines for categories not printed on the form.

EXHIBIT 5-6

CORPORATE FINANCIAL WORKSHEET

Name: _____ (1) _____

_____ (2) _____ Audited Financial Statements for the last three years were reviewed.

_____ CPA-prepared unaudited statements for the last three years were reviewed.

_____ Company-prepared financial statements for the last three years were reviewed.

_____ A credit report on the company was ordered and reviewed.

Three years' financial statements were not available for the following reason(s): __

_____ (3) _____

Statement Period: (4)			
Current Assets	____ (5) ____		
Current Liabilities	____ (6) ____		
Current Ratio	____ (7) ____		
Working Capital	____ (8) ____		
Intangible Assets	____ (9) ____		
Trade Accounts Payable	____ (10) ____		

EXHIBIT 5-6 (Cont'd.)

Total Liabilities   ____ (11) ____   _____   _____

Tangible Net Worth   ____ (12) ____   _____   _____

    Debt to Worth Ratio   ____ (13) ____   _____   _____

See attached worksheet, page 2, for computation of the following ratios:

Accounts Receivable   ____ (14) ____   _____   _____
    Turnover

Age of Receivables   ____ (15) ____   _____   _____
    in Days

Inventory Turnover   ____ (16) ____   _____   _____

Number of Days   ____ (17) ____   _____   _____
    Inventory on Hand

Turnover of Trade   ____ (18) ____   _____   _____
    Accounts Payable

Number of Days to Pay   ____ (19) ____   _____   _____
    Accounts Payable

Statement Period: ____ (20) ____   _____   _____

Turnover of Accounts Receivable: (21)

    The number of times receivables turn over during the period:

$$\frac{\text{Net Sales}}{\text{Receivables}} \quad = \quad \underline{\hspace{2cm}} \times \underline{\hspace{2cm}} \times \underline{\hspace{2cm}} \times$$

    Age of Receivables in Days: (22)

$$\frac{360}{\text{Number of Times Receivables Turnover}} \quad = \quad \underline{\hspace{1.5cm}} \text{ days} \quad \underline{\hspace{1.5cm}} \text{ days} \quad \underline{\hspace{1.5cm}} \text{ days}$$

Turnover of Inventory: (23)

    The number of times inventory turns during the period:

$$\frac{\text{Cost of Goods Sold}}{\text{Inventory}} \quad \underline{\hspace{2cm}} \times \underline{\hspace{2cm}} \times \underline{\hspace{2cm}} \times$$

    The number of Days Inventory on hand: (24)

$$\frac{360}{\text{Number of Times Inventory Turns}} \quad = \quad \underline{\hspace{1.5cm}} \text{ days} \quad \underline{\hspace{1.5cm}} \text{ days} \quad \underline{\hspace{1.5cm}} \text{ days}$$

Turnover of Trade Accounts Payable:

    The number of times trade accounts payables turn over during the period: (25)

$$\frac{\text{Cost of Goods Sold}}{\text{Trade Accounts Payable}} \quad \underline{\hspace{2cm}} \times \underline{\hspace{2cm}} \times \underline{\hspace{2cm}} \times$$

Number of Days to Pay Accounts Payable: (26)

$$\frac{360}{\text{Number of Times Payable Turnover}} \quad \underline{\hspace{1.5cm}} \text{ days} \quad \underline{\hspace{1.5cm}} \text{ days} \quad \underline{\hspace{1.5cm}} \text{ days}$$

Prepared by: _____ (27) _____ Date: _____ (28) _____

Reviewed by: _____ (29) _____ Date: _____ (30) _____

7. Liabilities should be reflected in the same manner as the assets.

8. Use this section of the spreadsheet to show total sales for the period under review, net profits, dividend or withdrawals, and changes in net worth.

9. Use this section to compute certain key ratios that are important to financial statement analysis. Unusual changes in these ratios can reflect problem areas that need closer review.

Using the Corporate Financial Worksheet to Enhance the Analysis of Key Areas

The corporate financial worksheet can be used along with the spreadsheet to enhance the analysis of key areas. Use of the form provides a quick review of the financial statements. It will also help less experienced officers by guiding them in their analysis.

A worksheet is reflected in Exhibit 5-6. Fill the form in as follows:

1. The name of the entity whose statements are being analyzed.

2. Indicate the type of financial statements that were provided and analyzed, and whether a credit report was ordered and reviewed.

3. Explain any shortcomings in the financial statements that were available for analysis.

4. Identify the financial statement period analyzed; for example, fiscal year end, six-month interim.

5. Fill in the current assets from the financial statements.

6. Fill in the current liabilities from the financial statements.

7. Compute the current ratio.

8. Compute working capital available.

9. Show the dollar amount of intangible assets reflected on the company's financial statements.

10. Show the dollar amount of trade accounts payable reflected on the company's financial statements.

11. Fill in the total liabilities from the financial statements.

12. Compute tangible net worth.

13. Compute the debt-to-worth ratio.

14. Bring forward the accounts receivable turnover from the worksheet portion on page 2.

15. Bring forward the day's receivables figure from page 2 of the worksheet.

16. Plug in the inventory turnover figure from page 2 of the worksheet.

17. Show the day's inventory figure from page 2 of the worksheet.

18. Show the turnover of accounts payable from page 2 of the worksheet.

19. Show the days required to pay off accounts payable from page 2 of the worksheet.

20. Put in the statement period at the start of page 2.

21. Compute the turnover of accounts receivable for each statement period by dividing net sales by trade receivables.

22. Compute the age of receivables in days by dividing 360 by the number of times receivables turn over. Some lenders prefer using 365 days, a calendar year, which will give a slightly less conservative answer.

23. Compute the turnover of inventory by dividing the cost of goods sold by the inventory figure.

24. Compute the days of inventory on hand by dividing 360 (or if you prefer, 365) by the number of times inventory turns.

25. Compute the number of times trade accounts payable turn over by dividing the cost of goods sold by the trade accounts payable.

26. Compute the number of days required to pay accounts payable by dividing 360 (or if you prefer, 365) by the number of times payables turn over.

27–28. The preparer of the worksheet should sign and date the form.

29–30. If review and approval is needed, then the reviewer should also sign and date the form.

How to Perform a Cash Flow Analysis

Cash flow pays back long-term loans. While the real estate can be foreclosed and sold in the event of a default, this is not a desirable or certain source of repayment for the loan. If the loan works as scheduled, repayment will come from cash flow generated from the operation of the real estate.

Exhibit 5-7 is a worksheet for use in analyzing cash flow, and for determining the adequacy of the cash flow to service the debts of the company. This worksheet can be attached to the loan approval and submitted for the review of the people approving the loan.

Complete the worksheet with the following information:

1. The date of the statements from which financial information will be taken; for example, fiscal year end.

2. Net profit after tax for each statement period analyzed, from the Profit and Loss Statement.

3. All interest payments on debt, taken from the Profit and Loss Statement.

4. All lease payments for the rental of real estate.

5. All lease payments other than real estate.

6. Depreciation expense.

7. Gross Available Cash Inflow is the sum of items 2 through 6.

8. Capital expenditures made for fixed assets during the statement period.

9. Net Available Cash Inflow can be computed by subtracting Fixed Asset Expenditures from Gross Available Cash Inflow.

10. Amortization of Long-Term Debt is principal payments made on debt (excluding interest).

11. Total Required Cash Payments is the sum of items 3, 4, 5, and 10.

12. Excess Cash Available is computed by subtracting Total Required Cash Payments from Net Available Cash Inflow.

13. The Fixed Obligation Coverage Ratio is computed by dividing Net Available Cash Inflow by Total Required Cash Payments. This ratio reflects the adequacy of cash flow to service fixed payment obligations. The ratio should be positive, but how much so depends on the requirements of your organization. Over time a ratio that is declining may indicate a company that is taking on too much fixed debt.

EXHIBIT 5-7

CASH FLOW WORKSHEET

Statement Date: (1)	_____	_____	_____
Profit After Tax (2)	_____	_____	_____
Interest on Debt (3)	_____	_____	_____
Real Estate Leases (4)	_____	_____	_____
Other Leases (5)	_____	_____	_____
Depreciation (6)	_____	_____	_____
Gross Available Cash Inflow (7)	_____	_____	_____
Fixed Asset Expenditures (8)	_____	_____	_____
Net Available Cash Inflow (9)	========	========	========
Required Payments For:			
Interest on Debt (3)	_____	_____	_____
Real Estate Leases (4)	_____	_____	_____
Other Leases (5)	_____	_____	_____
Amortization of Long-Term Debt (10)	_____	_____	_____
Total Required Cash Payments (11)	_____	_____	
Net Cash Available (12)	========	========	========
Fixed Obligation Coverage Ratio (13)	========	========	========

Sample Commitment Letter

A commitment letter is used to transmit the terms and conditions of loan approval to the borrower. Much of the language in and format of commitment letters does not vary from loan to loan. Standard letters can be amended with clauses specific to the particular transaction.

Exhibit 5-8 shows a standard commitment letter. This letter contains clauses applicable to construction lending. These can be deleted if the loan is a permanent loan. Also delete those clauses that do not apply to the loan you are committing.

Complete the Commitment Letter with the following information:

1. The date of the Commitment Letter.
2. The name and address of the party to whom the letter is addressed.
3. The street address of the property that will collateralize the loan.
4. A description of the property; for example, "Two office/warehouse buildings of 24,000 square feet total."
5. The name of your lending institution.
6. The type of loan, interim construction or permanent.

EXHIBIT 5-8

COMMITMENT LETTER

_____ (1) _____

_____
_____ (2) _____
_____

RE: The property at _____ (3) _____
_____
consisting of _____ (4)_____
_____

Dear _____:

_____ (5) _____ (hereinafter "Bank") agrees to make an
_____ (6) _____ loan to _____ (7) _____
(hereinafter "Borrower") upon the terms and conditions hereinafter mentioned:

Article I
BASIC TERMS

1.1   *Borrower.* _____ (7) _____

1.2   *Loan   Amount.*   The   Bank   shall   lend   to   the   Borrower
_____ (8) _____
_____ (hereinafter "Loan").

1.3   *Term   of   the   Loan.*   The   term   of   the   loan   shall   be
_____ (9) _____.

1.4   *Interest   Rate.*   The   interest   rate   shall   be   calculated   at
_____ (10) _____
_____.

1.5 *Required Payments.* _____
_____
_____ (11) _____
_____

1.6 *Loan Fee.* The loan fee shall be _____
_____ (12) _____ , or _____%. Of that
amount _____ (13) _____ shall be paid by Borrower to Bank
simultaneous with the delivery to Bank of Borrower's signed, accepted copy of this
Commitment Letter.

In the event that the terms, provisions, and conditions of this commitment letter
are not fulfilled by Borrower within the time limitations described in this letter, and
as a result thereof, Bank does not disburse the loan, Borrower shall be in default
hereunder, and Bank shall retain the deposit to compensate Bank for time spent,
labor and services performed, loss of interest and for any other action, it being
understood that Bank's damages as a result of such default are not fully capable of

EXHIBIT 5-8 (Cont'd.)

being ascertained at the time, and the deposit represents Borrower's and Bank's best estimation at this time of such damages, and Borrower shall then be released from any liability incurred as a result of such default.

The balance of the loan fee, _____ _____ (14) _____, shall be paid on the date funds are first advanced.

1.7 *Note, Deed of Trust, and Other Security.* The indebtedness shall be evidenced by a Promissory Note secured by a _____ (15) _____ and Assignment of Rents in a form provided by Bank, which shall be a valid _____ (16) _____ upon the above-referenced property more particularly described as set forth in Exhibit "A" attached hereto and incorporated herein by this reference (hereinafter referred to as the "Property"), and improvements to be constructed thereon (hereinafter the "Improvements").

A financing statement and Security Agreement in favor of Bank, as additional security to cover all machinery, equipment, material, appliances, furniture, or fixtures now or hereafter installed upon the Property or Improvements shall be signed and delivered by Borrower to Bank.

Among other items, the _____ (17) _____ shall refer to and incorporate the terms of the _____ (6) _____ Loan Agreement in a form provided by Bank which shall provide that Borrower shall not transfer or otherwise convey the Property during the term of the Loan without the prior written consent of the Bank. It is understood that the Loan is made upon the experience and credit of Borrower and Borrower's principals.

1.8 *Purpose.* The purpose of the loan is _____ _____ (18) _____ _____

1.9 *Title and Title Insurance.* Borrower shall have marketable title to the Property and shall furnish Bank, at Borrower's expense, an _____ (19) _____ policy of title insurance in the amount of the Loan. Said policy shall include such other endorsements as Bank may require. Title to the property, improvements, and personal property shall be subject to the approval of Bank's counsel.

1.10 *Other Insurance.* Borrower shall provide Bank with evidence of all-risk _____ (20) _____ insurance on the improvements and evidence of liability and worker's compensation insurance in amounts satisfactory to Bank. All policies shall name Bank as lender's loss payee. If required, flood insurance shall be provided by Borrower.

1.11 *Covenants, Conditions, and Restrictions.* All existing and future declarations and/or convenants, conditions, and restrictions limiting the use or otherwise restricting the Property shall be subject to Bank's prior approval.

1.12 *Tract Map.* A final tract map shall be submitted by Borrower and shall have been approved by Bank and the City of _____ (21) _____ prior to recordation.

1.13 *Legal Opinion.* Bank may require an opinion of its counsel at or prior to the

EXHIBIT 5-8 (Cont'd.)

closing as a condition of such closing, in scope and substance satisfactory to it, covering such matters as due authorization, execution and delivery, and legality, and any other matters incident to the loan as Bank may reasonably request.

Article II
CONSTRUCTION OF THE IMPROVEMENTS

As a condition precedent to recordation of the Loan:

2.1 *Plans and Specifications.* A complete and final set of plans and specifications for all improvements, including a site plan with legal description, shall have been submitted to and approved by Bank. Said plans and specifications shall reflect the approval of the governmental body having jurisdiction over the property. Said plans and specifications shall be signed by the Borrower and the general contractor.

2.2 *Cost Breakdown.* Borrower shall provide Bank with a detailed cost breakdown signed by the contractor and contractor's architect, in a form acceptable to the Bank.

2.3 *Evidence of Compliance.* Borrower shall provide Bank with a copy of the building permit, and any other evidence Bank may reasonably require demonstrating compliance with zoning, planning or subdivision restrictions, building codes, use and geologic hazard permits, and environmental or utility district regulations.

2.4 *Trade List.* Borrower shall prepare, initial, and deliver to Bank a complete list of all subcontractors and vendors to be employed on the project, including name, trade, scope of work, address, phone number, and name of principal. Borrower will provide the Bank a complete and true copy of all subcontracts let for the subject project.

2.5 *Proposed Budget.* Borrower shall provide a statement indicating the use of loan proceeds (Budget) to pay all closing costs and to pay the cost of completing the improvements, in a form acceptable to the Bank.

2.6 *Soils Report.* A soils report, by a licensed soils engineer, shall be provided by Borrower for Bank's approval. The report shall include test borings, recommended soil bearing pressure, type of foundations, excavation, fill and compaction, and all recommendations shall be followed in construction of the buildings. In addition, architectural approval on compaction test reports shall be submitted to the Bank.

2.7 *Retentions.* The Construction Loan Agreement shall provide for, among other things, retentions in the amount of _____ (22) _____ percent (_____ %), and that these retentions shall be released upon satisfactory completion of the project.

2.8 *Start of Construction.* Any obligation of Bank to fund this Loan shall terminate unless construction commences within _____ (23) _____ days of the date of Borrower's acceptance of this Commitment Letter and is continuously pursued through to completion of the project. Borrower warrants and covenants that construction has not begun and will not begin before the date funds are first advanced (hereinafter "Advance Date"). However, in the event that construction commences before the Advance Date, Bank will not have any obligation to fund the commitment hereunder until such time as Borrower provides Bank with an indemnification and endorsement to the title insurance policy acceptable to Bank in its sole discretion.

EXHIBIT 5-8 (Cont'd.)

2.9 *Inspection of Construction.* The Construction Loan Agreement shall provide that the improvements (including grading, landscaping, and any other site work) shall be completed in accordance with said approved plans and specifications, and shall be inspected periodically during the course of construction at Borrower's expense.

2.10 *Completion of Construction.* The Construction Loan Agreement shall provide that construction of the Improvements shall be deemed complete when the work provided for in the plans and specifications has been completed and accepted by Borrower and Bank, a valid Notice of Completion is filed of record, a valid Certificate of Occupancy is issued, Borrower has delivered a copy of the notice and certificate to the Bank, the title insurance company has issued to Bank a satisfactory Mechanic's Lien Endorsement, and has released any funds withheld in accordance with its Indemnity Agreement.

Article III
CONDITIONS PRECEDENT

In addition to the conditions precedent set forth above, Bank shall not be obligated to disburse any portion of the Loan unless and until the following conditions are met:

3.1 *Financial Statements.* Borrower shall furnish Bank with full and complete financial statements of Borrower on an annual basis, in a form acceptable to Bank.

3.2 *Completion Guarantors.* Completion Guarantees shall be signed and delivered to Bank by _____

_____ (24) _____.

3.3 *Title Insurance Issued.* The title insurance described above shall have been issued.

3.4 *Loan Documents.* All Loan Documents specified by the Bank shall be completed and signed by the appropriate parties.

3.5 *Commitment Compliance.* All other provisions of this Commitment Letter have been complied with.

3.6 *Special Conditions.* The following special conditions have been complied with:

_____
_____
_____ (25) _____
_____
_____

Article IV
REPRESENTATIONS AND WARRANTIES

4.1 Borrower hereby represents and warrants, which continuing representations and warranties shall fully survive the disbursement of the loan, as follows:

    4.1.1   The Borrower is an entity duly formed, in good standing and is authorized to do business in the State of _____ (26) _____ .

    4.1.2   The persons executing the Loan Documents on behalf of the Borrower are duly authorized to do so.

EXHIBIT 5-8 (Cont'd.)

4.1.3   This Commitment Letter, and all loan documentation executed in conjunction with the provisions of the Loan referenced herein, shall constitute a legal, valid, and binding obligation of the obligors.

Article V
TERMS OF COMMITMENT

5.1 *Term of Commitment.* Borrower shall have _____ (27) _____ days from the date of acceptance within which to meet the terms of this Commitment Letter. If the Loan has not been made by Bank within the _____ (27) _____ -day period, then Bank's obligation shall cease unless, at Bank's option, Bank extends this Commitment Letter in writing.

5.2 *Waivers.* A waiver of any of the terms or conditions of this Commitment Letter shall not constitute a continuing waiver of strict performance of any other provision in this Commitment Letter.

5.3 *Limitation on Assignment.* This Commitment Letter may not be assigned by the Borrower without the prior written consent of Bank and any such attempted assignment shall be void.

5.4 *Notice; Method of Service.* All notice permitted or required in this Commitment Letter must be in writing and shall be deemed to have been served when sent by United States certified or registered mail, return receipt requested, postage prepaid, and addressed to the party to whom such notice is intended as set forth herein. Such notices shall be effective _____ (28) _____ days after mailing. Such notices shall be mailed to the respective parties at the addresses set forth in this Commitment Letter. Any party may change such address by appropriate notice to all of the other parties hereto.

5.5 *Signs and Publicity Releases.* During the term of the Loan, Bank may place on the property and/or improvements such signs as are appropriate to evidence the placement of interim financing through the Bank. Bank may also issue publicity releases announcing the placement of interim financing through the Bank.

5.6 *Survival of Terms.* The terms of this Commitment Letter shall not be extinguished upon the execution of the Loan Documents, but shall survive the Advance Date and shall be incorporated into the terms of the Construction Loan Agreement.

5.7 *Power of Attorney.* No power of attorney shall be used unless it is recorded or in recordable form and is approved by Bank's counsel prior to the Advance Date.

5.8 *Amendment.* No modification of this Commitment Letter shall be binding unless it shall be in writing and signed by the party against whom any such modification is sought to be enforced. This Commitment Letter constitutes the entire agreement and understanding of the parties with respect to the transaction herein contemplated, and all prior negotiations shall be deemed of no effect.

5.9 *Nature of Documents: Time of the Essence.* This Commitment Letter, when accepted and agreed to by Borrower, shall be deemed to be a contract to be construed according to the laws of the state where the Property is located and all documents evidencing and securing the loan or relating in any way to the transaction contemplated herein shall be construed under the laws of that state. It is agreed that time shall be of the essence of this Commitment Letter.

EXHIBIT 5-8 (Cont'd.)

5.10 *Costs and Fees.* Borrower shall pay all costs, fees, and charges of every kind in connection with the Loan referenced herein, including without limitation the cost of obtaining, preparing, and furnishing to Bank all documents herein mentioned, surveys and title reports, the premium for title insurance, the fees for recording and filing documents, appraisal fee, legal fees, cost estimating and inspection fees, any costs and fees arising from Bank's monthly disbursement of funds, and any tax required to be paid at the time of recordation of the Security Instruments (but only to the extent permitted by law).

_____

Upon return to Bank of the signed copy of this Commitment Letter, together with the fee required under Section 1.6 above, within _____ (29) _____ days of the date of this letter, this letter agreement shall be deemed to be the binding obligation of each party hereto in respect to all matters herein required on the part of each said party to be done or performed.

Sincerely,

_____ (30) _____

By: _____ (31) _____

Agreed to and accepted this _____ (32) _____ day of _____ , 19___.

By: _____ (33) _____

By: _____ (33) _____

7. The name of the borrower.

8. The amount of the loan; for example, "One Hundred Thousand Dollars ($100,000)."

9. The term of the loan; for example, "Twenty-Four (24) Months."

10. The interest rate on the loan.

11. The payments that will be due during the term of the loan.

12. The amount of loan fee; for example, "Ten Thousand Dollars ($10,000), or 1%."

13. Use this space to indicate how much of the total loan fee will be collected up front as a commitment fee.

14. The balance of the loan fee, net of the amount collected up front.

15. The security instrument: deed of trust, or mortgage.

16. Describe the nature of the lien; for example, "First Lien" or "Second Lien."

17. Fill in the security instrument: trust deed, or mortgage.

18. Describe the purpose of the loan.

19. Describe the type of title insurance policy to be purchased by the borrower.

20. If the loan is a construction loan, fill in "course of construction." If the loan is a permanent loan, delete this space.

21. Fill in the city in which the property is located.

22. The percentage retention should be filled in here; for example, "five percent (5%)."

23. The number of days granted to the borrower before construction must begin.

24. Fill in the names of all parties from whom you want to obtain completion guarantees.

25. Use this space to put in any special conditions applicable to the particular loan. For example, if the loan is subject to an appraisal, use:

"This Commitment is subject to receipt and approval by the Bank of a satisfactory appraisal report showing a minimum appraised value for the subject property of $1,000,000."

If the loan is subject to a certain leasing requirement, the following language can be used:

"Loan funding is subject to receipt and approval by the Bank of signed leases acceptable to the Bank in form and content, showing minimum annual triple net rents of $25,000 from not more than 2,500 square feet of net rentable area."

26. The state in which the borrowing entity does business.

27. The number of days granted to the Borrower to meet the terms of the Commitment Letter.

28. Fill in the number of days after which mailed notices will become effective.

29. Fill in the number of days granted to the borrower to return the executed copy of the Commitment Letter and the commitment fee.

30. The name of the lending institution.

31. The signature of the person making the loan commitment on behalf of the lending organization.

32. The date the commitment Letter is accepted by the Borrower.

33. The borrower's signature.

Commitment Letter Modifications

Once a Commitment Letter is issued and accepted, it is a binding agreement on both parties. From time to time, however, it may be necessary or desirable to amend the terms of commitment. Perhaps more time is needed for the satisfaction of certain conditions, or conditions have been largely met and the lender is willing to waive the balance of the requirement.

Exhibit 5-9 shows a modification of a commitment letter. Complete the letter as follows:

1. The date of the Amendment.

2. The name and address of the party to whom the letter is addressed.

3. The name of the lending institution.

4. The date of the original Commitment Letter.

5. The name of the Borrower, which should be the same as the Borrower on the original Commitment Letter.

6. The number of the paragraph(s) of the original letter which are being amended.

7. The new language for the amended paragraph(s).

8. The signature of the authorized signer who is amending the Commitment Letter.

EXHIBIT 5-9

COMMITMENT LETTER AMENDMENT

_____ (1) _____

_____
_____ (2) _____
_____

Dear _____:

_____ (3) _____ (hereinafter "Bank") hereby modifies that certain Commitment Letter dated _____ _____ (4) _____ by and between the Bank and _____ _____ (5) _____ (hereinafter "Borrower").

    Paragraph ___ (6) ___ is hereby modified to read _____
_____
_____ (7) _____
_____.

    Paragraph ___ (6) ___ is hereby modified to read _____
_____
_____ (7) _____
_____.

All other terms of the Commitment Letter remain unchanged and in full force and effect.

This Amendment will be effective upon execution of this letter by the Borrower and return of the original to the Bank.

Sincerely,

_____ (3) _____

By:____ (8) _____

Acceptance is made of the foregoing terms and provisions of this Amendment this ___ (9) ___ day of _____ , 19___. Borrower acknowledges that all other terms and conditions of the original Commitment Letter dated _____ (4) _____ remain unchanged.

By: _____ (10) _____

By: _____ (10) _____

EXHIBIT 5-10

CHECKLIST

	Prepared by	Date
	_____	_____
Loan Approval/Writeup Prepared	_____	_____
Property Worksheet Prepared	_____	_____
Financial Statement Spreadsheet Prepared	____ (1) ____	____ (2) ____
Corporate Financial Analysis Prepared	_____	_____
Cash Flow Analysis Prepared	_____	_____

Loan was ( ) Approved   Date: _____ (3) _____
           ( ) Declined
Commitment Letter issued: _____ (4) _____
Commitment Letter accepted: _____ (5) _____

Declination Letter issued: _____ (6) _____
Response from Borrower, if any: _____

_____ (7) _____

_____

9. The date on which the amendment is accepted by the Borrower.
10. The signature of the Borrower.

End Note

Exhibit 5-10 is a checklist to use in documenting the loan approval process. Complete it as follows:

1. The name of the party preparing the checklist.
2. The date the checklist was prepared.
3. Indicate in the boxes whether the loan was approved or declined. Give the date of loan approval.
4. The date that a commitment letter was sent to the borrower.
5. The date the accepted letter was returned, along with the commitment fee.
6. If the loan was declined, a declination letter should be issued. Indicate the date the letter was sent out.
7. Space is provided for a summary of any response from the borrower.

Once the loan is approved, attention turns to the task of properly documenting it. The balance of this book will deal with issues surrounding that process.

6

How to Document the Borrowing Entity

The borrowing entity can take a number of forms, including partnership, corporation, and joint venture. For each, certain documents are obtained that define the entity, and, more importantly, describe the methods and means by which it can enter into real estate loan transactions. Unless the lender is clear on who can incur debt for the borrowing entity, and who can pledge assets as collateral for debt, there is a risk that later disputes may arise.

Individuals are not a problem. They sign and thereby become indebted. There is a need to make sure that they own the asset they propose to pledge, but title searches solve that problem. In community property states, care must be exercised about requiring spousal guarantees. The law is leaning towards the interpretation that either one of the spouses can pledge community assets, and that lenders cannot require that the other spouse guarantee the loan.

Uses of a Statement of Partnership

A Statement of Partnership is a document that is recorded to identify and define the principals of a partnership. Laws vary from state to state, so care should be taken as to the exact form to use in your state.

Exhibit 6-1 shows a sample Statement of Partnership form.

This document names the partnership, tells who the partners are and which of the partners can enter into the loan transaction. The document should be recorded, and, if the partners have not already done so, the lender can record it with the rest of the docouments.

How to Assemble a General Partnership Agreement

The General Partnership Agreement describes how the business of the partnership will function. From this document you can determine that the partnership is a valid borrowing entity that can own real estate and enter into mortgage loans.

EXHIBIT 6-1

STATEMENT OF PARTNERSHIP

This Statement of Partnership is made by the XYZ Partnership, a _____ partnership, which declares that it is a partnership and that:

1. The name of the partnership is:

XYZ Partnership

2. The name of each of the partners is:

Harold Smith

Robert Jones

3. The partners named above are all of the partners of the partnership.

4. Each of the partners acting alone is authorized to execute, acknowledge, and deliver, on behalf of and in the name of the partnership, any and all agreements, documents, and instruments of every kind and nature as any of the foregoing relate to financing of, encumbrances upon, or acquisitions of any real property or any interest therein.

Executed at _____ on the _____ day of _____ , 19 ____ .

XYZ PARTNERSHIP

By: _____

By: _____

Some of the clauses that are found in a typical partnership agreement include:

1. Principal Offices—A description of the principal business location of the partnership, to which correspondence can be directed.

2. Purpose of the Partnership—Comments as to why the partnership was formed and what it plans to do. For example, a statement might be made that: "The purpose for the formation of the partnership is to purchase, develop, lease, finance, own for investment, and sell certain real property that may from time to time come to the attention of the partnership."

3. Term of the Partnership—A statement of how long the partnership will stay in business. This might be a term of years; for example, "the partnership will operate for 20 years, or to the year 2007." Alternatively, expiration of the partnership might be tied to some event; for example, "the partnership will terminate when the property that is the subject of the partnership is sold."

It is important to make sure that there is sufficient time left in the partnership to cover the term of the real estate loan. If the loan term is 15 years and the partnership will terminate in 10 years, then the partners should be asked to amend the partnership termination date to coincide with loan maturity.

4. Partnership Capital—There will be language in the partnership agreement describing the percentage and dollar amount of contribution by the partners. There will also be statements as to the distribution of profits and the sharing of losses, which usually is in the same proportion as the capital contribution.

5. Management—The Agreement will specify which partner has day-to-day responsibility for the management of the partnership.

6. Hypothecation—This clause is crucial to the lender, a description of who can pledge partnership assets against the debts incurred. For example, it might read, "Unless consented to in writing by all partners, no partner shall voluntarily pledge, hypothecate, or encumber in any manner whatsoever all or any portion of partnership assets."

7. Sale or Transfer—There will be language covering the sale or transfer of a partner's share of ownership in the partnership. Usually this cannot be done without the consent of the other partners, or without other partners being given the right to purchase the share of the partner who desires to sell.

Other clauses may cover:
- when financial statements will be prepared,
- who will prepare financial statements,
- who will pay attorney's costs,
- additional capital contributions.

What to Include in a Joint Venture Agreement

A Joint Venture Agreement is a form of partnership agreement. Usually it is used when two corporate or partnership entities are entering into a partnership. Such an agreement is very often specifically for one venture.

Since a venture is a partnership, the agreement will contain the same kinds of clauses as those outlined above for partnership agreements. The venture agreement may be more detailed as to the duties of the venture partners, since each entity is usually bringing some specific expertise to the venture.

For example, an architectural firm and a general contractor might form a joint venture to develop a project. In this case the venture agreement might give the architectural partner responsibility for developing all of the plans and securing the permits, while charging the contractor partner with responsibility for construction.

Drawing Up a Limited Partnership Certificate

Because securities laws govern the selling of shares in certain limited partnerships, extra care should be used when dealing with such an entity. You should check the laws of your state to determine whether a specific certificate form needs to be recorded.

If there is no particular format, then the form in Exhibit 6-2 can be used as a Certificate of Limited Partnership. Complete it with the following information:

1. The name of the limited partnership entity.
2. The street address of the principal office of the limited partnership.
3. The names and addresses of all of the general partners in the limited partnership.
4. The name and address of the person or company who will accent service of legal documents for the limited partnership.
5. The term of years for which the limited partnership will remain active.

EXHIBIT 6-2

CERTIFICATE OF LIMITED PARTNERSHIP

Name of Limited Partnership:

(1)

Street Address of Principal Office: City and State   Zip Code

(2)

Names and Addresses of All General Partners:
Name:
Address: (3)
City: State: Zip:

Name:
Address:
City: State   Zip

Name:
Address:
City: State: Zip:

Name and Address of Agent for Service:
Name:
Address: (4)
City: State: Zip:

Term for Which This Partnership Is to Exist:

(5)

For the Purpose of Filing Amendments, Dissolution, and Cancellation Certificates Pertaining to This Certificate, the Acknowledgment of ____ (6) ____ General Partners Is Required.

It is hereby declared that I am (We are) the person(s) who executed this certificate of limited partnership:

By: _____ (7) _____   Date: _____

By:_____   Date:_____

6. The number of general partners who are needed to amend or change the certificate.

7. All of the general partners should sign and date the certificate.

This document gives the same kind of information obtained from the statement of partnership used for a general partnership. It is useful for a quick identification of the key members of the partnership and as a way of having those partners certify as to their membership in the partnership.

Clauses to Review in a Limited Partnership Agreement

The limited partnership agreement establishes the partnership and the terms and conditions under which it will run. It is similar in content to a general partnership agreement and many of the key clauses that are found in one will be found in the other.

Clauses in a limited partnership agreement that you should review include:

1. General Partners—The duties and responsibilities of the general partners should be clearly stated. A major problem that arises in this kind of venture is limited partner complaints, that the general partner was not authorized to take whatever action he took, or that he acted in an irresponsible manner.

2. Limited Partners—The attraction of this partnership vehicle is the limited liability of the investor partners who are classified as "limited." Their exposure is restricted to specific capital investment requirements. In return limited partners usually give up most of the control of the partnership to the general partner(s).

There should be clauses in the partnership document defining what powers, if any, the limited partners have. At a minimum they can usually vote to remove the general partner if they feel that performance is lacking.

3. Distribution to the General Partner—Attention should be paid to the payments made to the general partner. Is he taking unreasonably large fees that may hurt the operation of the partnership by depleting capital resources?

As with general partnerships, you need to be concerned with how the limited partnership borrows and pledges assets, and who is authorized to enter into such transactions.

Sample Articles of Incorporation

Articles of Incorporation are filed by corporate entities. They contain information that is similar to that found in statements of partnership.

Exhibit 6-3 is a sample.

How to Use Corporate By-Laws

Corporate By-Laws define how the company will operate, and appoint those parties who are authorized to take action in the conduct of corporate affairs. You

EXHIBIT 6-3

ARTICLES OF INCORPORATION
OF
UNIVERSAL PRODUCTS COMPANY

The undersigned, desiring to form a corporation under the laws of the State of _____ , declare:

First: The name of the corporation is: Universal Products Company.

Second: The purpose of the corporation is to engage in any lawful act or activity for which a corporation may be organized under the laws of the state.

Third: The name and address of the corporation's agent for service of process is: _____.

Fourth: This corporation is authorized to issue only one class of shares of stock, and the total number of shares that this corporation is authorized to issue is _____ .

IN WITNESS WHEREOF, the undersigned has executed these Articles of Incorporation on this _____ day of _____ , 19 ___ .

_____
James M. Smith

_____
Frederick S. Smith

We, James M. Smith and Frederick S. Smith hereby declare that we are the persons who executed the foregoing Articles of Incorporation of Universal Products Company and that said Articles of Incorporation are our own act and deed.

should determine who can borrow on behalf of the corporation, and who can pledge the corporation's assets to secure the debt.

The by-laws contain clauses such as:

1. Shareholders' Meetings—This clause defines when such meetings take place, where, how often, and who can attend. Also defined would be each shareholder's right to vote and how votes can be cast.

2. Board of Directors—The duties of each member of the Board are set, and the time for Board meetings is established. This clause will also state how Board members are elected and the length of their term of office.

3. Officers—There will be a clause that will identify corporate officers; for example, Chairman of the Board, President, Vice-President. The By-Laws establish the procedures for choosing and removing officers, and define the duties of each position.

Other clauses may discuss books and records, how corporate business will be conducted, and who is authorized to act on behalf of the corporation.

EXHIBIT 6-4

CHECKLIST

Borrowing Entity Is: (1)
( ) Individual
( ) Partnership
   ( ) General Partnership
   ( ) Joint Venture
   ( ) Limited Partnership
( ) Corporation
If borrowing entity is a partnership: (2)
   ( ) Statement of Partnership Reviewed
      Date: _____
   Partnership Agreement Reviewed
      Date: _____
   Partners authorized to incur debt are:
_____ (3) _____

_____

   Partners authorized to pledge real estate owned are:
_____ (4) _____

_____

If borrowing entity is a corporation: (5)
   ( ) Articles of Incorporation Reviewed
      Date: _____
   ( ) Corporation By-Laws Reviewed
      Date: _____
Persons authorized to incur debt on behalf of the corporation are:
   Name: _____ (6) _____   Title: _____
   Name: _____   Title: _____
Persons authorized to pledge real estate assets owned to secure the corporation's
debt are:
   Name: _____ (7) _____   Title: _____
   Name: _____   Title: _____

End Note

Use the checklist in Exhibit 6-4 to make sure that all the appropriate documents have been received and reviewed. Fill it in as follows:

1. Check the appropriate box to indicate the nature of the borrowing entity.

2. If the borrowing entity is a partnership, check the boxes to indicate receipt and review of the statement of partnership and partnership agreement and the date of review.

3. The partners who can incur debt on behalf of the partnership.

4. The partners who can pledge real estate owned by the partnership as security for debt incurred.

5. If the borrowing entity is a corporation, check the boxes to indicate receipt and review of the Articles of Incorporation and Corporation By-Laws, and give the date that each was reviewed.

6. The name and title of the person(s) authorized to borrow on behalf of the corporation.

7. The name and title of the person(s) authorized to pledge real estate owned to secure corporate debt.

7

How to Document
the Indebtedness

Documenting a loan begins with documentation of the indebtedness. These documents establish the agreement between lender and borrower regarding loan amount, terms of the loan, repayment schedule, and interest rate.

Additional documentation insures that the borrower is properly authorized to incur the debt, and that the individuals signing on behalf of the borrower are authorized to do so.

Types of Promissory Notes

A promissory note is the evidence of indebtedness, a promise by a borrower to repay a sum of money under certain specific terms. It documents loan amount, interest rate, and repayment schedule. Different lending situations may dictate the form of the note. For example, interest may be included in the payment, separate from the payment or paid at the end of the note. Clauses may be included regarding prepayment options, whether the loan is due if the property is sold, and tying one note into other notes.

Using the Interest Only Note

Exhibit 7-1 is an example of an Interest Only Note, with principal due at maturity. It should be completed as follows:

1. The dollar amount of the loan; for example, "$100,000.00."
2. The city and state in which the note is being executed.
3. The date of the note.
4. The term of the loan; for example, "Six (6) Months."
5. The name of the lending institution.

EXHIBIT 7-1

$ _____(1)_____ _____(2)_____ _____(3)_____ , 19 _____

_____(4)_____ after date, for value received, the undersigned promise to pay to

_____(5)_____ banking association, or order, at _____(6)_____

the sum of _____(7)_____ DOLLARS

with interest from _____(8)_____ until paid,

at the rate of _____(9)_____ per cent per annum (computed on the basis of a 360 day year and actual days elapsed),

payable _____(10)_____

Should default be made in payment of interest when due, or in the event of default other than in the non-payment of interest when due, the whole sum of principal and interest shall become immediately due and payable without notice, at the option of the holder of this note. Also, the interest rate provided for under this note shall, at the option of the holder hereof, and without notice, increase to 2% in excess of the contractual rate, but not less than 10% per year effective from the day following the agreed or accelerated date of maturity and continuing until principal and interest shall have been fully paid. Principal and interest payable in lawful money of the United States. Should the undersigned (or the successor in interest to the undersigned) without the consent in writing of the holder hereof sell, transfer, convey, or permit, or suffer to be sold, transferred, or conveyed, the interest of the undersigned in the property (or any part thereof) which secures this note, then such holder may at its election declare the whole sum of principal and interest (and all other sums secured by any deed of trust taken in connection with this note) immediately due and payable. This provision shall apply to each and every sale, transfer, or conveyance, regardless whether or not the holder has consented to, or waived, its right hereunder, whether by action or non-action, in connection with any previous sale, transfer, or conveyance, whether one or more. If this note is not paid when due, the undersigned promise to pay, in addition, all costs and expenses of collection and reasonable attorney's fees on account of such collection, whether or not suit is filed thereon.

The undersigned shall pay to the holder hereof a late charge of 6% or $5.00 whichever is greater of any provided for payment of principal or interest not received by the holder hereof on or before the 10th day after such payment is due.

Should this note be signed by more than one person and/or firm and/or corporation, all of the obligations herein contained shall be considered joint and several obligations of each signer hereof.

This note is secured by a Deed of Trust/Mortgage in favor of (11)

(12)

_____   _____

_____   _____

DO NOT DESTROY THIS NOTE

6. The location at which payments are to be made.

7. The amount of the loan in written form; for example, "One Hundred Thousand and No/100."

8. Language detailing the date at which interest starts to accrue, usually "The date funds are disbursed."

9. The interest rate; for example, "Ten (10%)."

10. The terms under which interest is payable. Interest may be payable "Monthly, on the first day of every month following disbursement" or "Quarterly," or "Semi-annually."

11. Fill in the type of security instrument, either Trust Deed, with name of Trustee, or Mortgage.

12. The borrower should sign the note. Be sure that everyone who needs to sign does so.

Using a Regular Installment Payment Note

Exhibit 7-2 is an example of a Promissory Note requiring regular installment payments on the loan. In this case the principal portion is fixed and the interest is extra.

The form can be completed with the following information:

1. The dollar amount of the loan; for example, "$100,000.00."

2. The city and state in which the note is being executed.

3. The date of the note.

4. The name of the lending institution.

5. The location at which payments are to be made, usually the office of the institution that originated the loan.

6. The amount of the loan in written form; for example, "One Hundred Thousand and No/100."

7. Language detailing the date at which interest starts to accrue, usually "The date funds are disbursed."

8. The interest rate; for example, "Ten (10%)."

9. The timing for interest payments; for example, "Monthly" or "Quarterly."

10. The dollar amount of principal payments; for example, "Two Hundred Fifty and No/100 ($250.00)."

11. The day of the month when principal payments are to be made; for example, the "1st."

12. Put language in this space if payments are not to be made every month. You might use "second loan" or "and every."

13. The date on which principal payments are to commence.

14. The date on which payments are to end and all unpaid principal is due and payable.

15. Fill in the type of security instrument, either Trust Deed, with name of Trustee, or Mortgage.

16. The borrower should sign the note. Be sure that everyone who needs to sign does so.

EXHIBIT 7-2

$ ____(1)____ ____(2)____ ___, ____(3)____ , 19 ____

In installments as herein stated, for value received, the undersigned promise to pay to

____(4)____ at ____(5)____

the sum of ____(6)____ DOLLARS,

with interest from ____(7)____ on unpaid principal at the

rate of ____(8)____ per cent per annum (computed on the basis of a 360 day year and actual

days elapsed), payable ____(9)____

principal payable in installments of ____(10)____

_____ DOLLARS

on the ____(11)____ day of each ____(12)____ month,

beginning on the ____(13)____ day of _____, 19 ____ and continuing until

the ____(14)____ day of _____, 19 ____, on which day the unpaid balance of

said principal sum, with the unpaid interest due thereon, shall become due and payable.

Should default be made in payment of any installment of principal or interest when due, or in the event of default other than in the non-payment of principal or interest when due, the whole sum of principal and interest shall become immediately due and payable without notice, at the option of the holder of this note. Also, the interest rate provided for under this note shall, at the option of the holder hereof, and without notice, increase to 2% in excess of the contractual rate, but not less than 10% per year effective from the day following the agreed or accelerated date of maturity and continuing until principal and interest shall have been fully paid. Principal and interest payable in lawful money of the United States. Should the undersigned (or the successor in interest to the undersigned) without the consent in writing of the holder hereof sell, transfer, convey, or permit, or suffer to be sold, transferred, or conveyed the interest of the undersigned in the property (or any part thereof) which secures this note, then such holder may at its election declare the whole sum of principal and interest (and all other sums secured by any deed of trust taken in connection with this note) immediately due and payable. This provision shall apply to each and every sale, transfer, or conveyance, regardless whether or not the holder has consented to, or waived, its right hereunder, whether by action, or non-action, in connection with any previous sale, transfer, or conveyance, whether one or more. If this note is not paid when due, the undersigned promise to pay, in addition, all costs and expenses of collection and reasonable attorney's fees on account of such collection, whether or not suit is filed thereon.

The undersigned shall pay to the holder hereof a late charge of 6% or $5.00 whichever is greater of each and every monthly installment not received by the holder hereof on or before the 10th day after each such installment is due.

Should this note be signed by more than one person and/or firm and/or corporation, all of the obligations herein contained shall be considered joint and several obligations of each signer hereof.

This note is secured by a Deed of Trust/Mortgage in favor of (15)

____(16)____ _____

DO NOT DESTROY THIS NOTE

Using a Principal and Interest Payment Note

Exhibit 7-3 is a note where the payments made include both principal and interest. Fill it in with the following information:

1. The dollar amount of the loan; for example, "$100,000.00."
2. The city and state in which the note is being executed.
3. The date of the note.
4. The name of the lending institution.
5. The location at which payments are to be made, usually the office of the institution that originated the loan.
6. The amount of the loan in written form; for example, "One Hundred Thousand and No/100."
7. Language detailing the date at which interest starts to accrue, usually "The date funds are disbursed."
8. The interest rate; for example, "Ten (10%)."
9. The amount of the payment to be made; for example, "One Thousand Four Hundred Fifty and No/100 ($1,450.00) Dollars."
10. The day of the month on which payments are to be made.
11. Put language in this space if payments are not to be made every month. You might use "second loan" or "and every."
12. The date on which principal payments are to commence.
13. The date on which payments are to end and all unpaid principal is due and payable.
14. Fill in the type of security instrument, either Trust Deed, with name of Trustee, or Mortgage.
15. The borrower should sign the note. Be sure that everyone who needs to sign does so.

Optional Clauses for Promissory Notes

Additional clauses can be added to the promissory note to accommodate peculiarities of a particular loan. One such clause is a "due on sale" clause. This clause allows the lender to accelerate the loan by calling the entire balance due and payable if there is a transfer of property ownership. It might read: "Should borrower sell, enter into a contract of sale, convey or alienate said property or any part thereof, or suffer his title or any interest therein to be divested, whether voluntarily or involuntarily, or lease said property or any part thereof, or lease with an option to sell, or change or permit to be changed the character or use of said property without the written consent of Lender being first obtained, Lender shall have the right, at its option, to declare all sums secured hereby due and payable within 30 days after such declaration."

The "due on encumbrance" clause is similar to the due on sale clause. It allows acceleration if additional financing creates new liens against the property.

Prepayment penalties are also a part of the promissory note. Penalties are assessed if the loan is paid off earlier than anticipated. Such penalties are viewed as additional yield to the lender and compensation for the work and effort that goes into

EXHIBIT 7-3

$ ___(1)___ ___(2)___, ___(3)___

In installments as herein stated, for value received, the undersigned promise to pay to

(4)   at ___(5)___

the sum of ___(6)___ DOLLARS,

with interest from ___(7)___ on unpaid principal at the

rate of _(8)_ per cent per annum (computed on the basis of a 360 day year and actual days elapsed); principal

and interest payable in installments of ___(9)___ Dollars

on the ___(10)___ day of each ___(11)___ month, beginning

on the ___(12)___ day of ___, 19 ___,

and continuing until the ___(13)___ day of ___, 19 ___,

on which day the unpaid balance of said principal sum, with the unpaid interest due thereon, shall become due

and payable.

Each payment shall be credited first on interest then due and the remainder on principal; and interest shall thereupon cease upon the principal so credited. Should default be made in payment of any installment of principal or interest when due or in the event of default other than in the non-payment of principal or interest when due, the whole sum of principal and interest shall become immediately due and payable without notice, at the option of the holder of this note. Also, the interest rate provided for under this note shall, at the option of the holder hereof, and without notice, increase to 2% in excess of the contractual rate, but not less than 10% per year effective from the day following the agreed or accelerated date of maturity and continuing until principal and interest shall have been fully paid. Principal and interest payable in lawful money of the United States. Should the undersigned (or the successor in interest to the undersigned) without the consent in writing of the holder hereof sell, transfer, convey, or permit, or suffer to be sold, transferred, or conveyed, the interest of the undersigned in the property (or any part thereof) which secures this note, then such holder may at its election declare the whole sum of principal and interest (and all other sums secured by any deed of trust taken in connection with this note) immediately due and payable. This provision shall apply to each and every sale, transfer, or conveyance, regardless whether or not the holder has consented to, or waived, its right hereunder, whether by action or non-action, in connection with any previous sale, transfer, or conveyance, whether one or more. If this note is not paid when due, the undersigned promise to pay, in addition, all costs and expenses of collection and reasonable attorney's fees on account of such collection, whether or not suit is filed thereon.

The undersigned shall pay to the holder hereof a late charge of 6% or $5.00 whichever is greater of each and every monthly installment not received by the holder hereof on or before the 10th day after the installment is due.

Should this note be signed by more than one person and/or firm and/or corporation, all of the obligations herein contained shall be considered joint and several obligations of each signer hereof.

This note is secured by a Deed of Trust/Mortgage in favor of (14)

___(15)___

_____   _____

_____   _____

DO NOT DESTROY THIS NOTE

making an income property loan. Early payoff might deprive the lender of yield anticipated when he made the loan decision.

If there is no penalty, then the clause can read: "Privilege is reserved to pay all or any part of this Note at any time during the term hereof without penalty."

If there is a prepayment penalty, then language should be inserted into the note to define the terms of the penalty.

For example:

"This note cannot be prepaid in any way during the first five (5) loan years. After the 5th loan year the note can be prepaid upon the payment of a penalty equal to 5% in the 6th loan year, the penalty declining 1/2% per loan year thereafter."

There are times when you may choose to allow some level of payoff without necessarily permitting the entire loan to be prepaid. Then language such as the following can be included in the note:

"Notwithstanding any other terms of this prepayment penalty clause, the borrower can pay off a sum equal to ten (10%) of the then outstanding loan balance in any loan year after the 5th loan year without penalty."

The language in these clauses can be modified to suit the individual loan transaction.

If the borrower is granted the right to extend the note for an additional period of time, a clause regarding the extension should be included in the promissory note. Use language such as the following:

"Provided the maker is not then in default under the terms of this Note, or in the provisions of the loan security documents, including, but not limited to, the Deed of Trust, and Assignment of Rents and Leases, Lender shall grant Borrower a six-month extension of the Note from June 1, 19— to December 1, 19—, upon the payment of an extension fee equal to 1/2 of 1% of the principal balance then outstanding."

Sometimes lenders are asked to grant a "nonrecourse" loan. Nonrecourse means that in a default the lender agrees to look only to the real estate for repayment, not the personal assets of the borrower(s) or guarantor(s). Language such as the following can be inserted into the note:

"All payments of principal and interest to be made by the Borrower on the Note shall be made only from the Collateral and the income and proceeds thereof, and the holder of this Note by its acceptance hereof agrees that it will look solely to the Collateral and the income and proceeds thereof for the payment of this Note and that neither the Borrower nor any of its partners shall be personally liable to the holder hereof for any amounts payable under this Note."

How to Make Modifications to a Note

Sometimes a modification of the terms of a note is warranted. Any changes from the original note should be documented with a Modification Agreement. Exhibit 7-4 is such an agreement and it can be completed in the following manner:

1. Fill in the dollar amount of the original note; for example, "Two Hundred Fifty Thousand and No/100 Dollars ($250,000.00)."

EXHIBIT 7-4

NOTE MODIFICATION AGREEMENT

WHEREAS there is a certain Promissory Note ("Note") in the amount of _____ (1) _____ and dated _____ (2) _____, made by _____ (3) _____ ("Borrower") to _____ (4) _____ ("Lender"), and

WHEREAS Borrower and Lender desire and agree to modify the terms of that Note,

NOW, THEREFORE, Borrower and Lender agree to the following modifications:

(5)

Borrower's default under any of the obligations hereunder not cured within any applicable notice or grace periods in the Note, is a default of the Note. The remaining terms and conditions of the Note shall remain in full force and effect and unmodified.

_____ (6) _____
By:_____ (7) _____
By:_____
_____ (8) _____
By:_____ (9) _____
By:_____

2. The date of the original note.
3. The name of the borrower under the original note.
4. The name of the lender under the original note.
5. Put in language to detail the modifications to which borrower and lender agree.
6. The name of the borrowing entity, if corporation or partnership.
7. The signature(s) of the borrower.
8. The name of the lending institution.
9. The signature(s) of the authorized parties at the lending institution.

Use and Example of a Loan Revision Agreement

Another form of modification to the original agreement between borrower and lender is the Loan Revision Agreement. This document should be used when changes are of such a nature that the recorded security instrument, whether Deed of Trust or Mortgage, will be affected by the change.

Exhibit 7-5 is a Loan Revision Agreement. Note that the agreement should be recorded in the same manner as the original security instrument. Fill the document in as follows:

1. The name and address to which the recorded document should be returned.
2. The loan number, if desired.
3. The name of the lending institution issuing the revision.
4. The date of the original promissory note.
5. The name of the lending institution.
6. The name of the borrowing entity.
7. The dollar amount of the original loan.
8. The maturity date of the original note.
9. The type of recorded security instrument: deed of trust, or mortgage.
10. The date of the original security instrument.
11. The recording information giving the location in the official records of the security instrument.
12. The county and state in which the security instrument is recorded.
13. The date on which the principal balance was taken for purposes of reflecting it on the revision form.
14. The current principal balance of the loan corresponding to the date shown on the revision form.
15. The date to which interest is paid.
16. The terms of the original note which are being modified.
17. The location at which the revision document is signed.
18. The date on which the revision document is executed.
19. Type in the name of the borrowing entity.
20. The signature of the borrower.
21. The date on which the revision document is accepted by the lender.
22. The name of the lending institution.
23. Signature(s) of the authorized representatives of the lending institution.

As with all recorded documents, signatures must be notarized for proper recording to take place.

Proper Use of Guarantees

The question of whether to take guarantees as part of a commercial real estate transaction is a complex one depending a great deal on the laws in your state. These laws will dictate whether guarantees can be effectively pursued in a default situation. Guarantees are most useful for their moral impact on the guarantor, and, therefore, should probably be taken only when you know the guarantor well.

Exhibit 7-6 is a Continuing Guaranty form. Complete it with the following information:

1. The name of your lending institution.
2. The name of the borrowing entity, the one whose debt is being guaranteed.
3. Write out the amount of the real estate loan; for example, "Two Hundred Thousand and No/100."

———— SPACE ABOVE THIS LINE FOR RECORDER'S USE ————

LOAN REVISION AGREEMENT

TO: (3)   LOAN NO. _____(2)_____

This Revision Agreement refers to the loan evidenced by a promissory note dated _____(4)_____,19_____,
in favor of   (5)   ("Bank") executed by _____(6)_____
(hereinafter referred to as "Borrower") in the amount of $ _____(7)_____, payable in full on ____(8)____, 19 ____,
subject to the installment maturities therein, if any. Said note is secured by _____(9)_____
dated _____(10)_____,19_____ (hereinafter referred to as the "encumbrance"), recorded on _____,
19 _____, in book _____(11)_____, Page _____, instrument number _____, in the Recorder's
                    (12)
Office of _____County, State of
The principal balance of said note as of _____(13)_____, 19 _____, is $ ____(14)____ on which interest is
paid to _____(15)_____, 19 _____.

The undersigned Borrower hereby requests that Bank revise the terms of said note and that such Bank accept payment thereof at the time, or times, and in the manner following:

(16)

In consideration of Bank's acceptance of the revision of said note, including the time for payment thereof, all as set forth above, the Borrower does hereby acknowledge and admit to such indebtedness, and further does unconditionally agree to pay such indebtedness together with interest thereon within the time and in the manner as revised in accordance with the foregoing, together with any and all attorney's fee, costs of collection, and any other sums secured by the encumbrance.

Any and all security for said principal obligation held by Bank, including the encumbrance, may be enforced by Bank concurrently or independently of each other and in such order as Bank may determine; and with reference to any such security in addition to the encumbrance Bank, may without consent of or notice to Borrower, exchange, substitute or release such security without affecting the liability of the Borrower, and Bank may release any one or more parties hereto or to the above obligation or permit the liability of said party or parties to terminate without affecting the liability of any other party or parties liable thereon.

This agreement is a revision only, and not a novation; and except as herein provided all of the terms and conditions of said note and said encumbrance shall remain unchanged and in full force and effect.

When more than one Borrower signs this agreement, all agree:
    a.   That where in this agreement the word "Borrower" appears, it shall read "each Borrower"
    b.   That breach of any convenant by any Borrower may at the Bank's option be treated as breach by all Borrowers;
    c.   That the liability and obligations of each Borrower are joint and several.

Dated at _____(17)_____,   this ____(18)____ day of _____, 19 ____.

_____(19)_____

_____(20)_____
Borrower

The foregoing agreement is accepted this

_____ day of _____(21)_____, 19 ____.
        (22)

By _____(23)_____

(ALL OF THE ABOVE SIGNATURES MUST BE ACKNOWLEDGED)

EXHIBIT 7-6

CONTINUING GUARANTY

For valuable consideration, the undersigned (hereinafter called Guarantors) jointly and severally unconditionally guarantee and promise to pay (1) (hereinafter called Bank), or order, on demand, in lawful money of the United States, any and all indebtedness

of _____(2)_____

_____ (hereinafter called Borrowers) to Bank. The word "indebtedness" is used herein in its most comprehensive sense and includes any and all advances, debts, obligations and liabilities of Borrowers or any one or more of them, heretofore, now, or hereafter made, incurred or created, whether voluntary or involuntary and however arising, whether due or not due, absolute or contingent, liquidated or unliquidated, determined or undetermined, and whether Borrowers may be liable individually or jointly with others, or whether recovery upon such indebtedness may be or hereafter become barred by any statute of limitations, or whether such indebtedness may be or hereafter become otherwise unenforceable.

The liability of Guarantors shall not exceed at any one time the sum of _____(3)_____

_____ Dollars ($ _____(4)_____) for principal, plus all interest thereon. Notwithstanding the foregoing, Bank may permit the indebtedness of Borrowers to exceed Guarantors' liability. This is a continuing guaranty relating to any indebtedness, including but not limited to that arising under successive transactions which shall continue the indebtedness or create new indebtedness after satisfaction, payment or reduction of previous indebtedness. The amount of Guarantors' liability hereunder and under any other agreement now or at any time hereafter in force between Guarantors and Bank including any other guarantee executed by Guarantors relating to any indebtedness of Borrower to Bank shall be cumulative and not alternative. This guaranty shall not apply to any new indebtedness created after actual receipt by Bank of written notice of its revocation as to future transactions. Any payment by Guarantors shall not reduce their maximum obligation hereunder, unless written notice to that effect be actually received by Bank at or prior to the time of such payment. This is a continuing guaranty and Guarantors agree that it shall remain in full force until and unless Guarantors deliver to Bank written notice that it has been revoked as to credit granted or indebtedness incurred subsequent to the effective time of revocation as herein provided. Delivery of such notice shall not affect any of Guarantors' obligations hereunder with respect to credit extended prior to the effective date of such revocation nor shall it affect any of the obligations of any other guarantor for the credit granted to or indebtedness incurred by Borrower.

The obligations hereunder are joint and several, and independent of the obligations of Borrowers, and a separate action or actions may be brought and prosecuted against Guarantors whether action is brought against Borrowers or whether Borrowers be joined in any such action or actions; and Guarantors waive the benefit of any statute of limitations affecting their liability hereunder or the enforcement thereof.

Either before or after revocation hereof, Guarantors authorize Bank, without notice or demand and without affecting their liability hereunder, from time to time to (a) renew, compromise, extend, accelerate or otherwise change the time for payment of, or otherwise change the terms of the indebtedness or any part thereof, including increase or decrease of the rate of interest thereon; (b) take and hold security for the payment of this guaranty or the indebtedness guaranteed, and exchange, enforce, waive and release any such security; (c) apply such security and direct the order or manner of sale thereof as Bank in its discretion may determine; and (d) release or substitute any one or more endorsers or guarantors. Bank may without notice assign this guaranty in whole or in part.

Guarantors waive any right to require Bank to (a) proceed against Borrowers; (b) proceed against or exhaust any security held from Borrowers; or (c) pursue any other remedy in Bank's power whatsoever. Guarantors waive any defense arising by reason of any disability or other defense of Borrowers or by reason of the cessation from any cause whatsoever of the liability of Borrowers. Until all indebtedness of Borrowers to Bank shall have been paid in full, even though such indebtedness is in excess of Guarantors' liability hereunder, Guarantors shall have no right of subrogation, and waive any right to enforce any remedy which Bank now has or may hereafter have against Borrowers, and waive any benefit of, and any right to participate in any security now or hereafter held by Bank, and without limiting the generality of the foregoing, Guarantors specifically waive and relinquish as against Bank any defense or benefit otherwise available to them should Bank make an election of remedies as against Borrowers (and irrespective of the circumstances or manner in which or whereby such election is made) which destroys or impairs Guarantors' subrogation rights or rights to proceed against the Borrowers for reimbursement. Guarantors waive all presentments, demands for performance, notice of non-performance, or other default, protests, notices of protest, notices of dishonor, and notices of acceptance of this guaranty and of the existence, creation, or incurring of new or additional indebtedness. Guarantors assume the responsibility for being and keeping themselves informed of the financial condition of Borrowers and of all other circumstances bearing upon the risk of nonpayment of the indebtedness which diligent inquiry would reveal, and agree that Bank shall have no duty to advise Guarantors of information known to it regarding such condition or such circumstances.

In addition to all liens upon, and rights of setoff against the moneys, securities or other property of Guarantors given to Bank by law, Bank shall be hereby granted a security interest in and shall have a right of setoff against all moneys, securities and other property of Guarantors now or hereafter in the possession of or on deposit with Bank, whether held in a general or special account or deposit, or for safekeeping or otherwise; and every such lien and right of setoff may be exercised without demand upon or notice to Guarantors. No lien or right of setoff shall be deemed to have been waived by any act or conduct on the part of Bank, or by any neglect to exercise such right of setoff or to enforce such lien, or by any delay in so doing; and every right of setoff and lien shall continue in full force and effect until such right of setoff or lien is specifically waived or released by an instrument in writing executed by Bank.

EXHIBIT 7-6 (Cont'd.)

Any indebtedness of Borrowers now or hereafter held by Guarantors is hereby subordinated to the indebtedness of Borrowers to Bank; and such indebtedness of Borrowers to Guarantors if Bank so requests shall be collected, enforced and received by Guarantors as trustees for Bank and be paid over to Bank on account of the indebtedness of Borrowers to Bank but without reducing or affecting in any manner the liability of Guarantors under the other provisions of this guaranty.

Where any one or more of Borrowers are corporations or partnerships it is not necessary for Bank to inquire into the powers of Borrowers or the officers, directors, partners or agents acting or purporting to act on their behalf, and any indebtedness made or created in reliance upon the professed exercise of such powers shall be guaranteed hereunder.

Guarantors have entered into this guaranty with the understanding that Bank may rely upon it to the exclusion of any other guarantees. Bank has not, nor has Borrower represented that there are or may be other guarantors. However, nothing in this guaranty shall bind Bank to seek other guarantors, separate and apart from the undersigned. Guarantors understand that Bank may already have, or concurrently herewith may have obtained or hereafter may obtain other guarantors (one or more, several or joint) of the indebtedness hereinabove referred to. Such guarantors, heretofore, herewith, or hereafter obtained, shall in no way affect Guarantors' complete joint and several liability hereunder for the full amount of said indebtedness. Nothing herein shall require Bank to sue all of said Guarantors severally or together or to sue more than one or to pro rate the above liability among the Guarantors or any of them. Guarantors agree that Bank may, in its sole and uncontrolled discretion, sue any one or more of the Guarantors for the whole of said indebtedness; and within its sole and uncontrolled discretion Bank may take judgment against any one of the Guarantors for the whole of the indebtedness above referred to, plus interest costs and attorney's fees, or within its sole and uncontrolled discretion Bank may pro rate such judgment between or among one or more of such Guarantors.

Guarantors agree to pay reasonable attorney's fees and all other costs and expenses which may be incurred by Bank in the enforcement of this guaranty, irrespective of whether suit is filed thereon.

Guarantors agree that recourse may be had against their separate property for all their obligations under this guaranty.

In all cases where there is but a single Borrower or a single Guarantor, then all words used in the plural shall be deemed to have been used in the singular where the context and construction so require; and when there is more than one Borrower named herein, or when this guaranty is executed by more than one Guarantor, the word "Borrowers" and the word "Guarantors" respectively shall mean all and any one or more of them.

This guaranty shall benefit the Bank, its successors and assigns, and shall bind Guarantors' successors and assigns. This guaranty is assignable by Bank with respect to all or any portion of the indebtedness and obligations guaranteed hereunder, and when so assigned Guarantors shall be liable to the assignees under this guaranty without in any manner affecting Guarantors' liability hereunder with respect to any indebtedness or obligations retained by Bank.

If any term, provision, covenant or condition of this agreement is held by a court of competent jurisdiction to be invalid, void or unenforceable, the remainder of the provisions shall remain in full force and effect and shall in no way be affected, impaired or invalidated.

This Continuing Guaranty is executed by Guarantors this _____ day of _____ **(5)** ,

19 _____ .

(6)

_____   _____
(S. S. or TAX I. D. NO. _____)   (S. S. or TAX I. D. NO. _____**(7)**_____)

_____   _____
(S. S. or TAX I. D. NO. _____)   (S. S. or TAX I. D. NO. _____)

4. The amount of the loan in numerical form, "$200,000.00."

5. The date that the guaranty form is executed by the guarantor.

6. The signature of the guarantor(s). Use a separate guarantee form for each guarantor.

7. The social security number (if an individual) or tax identification number (if partnership or corporation) of the guarantor.

Supplementing a Note with a Loan Agreement

There are times when the terms of a loan are too complex to be covered by a form note. A Loan Agreement can supplement the note by describing and detailing additional terms and conditions that are a part of the indebtedness.

A loan agreement can be set up with the following sections spelling out the terms by which the borrower will be bound:

1.Definitions. All terminology should be defined so that no confusion will result later as to the specific meaning implied by the use of certain language.

2. Amount and Terms of the Loan. The loan amount should be indicated and reference made to the attached note, of which the loan agreement is a part. Procedures should be established for borrowings under the note and repayment of the loan. Prepayment conditions and penalties can be explained. The interest rate should be defined.

3. Representations and Warranties. Representations and warranties by the borrower assure the lender about facts the lender needs to know in order to make the loan. These can be as detailed as the lender feels is needed.

4. Conditions Precedent. Conditions precedent must be met before the lender loans funds. Examples of typical conditions are proper title insurance, legal opinion, copies of exhibits still needed for the file, and necessary permits or licenses.

5. Affirmative Covenants. These covenants define the borrower's agreement to perform during the course of the loan. An example would be an agreement to provide regular financial statements on an annual basis.

6. Negative Covenants. These covenants require that the borrower agree not to engage in certain activities during the loan term. For example, the borrower might agree not to allow his net worth to decline below a certain figure, or to refrain from additional financing using the subject property as collateral without the prior consent of the original lender.

7. Events of Default. Clauses will be written into the agreement defining default, and listing the various incidents that would be interpreted as a default.

Loan agreements are not necessary for the average loan. They are used when the dollars to be lent are unusually high for the institution, or where the nature of the loan demands a more detailed agreement.

How to Complete a Construction Loan Agreement

The construction loan agreement explains the terms and conditions under which funds will be disbursed as work progresses. This document can be as complex and thorough as needed for the particular transaction.

Exhibit 7-7 is a Construction Loan Agreement form. Complete it with the following information:

1. The name of the borrower or borrowing entity.
2. The name of the lending institution.
3. The dollar amount of the construction loan.

EXHIBIT 7-7

CONSTRUCTION LOAN AGREEMENT

The agreements herein contained are entered into in connection with a construction loan which the undersigned borrower(s)

(1)

(hereinafter referred to as the "Borrower", whether one or more), has applied for from

(2)

(hereinafter referred to as the "Bank"), for the purpose of, among other things, defining the use and disposition which shall be made of the proceeds of such construction loan (and such other moneys if any as may be deposited by the Borrower with the Bank for similar use). Said construction loan is to be evidenced by the promissory note of the Borrower in favor of the Bank (which promissory note is hereinafter referred to as the "Note") for the principal sum of $ _____(3)_____ , bearing simple interest at the rate of __(4)__ percent per annum, dated _____(5)_____ , 19____ , and secured by a (6) of the same date to _____(7)_____ , covering, and which is to be a first lien or charge upon, the Borrower's real property, including all buildings and improvements now or hereafter constructed thereon, in ____(8)____ County, described as

(9)

(hereinafter referred to as the "Property").

NOW, THEREFORE, IN CONSIDERATION of the mutual covenants and promises of the parties and in further consideration for the making of such construction loan, the parties hereto agree as follows:

1. The Borrower contemplates constructing and hereby promises and agrees to construct (and the said construction loan is being obtained for the purpose of obtaining funds for such construction), on the Property, a building or buildings and improvements (hereinafter for convenience called the "Structure", whether one or more) according to certain plans and specifications, a copy of which has been heretofore furnished to the Bank or is attached hereto bearing Borrower's signature or initials and made a part hereof.

2. Borrower hereby certifies that he has examined and is familiar with all conditions, restrictions, reservations and zoning ordinances affecting the Property and that said Structure will in all respects conform to and comply with all the requirements of said conditions, restrictions, reservations, and zoning ordinances.

3. In addition to the net proceeds of said construction loan, the Borrower herewith delivers to Bank the sum of _____

(10)

_____ Dollars

(Insert Amount or State "None")

for deposit with the funds constituting the proceeds of said loan. Such net proceeds of said construction loan and such sums as delivered herewith (or hereafter for like purpose) to be held in and handled as a special non-interest bearing account (hereinafter referred to as the "Account") and disbursed in accordance with this agreement. Borrower represents that the total of said moneys (to wit: such construction loan funds and such sums as are delivered herewith) is sufficient to pay the customary charges and expenses in connection with said construction loan and to complete said Structure and pay all costs of construction thereof. Should it appear at any time that in the reasonable judgment of Bank, further or additional funds are required for said purposes, the Borrower agrees to promptly deposit the required sums with said Bank. The Borrower hereby irrevocably authorizes and empowers said Bank to use and/or dispose of the whole of said moneys, to wit, the proceeds of said construction loan and the herewith delivered additional sum if any (and any further or additional sums hereafter deposited with said Bank for like purposes), and the Borrower and the Bank hereby agree that the same shall be used and/or disposed of, in the following manner and for the following purposes, the Borrower hereby irrevocably assigning, transferring and pledging to said Bank the said moneys for said purposes, namely:

First: To pay all costs and charges heretofore or hereafter incurred in connection with the making of said loan, including Bank's loan fee, cost of policy of title insurance, tax and lien service, recording and any other necessary items, and if it is contemplated that said loan will be guaranteed under the Servicemen's Readjustment Act, or insured under the National Housing Act, to impound such funds as may be necessary to cover taxes, fire insurance, mortgage insurance, and any other items mentioned in the law or regulations in reference thereto; such costs and charges are as follows:

(11)

Second: The remainder in the Account shall be released (subject to the terms and provisions of this construction loan agreement) in installments from time to time, during progress of construction of said Structure and/or following completion thereof, in accordance with the following Schedule:

(12)

EXHIBIT 7-7 (Cont'd.)

4. Bank may, in its sole discretion, change the amounts and manner of disbursement of any funds, provided such changes shall not delay in time or diminish the total to be disbursed in the foregoing Schedule. Borrower agrees, when requested by Bank so to do, to furnish, as a condition to disbursement, receipted invoices and releases of mechanic's lien rights covering work done and/or materials furnished in respect of the then requested disbursement, and also evidencing the expenditure of an amount equal to the total of funds at such time disbursed from the Account.

5. Borrower warrants that he has not received other financing for either the acquisition of the Property or the construction and installation of the Structure except as has been specifically disclosed in writing to the Bank prior to recordation of the aforesaid Deed of Trust.

6. If it is contemplated that said construction loan will be guaranteed under the Servicemen's Readjustment Act or insured under the National Housing Act the release of said installments shall, in addition to the requirements set forth in said Schedule, be subject to the construction having been approved by the governmental agency concerned when required under its applicable rules and regulations, and Borrower agrees to comply with the statutes and regulations relating thereto, and further agrees to perform each and every condition provided in any commitment to insure or guarantee the payment of such construction loan as issued by any agency established pursuant to the foregoing Acts.

7. All moneys in the Account and/or so held by the Bank (including any additional moneys hereafter placed therein) shall be construed to be and are hereby made security for the payment and performance of each and every of the Borrower's obligations in favor of or held by the Bank; and the Bank is authorized, notwithstanding any provision to the contrary herein, to use said moneys or any portion thereof, in or toward the payment or performance of any obligation of the Borrower herein or in said (6) contained including the obligation of the Borrower to complete said Structure, and if said moneys are so used and shall be insufficient to remedy any default of the Borrower and/or complete said Structure, the Borrower promises and agrees to pay at once the deficiency, or to deposit at once with the Bank a sufficient sum in cash to cover such deficiency, and should the Borrower fail so to do the Bank may at its option, but without any obligation upon it so to do, employ workmen and purchase materials to protect or complete said Structure and may advance its own funds for any such purpose, in which event all such advancements shall be construed to be secured by said (6), it being expressly understood and agreed that the Bank shall not be liable for the construction of or failure to construct or complete or protect said Structure nor for the payment of any bills incurred in connection with such construction, nor for the performance or non-performance of any other obligation of the Borrower herein or in said (6) mentioned.

8. In the event Bank exercises its option to complete said Structure by using its own funds for such purposes, Borrower agrees to pay to Bank the amounts so expended forthwith, together with interest from the date of the Bank's expenditures at the rate of (13) per annum.

9. Borrower shall diligently proceed with construction and completion of the Structure in accordance with the aforesaid plans and specifications. The Structure shall be completed on or before (14) ; provided, however, that the time within which the Structure must be completed shall be extended for a period equal to the period of any delay caused by fire, earthquake, or other acts of God, riot, insurrection, governmental regulations of the sales of material and supplies or the transportation thereof, or strikes, directly affecting the work of construction or shortages of material or labor resulting directly from governmental controls or diversions. In no event, however, shall the time for completion of the Structure be extended beyond (15)

10. Bank, through its officers, agents or employees, shall have the right at all reasonable times:
    (a) To enter upon the Property and inspect the improvements and the work of construction to determine that the same is in conformity with the plans and specifications and all of the requirements hereof, and if said work is not deemed to be in conformance with said plans and specifications, or is not otherwise satisfactory to Bank, it shall have the right to stop such work and order its replacement whether or not unsatisfactory work has therefore been incorporated in said Structure, and the Bank shall not be obligated to make any releases of funds in said account unless or until said construction work is satisfactory to it; and
    (b) To examine the books, records, accounting data and other documents of Borrower, pertaining to construction of the Structure and to make extracts therefrom or copies thereof. Said books, records and documents shall be made available to Bank, its officers, agents or employees promptly upon written demand therefor.

It is expressly understood and agreed, however, that Bank is under no duty to supervise the work of construction or inspect the work in process or Borrower's books and that any such inspection is for the sole purpose of preserving Bank's rights hereunder. No such inspection on the part of Bank shall constitute a representation by Bank that there has been or will be compliance with the plans and specifications or that the construction is free from defective materials or workmanship.

11. Borrower promises and agrees that no change in the plans and/or specifications will be made after the same have been filed with the Bank, without first obtaining the written consent of said Bank to such changes, and the Borrower further promises and agrees that all contracts let by Borrower or the contractor of Borrower in connection with said construction will contain this provision. In the event Borrower has obtained a commitment from another lender to provide the permanent financing of said Structure, Borrower warrants that the plans and specifications submitted to said lender are true copies of the plans and specifications that have been heretofore approved by Bank. Borrower agrees to comply fully with all requirements and conditions provided in said commitment, and no changes in the plans and specifications approved by said lender shall be made by Borrower without first obtaining the written consent of said lender. Should such changes be made which involve additional cost, Borrower agrees to deposit with the Bank immediately and prior to the commencement of any work in connection with such change an amount equal to the cost thereof for disposition pursuant hereto. Borrower promises and agrees that the construction of said Structure will be continued and carried on to completion with reasonable dispatch.

12. Borrower promises and agrees that no materials, equipment, fixtures or any other part of said improvements shall be purchased and/or installed under conditional sales or lease agreement or other arrangements wherein the right is reserved or accrues to anyone to remove or repossess any such items or consider them as personal property.

13. Bank shall have the right to commence, appear in or defend any action or proceeding purporting to affect the rights, duties or liabilities of the parties hereunder, or the disbursement of any funds in the account. In connection therewith, Bank may incur and pay costs and expenses, including a reasonable attorney's fee. Borrower agrees to pay to Bank on demand all such expenses and Bank is authorized to disburse funds from the account for said purpose.

14. Notwithstanding that the proceeds of said construction loan are placed in said assigned Account and are to be disbursed in installments, Borrower shall pay interest at the rate specified in the Note only upon sums disbursed from the time of each disbursement.

15. Borrower agrees to obtain and deliver to the Bank upon the recording of the aforesaid (6) a policy of title insurance satisfactory to the Bank and showing (6) to be a first lien or charge on said Property subject only to such items as may be waived in writing by the Bank, and shall do all acts and take all steps necessary to maintain said (6) as such first lien or charge. Also Borrower shall, prior to disbursement of any construction loan funds furnish to the Bank upon the commencement of construction adequate Workmen's Compensation insurance and insurance covering fire (with extended coverage and course of construction endorsement), public liability, vandalism, malicious mischief, in amounts and in companies satisfactory to the Bank and with loss payable to the Bank, and receipted bills showing payment of premiums therefor. Bank shall be furnished a Certificate of Liability Insurance including a clause giving the Bank a minimum of ten (10) days notice in the event of cancellation of such liability insurance.

16. The provisions of this agreement are not intended to supersede the provisions of said (6) in any particular, but merely to supplement the latter, and the provisions hereof and of said (6) are intended to be harmonious. Borrower further agrees and acknowledges that his only right in and to the moneys in the said Account is to have the same used and/or disbursed by the Bank in accordance with this agreement, which use and/or disbursement the Bank, upon its acceptance of this agreement hereon, agrees to make for the purpose, at the times and upon the conditions herein set out.

EXHIBIT 7-7 (Cont'd.)

17. THE BORROWER PROMISES THAT NO WORK OF ANY CHARACTER WILL BE COMMENCED NOR WILL ANY MATERIALS BE DELIVERED OR CAUSED TO BE DELIVERED UPON THE PROPERTY UNTIL THE BORROWER HAS RECEIVED WRITTEN NOTICE FROM THE BANK THAT (i) SAID POLICY OF TITLE INSURANCE (IN FORM AND CONTENT SATISFACTORY TO BANK) HAS BEEN RECEIVED BY THE BANK, (ii) VALID BUILDING PERMIT OR PERMITS (IF MORE THAN ONE) HAVE BEEN OBTAINED FROM THE PROPER REGULATORY AUTHORITIES, AND (iii) SUCH CONTRACT BONDS AS MAY BE REQUIRED BY BANK HAVE BEEN RECEIVED BY IT.

18. If any of the following events should occur: (a) If Borrower or the contractor of Borrower does not proceed continuously with the erection and completion of said Structure or if work of construction is otherwise discontinued for a period of fifteen (15) days, except as such interruption or delay is excused under the provisions of paragraph 9 above; (b) if any of the promises, warranties or representations made by Borrower herein are or should the same become untrue; (c) if Borrower should default in the performance of or breach any of the terms, covenants and provisions contained in this agreement or in any lease agreement in the event the property constitutes a leasehold estate; (d) if Borrower should commit an act of bankruptcy or if any relief under the Bankruptcy Act is sought by or against Borrower, or if a receiver is appointed to take charge of the assets or affairs of Borrower, or if Borrower should make an assignment for the benefit of creditors or if Borrower should become insolvent; then and upon the occurrence of each or any such event the same shall be considered an event of default for the occurrence of which Bank shall be entitled at its option and without prior demand or presentment and without any notice to Borrower to (i) declare the unpaid balance of the Note to be due and payable; (ii) terminate any obligation of Bank to disburse the remainder of the loan proceeds (and/or other sums or funds) under the provisions of said paragraph 3, and Bank may, at its option, apply all or any part of said funds and proceeds to payment of principal and/or accrued interest (or both) under the Note; (iii) proceed as authorized by law to satisfy the indebtedness of Borrower to Bank and, in that regard, Bank shall be entitled to all of the remedies, rights, privileges and benefits as are provided in said **(6)** and/or to which Bank may be otherwise entitled for its protection or the enforcement of its rights.

19. All remedies of the Bank provided for herein are cumulative (and no one remedy exclusive of any other remedy) and shall be in addition to any and all other rights and remedies provided by law, including banker's lien and right of set-off. The exercise of any right or remedy by Bank hereunder shall not in any way constitute a cure or waiver of default hereunder or under the **(6)**, or invalidate any act done pursuant to any notice of default, or prejudice Bank in the exercise of any of its rights hereunder or under the **(6)**

20. A receipt, request or instruction in relation to said construction loan or for any advance or release may be made by any one of the parties constituting the Borrower, if more than one person, with the same effect as if signed by all of such parties.

21. In the event that Borrower is organized as a partnership, joint venture or sole proprietorship, the operation of this agreement shall not be affected by the death of any of the general partners or joint venturers comprising the Borrower or of the Borrower himself prior to the completion of said Structure or prior to the disbursement of the balance of said account. Bank is empowered to use and disburse the moneys in said account for the purposes and upon the terms and conditions provided herein, notwithstanding the occurrence of such event.

22. The Borrower does hereby irrevocably empower and authorize the Bank, as agent, to file for record any notices of completion, cessation of labor, or any other notice that said Bank deems necessary to file for record to protect any of the interests of the Bank under the provisions of this Agreement or the Note and **(6)** hereinbefore mentioned. The appointment of the Bank as agent, as herein provided, is expressly declared to be that of an agent coupled with an interest and as such shall be irrevocable and each of the power and authorities given Bank herein are irrevocable and coupled with an interest.

23. Borrower agrees that no lien or encumbrance, voluntary or involuntary, will be imposed upon the Property and no conveyance or transfer will be made of the title thereto without the written consent of Bank.

24. Borrower agrees to notify Bank immediately on completion of the foundation of the Structure and Borrower agrees to furnish to Bank a foundation endorsement, without exceptions, from the title company issuing such policy of title insurance guaranteeing in effect that the foundations have been located and constructed within the boundary lines of the property included in the Bank's **(6)** ; in that regard, Borrower agrees to furnish to said title company surveys and any other information in order to enable said title company to furnish said foundation endorsement to Bank.

25. Borrower agrees that nothing contained in this agreement shall be construed to vest in any contractor or the successors or assigns of any contractor, or any materialman or any laborer, any interest in or claim upon the funds or account so set aside by this agreement.

26. This agreement shall inure to the benefit of Bank, its successors and assigns and in the event Borrower is a natural person, this agreement shall bind his heirs, executors and administrators.

27. This agreement is made for the sole protection of Borrower and Bank, their successors and assigns, and no other person or persons shall have any right of action hereon.

28. Borrower agrees to hold Bank free and harmless from any responsibility and/or liability for the payment of any commission, charge or brokerage fees to anyone which may be payable in connection with the purchase or refinance of said construction loan, it being understood that any such commission, charge or brokerage fees will be paid direct by Borrower to that party or parties entitled thereto.

29. The Borrower agrees that Bank may place sign or signs appropriate to the construction project on the Structure evidencing that construction financing is being made by Bank.

30. Time is of the essence of this agreement.

IN WITNESS WHEREOF, the parties hereto have executed this Agreement this _____ day of _____ **(16)** _____ , 19 ___ .

(17)
_____
BORROWER

_____
BORROWER

Accepted; **(18)**

By ___ **(19)** ___

The undersigned, being the contractor for the construction of the Structure covered by the foregoing Construction Loan Agreement, hereby consents thereto and agrees that all money disbursed hereunder or otherwise received from Borrower in connection therewith shall be received and used as trust funds solely for the payment of materials, labor, services and other costs involved in said construction and for no other purpose until all bills, claims and demands for said materials, labor, services and other costs have been paid in full. The undersigned agrees to be bound by the provisions of the foregoing agreement to the extent they are applicable to the undersigned, including, but without limiting the generality of the foregoing, the provisions regarding changes in plans and specifications set forth in paragraph 11 thereof.

Dated: _____ **(20)** _____ 19 ___ at _____ _____
CONTRACTOR

4. The rate of interest to be charged on the loan.

5. The date of the note, of which the loan agreement is a part.

6. The nature of the security instrument: Deed of Trust or Mortgage.

7. If the security instrument is a Deed of Trust, fill in the name of the Trustee. If a mortgage, this portion can be crossed out.

8. The county and state in which the subject property is located.

9. The address and legal description of the subject property. Lengthy legal descriptions can be attached as "Exhibit A" and language such as the following can be put in the space: "See attached Exhibit A which is made a part hereof by this reference."

10. Fill in the amount of additional funds, if any, which the borrower must put up along with the loan amount to cover the cost of construction.

11. In this section fill in the items which will be paid from loan proceeds before construction funds are disbursed. Items in this section would include loan fees, title insurance, loans to be paid off from proceeds of your loan, and costs of putting the loan on the books.

12. In this section list all of the funds that will be disbursed during the course of construction. The lender should give the terms under which the funds will be disbursed, and any supporting information which must be provided before disbursement.

13. Identify the penalty rate of interest which will be charged in the event of default.

14. The date by which construction should be completed.

15. The final date acceptable by which construction should be completed, usually 30 or 60 days after the first date.

16. The date the document is executed.

17. The borrower(s) should sign the document.

18. The name of the lending institution.

19. The signature of the authorized representative of the lending institution.

20. The general contractor should sign and date the document.

Borrowing Resolutions

Borrowing Resolutions are used with partnership or corporate entities to document the organization's approval of the loan transaction. Resolutions also establish the right of the individuals signing to execute documents on behalf of the organization.

Exhibit 7-8 is a Corporate Resolution to Borrow. Complete it with the following information:

1. The name of the corporate entity that will be the borrower.

2. Your bank's name.

3. The dollar amount of borrowing being authorized. Write this amount out in the first section, then follow with the numbers; for example, Three Million Five Hundred Thousand Dollars ($3,500,000).

4. The names and titles of the corporate officers being authorized to sign documents evidencing loans to the corporation.

5. The name of the Corporate Secretary. This officer is usually the one who certifies the various actions of the Board of Directors.

EXHIBIT 7-8

CORPORATE RESOLUTION TO BORROW

RESOLVED, that this corporation, _____ (1) _____
borrow from _____ (2) _____ hereinafter referred to as 'Bank' from time to time, such sum or sums of money as, in the judgment of the officer or officers hereinafter authorized, this corporation may require; provided that the aggregate amount of such borrowing, pursuant to this resolution, shall not at any one time exceed the sum of:

_____ (3) _____

_____ Dollars ($ _____),

in addition to such amount as may be otherwise authorized:
    RESOLVED FURTHER, that

_____ the _____

or _____ (4) _____ the _____

or _____ the _____

or _____ the _____

of this corporation (the officer or officers, or officers acting in combination, authorized to act pursuant hereto being designated as 'authorized officers'), be and they are hereby authorized, directed and empowered, in the name of this corporation, to execute and deliver to Bank, and Bank is requested to accept, the note or notes, or other instruments or agreements evidencing the indebtedness of this corporation for the monies so borrowed, or to be borrowed, with interest thereon, and said authorized officers are authorized from time to time to execute renewals or extensions of such note or notes, or other instruments or agreements evidencing such indebtedness;

    RESOLVED FURTHER, that said authorized officers be and they are hereby authorized, directed and empowered, as security for any note or notes or any other indebtedness of this Corporation to Bank, whether arising pursuant to this resolution or otherwise, to grant a security interest in, transfer, pledge, mortgage or otherwise hypothecate to Bank or deed in trust for its benefit, any property belonging to this corporation, and to execute and deliver to Bank any and all security agreements, trust receipts, mortgages, pledge agreements, deeds of trust and other hypothecation agreements, including such agreements as required by the notes or other instruments and evidences of indebtedness referred to in the preceding paragraph, and such other agreements as Bank may otherwise require, and said authorized officers may approve, and the execution thereof by said authorized officers, shall be conclusive evidence of such approval;

    FURTHER RESOLVED, that said authorized officers be and they are hereby authorized, directed and empowered (a) to discount with or sell to Bank, Conditional Sale Contracts, security agreements, leases, bailment agreements, notes, acceptances, drafts, receivables and evidences of indebtedness payable to this corporation, upon such terms as may be agreed upon by them and Bank, and to endorse in the name of this corporation said notes, acceptances, drafts, agreements, contracts, receivables and evidence of indebtedness so discounted, and to guarantee the payment of the same to Bank and (b) to apply for and obtain from Bank letters of credit and in connection therewith to execute agreements, applications, trust receipts, security agreements, guaranties, indemnities and other financial undertakings as bank may require;

    RESOLVED FURTHER, that Bank is authorized to act upon this resolution until written notice of its revocation is delivered to Bank, and that the authority hereby granted shall apply with equal force and effect to the successors in office of the officers herein named. The authority given hereunder shall be deemed retroactive and any and all acts authorized hereunder performed prior to the passage of this resolution are hereby ratified and affirmed.

I, _____ (5) _____ , Secretary

_____ (6) _____ , a corporation, incorporated

under the laws of the State of _____ (7) _____ do hereby certify that the foregoing is a full, true and correct copy of a resolution of the Board of Directors of said corporation, duly and validly adopted by the Board of Directors of said corporation as required by law, and by the by-laws of said corporation.

    I further certify that said resolution is still in full force and effect and has not been amended or revoked, and that the specimen signatures appearing below are the signatures of the officers authorized to sign for this corporation by virtue of this resolution.

    IN WITNESS WHEREOF, I have hereunto set my hand as such Secretary, and affixed the corporate seal of said corporation,

this _____ day of _____ (8) _____ , 19 _____ .

    AUTHORIZED SIGNATURES:

_____
(SIGNATURE)
(9)

_____
(SIGNATURE)

_____
(SIGNATURE)

Affix corporate seal here

_____ (10) _____
(SIGNATURE)

SECRETARY OF

_____ (11) _____

A CORPORATION

_____
(SIGNATURE)

6. The name of the corporation.

7. The state in which the company is incorporated.

8. The date the resolution was signed.

9. The signatures of the Board members approving the resolution. Be sure to check the corporate by-laws to make sure the correct number of directors sign and that the ones signing are authorized to do so.

10. The signature of the Corporate Secretary.

11. The name of the corporation.

End Note

The documents discussed in this chapter will help you establish the terms of the loan. Documenting the indebtedness is part of the task. You must also make sure that there is a proper security interest in the property taken as collateral. That is the subject of the next chapter.

8

How to Document
Security Interests

A security interest is a lien taken by the lender on collateral. In real estate lending, the security interest is a key element of the lender's loan decision. Real estate lending is secured lending, with a security interest taken in property or properties against which the borrower is seeking a loan.

A commercial real estate lender may also take a security interest in rents, leases, and personal property. The instruments used to document these liens are the topic of this chapter.

How and When to Use Trust Deeds and Mortgages

The trust deed or mortgage is the instrument used to perfect a lien on a piece of real estate. By recording this document the lender's position becomes a matter of public record, and his position relative to other claimants against the property can be determined.

The trust deed is used in most western states. It has three parties of interest, the trustor, beneficiary, and trustee. The trustor is the borrower/property owner, the party who is pledging the property as collateral for the loan. The beneficiary is the lender, the party making the loan to be secured by the property. It is for the lender's benefit that a trust deed is taken. The trustee is a third party designated by the lender who holds the trust deed and who will act upon it if the need arises to protect the interests of the beneficiary.

This third party, the trustee, is the major differentiating factor between trust deeds and mortgages. Mortgages can be used just the same as trust deeds to perfect an interest in real estate. They are largely found in midwestern or eastern regions of the country. A mortgage has two parties, the mortgagor and the mortgagee. The mortgagor is the borrower, the party pledging an interest in the real estate. The mortgagee is the lender, the one who is advancing the funds.

Sample Deed of Trust

Exhibit 8-1 is a standard Deed of Trust used to secure an interest in commercial real estate. Complete the form as follows:

1. Fill in the name and address to which the recorded instrument should be sent. Usually this will be your real estate department, but it might be your attorneys, loan servicing area, or other designees.

2. The order number of the title insurance policy.

3. The escrow number if your state uses escrows and an escrow is involved.

4. The date of the Deed of Trust. This date should be consistent with the date of the other loan documents.

5. The name of the entity in whom title to the property vests. This will usually be the borrower. Include the designation for the entity, such as corporation or partnership; for example, 45th Street Venture, a California general partnership.

6. The address of the vesting entity.

7. The name of the trustee; usually a title company with which you do business.

8. The name of the beneficiary; for example, "First National Bank, a national banking association."

9. The city and county in which the property is located.

10. The legal description of the property. If the description is too long to fit in the space provided, then type it on a separate sheet headed "Exhibit A" and attach it to the Deed of Trust. In the space provided type "See Exhibit A attached hereto and by this reference made a part hereof" or similar phrasing.

11. If the street address is known the following can be added: "Also known as: 123 East Main Street, San Diego, California"

12. The loan amount.

13. On these lines type in a signature block for use by those principals of the trustor who will sign the document.

Since the document is to be recorded, the Notary Acknowledgment should be filled in by your Notary Public at the time the documents are signed. The Notary's stamp can be put in the box provided. A separate acknowledgment can be attached if the one provided on the document is not appropriate.

Sample Mortgage Document

Exhibit 8-2 is a Mortgage Document. The clauses included and the powers granted to the lender are similar to those in the trust deed. This document can be completed as follows:

1. The date of the mortgage instrument, which should correspond to the date of the rest of the loan documents.

2. The name of the mortgagor (the borrower or property owner).

3. The name of the mortgagee (the lender).

4. The amount of the loan.

5. The date of the Note.

6. The county and state in which the property to be secured is located.

7. The state in which the property is located.

EXHIBIT 8-1

EXHIBIT 8-1

DEED OF TRUST AND ASSIGNMENT OF RENTS (LONG FORM)/DUE-ON CLAUSE

BY THIS DEED OF TRUST, made this   4   day of   , 19   , between

5
6
, herein called **Trustor**, whose address is

(number and street)   (city)   (zone)   (state)

and   7   herein called **Trustee**, and

8
, herein called **Beneficiary**.

Trustor grants, transfers, and assigns to trustee, in trust, with power of sale, that property in

described as: 9   County,

10

11

SHOULD THE TRUSTOR OR HIS SUCCESSOR IN INTEREST WITHOUT THE CONSENT IN WRITING OF THE BENEFICIARY SELL, TRANSFER, OR CONVEY, OR PERMIT, OR SUFFER TO BE SOLD, TRANSFERRED OR CONVEYED, HIS INTEREST IN THE PROPERTY (OR ANY PART THEREOF), THEN BENEFICIARY MAY AT ITS ELECTION DECLARE ALL SUMS SECURED HEREBY IMMEDIATELY DUE AND PAYABLE. THIS PROVISION SHALL APPLY TO EACH AND EVERY SALE, TRANSFER, OR CONVEYANCE, REGARDLESS WHETHER OR NOT BENEFICIARY HAS CONSENTED TO, OR WAIVED, ITS RIGHT HEREUNDER, WHETHER BY ACTION OR NON-ACTION, IN CONNECTION WITH ANY PREVIOUS SALE, TRANSFER, OR CONVEYANCE, WHETHER ONE OR MORE.

Trustor also assigns to Beneficiary all rents, issues and profits of said realty reserving the right to collect and use the same except during continuance of default hereunder and during continuance of such default authorizing Beneficiary to collect and enforce the same by any lawful means in the name of any party hereto.

For the purpose of securing:

(1) Performance of each agreement of Trustor incorporated by reference or contained herein; (2) payment of the indebtedness evidenced by one promissory note of even date herewith and any extensions or renewals thereof in the principal sum of $ 12   payable to Beneficiary; (3) the payment of any money that may be advanced by the Beneficiary to Trustor, or his successors, with interest thereon, evidenced by additional notes (indicating they are so secured) or by endorsement on the original note, executed by Trustor or his successor.

A. TO PROTECT THE SECURITY HEREOF, TRUSTOR AGREES:

(1) To keep said property in good condition and repair, preserve thereon the buildings, complete construction begun, restore damage or destruction, and pay the cost therof; to commit or permit no waste, no violation of laws or covenants or conditions relating to use, alterations or improvements; to cultivate, irrigate, fertilize, fumigate, prune, and do all other acts which the character and use of said property and the estate or interest in said property secured by this Deed of Trust may require to preserve this security.

(2) To provide, maintain and deliver to Beneficiary fire insurance satisfactory to and with loss payable to Beneficiary. The amount collected under any fire or other insurance policy may be applied by Beneficiary upon any indebtedness secured hereby and in such order as Beneficiary may determine, or Beneficiary may release all or any part thereof to Trustor. Such application or release shall not cure or waive any default or notice of default hereunder or invalidate any act done pursuant to such notice.

(3) To appear in and defend any action or proceeding purporting to affect the security hereof or the rights or powers of Beneficiary or Trustee; and to pay all costs and expenses, including cost of evidence of title and attorney's fees, in a reasonable sum, in any such action or proceeding in which Beneficiary or Trustee may appear.

(4) To pay: at least ten days before delinquency all taxes and assessments affecting said property, including assessments on appurtenant water stock; when due, all incumbrances, charges and liens, with interest, on said property or any part thereof, which appear to be prior or superior hereto; all costs, fees and expenses of this Trust.

Should Trustor fail to make any payment or to do any act as herein provided, then Beneficiary or Trustee, but without obligation so to do and without notice to or demand upon Trustor and without releasing Trustor from any obligation hereof, may: make or do the same in such manner and to such extent as either may deem necessary to protect the security hereof, Beneficiary or Trustee being authorized to enter upon said property for such purposes; appear in and defend any action or proceeding purporting to affect the security hereof or the rights or powers of the Beneficiary or Trustee; pay, purchase, contest or compromise any incumbrance, charge or lien which in the judgment of either appears to be prior or superior hereto; and, in exercising any such powers, pay necessary expenses, employ counsel and pay his reasonable fees.

(5) To pay immediately and without demand all sums so expanded by Beneficiary or Trustee, with interest from date of expenditure at the amount allowed by law in effect at the date hereof, and to pay for any statement provided for by law regarding the obligations secured hereby in the amount demanded by Beneficiary, not exceeding the maximum permitted by law at the time of the request therefore.

EXHIBIT 8-1 (cont'd.)

B. IT IS MUTUALLY AGREED THAT:

(1) Any award of damages in connection with any condemnation for public use of or injury to said property or any part therof is hereby assigned to Beneficiary, who may apply or release such moneys received by him in the same manner and with the same effect as provided for disposition of proceeds of fire or other insurance.

(2) By accepting payment of any sum secured hereby after its due date, Beneficiary does not waive his right either to require payment when due of all other sums so secured or to declare default for failure so to pay.

(3) At any time or from time to time, without liability therefor and without notice, upon written request of Beneficiary and presentation of this Deed and such note for endorsement, and without affecting the personal liability of any person for payment of the indebtedness secured hereby, Trustee may: reconvey any part of said property; consent to the making of any map thereof; join in granting any easement thereon; or join in any agreement extending or subordinating the lien or charge hereof.

(4) Upon written request of Beneficiary stating that all sums secured hereby have been paid, and upon surrender of this Deed and said note to Trustee for cancellation and retention and upon payment of its fees, Trustee shall reconvey without warranty, the property then held hereunder. The recitals in such reconveyance of any matters or facts shall be conclusive proof of the truthfulness thereof. The grantee in such reconveyance may be described as "the person or persons legally entitled thereto".

(5) Upon default by Trustor in payment of any indebtedness secured hereby or in performance of any agreement hereunder, Beneficiary may declare all sums secured hereby immediately due and payable by delivery to Trustee of written declaration of default and demand for sale and of written notice of default and of election to cause said property to be sold, which notice Trustee shall cause to be duly filed for record. Beneficiary also shall deposit with Trustee this Deed, said note and all documents evidencing expenditures secured hereby.

Trustee shall give notice of sale as then required by law, and without demand on Trustor, at least three months having elapsed after recordation of such notice of default, shall sell said property at the time and place of sale fixed by it in said notice of sale, either as a whole or in separate parcels and in such order as it may determine, at public auction to the highest bidder for cash in lawful money of the United States, payable at time of sale. Trustee may postpone sale of all or any portion of said property by public announcement at such time and place of sale, and from time to time thereafter may postpone such sale by public announcement at the time fixed by the preceding postponement. Trustee shall deliver to such purchaser its deed conveying the property so sold, but without any covenant or warranty, expressed or implied. The recitals in such deed of any matters or facts shall be conclusive proof of the truthfulness thereof. Any person, including Trustor, Trustee or Beneficiary as hereinafter defined, may purchase at such sale.

After deducting all costs, fees and expenses of Trustee and of this Trust, including cost of evidence of title in connection with sale, Trustee shall apply the proceeds of sale to payment of: all sums expended under the terms hereof, not then repaid, with accrued interest at the amount allowed by law in effect at the date hereof; all other sums then secured hereby; and the remainder, if any, to the person or persons legally entitled thereto.

(6) This Deed applies to, inures to the benefit of, and binds all parties hereto, their legal representatives and successors in interest. The term Beneficiary shall include any future owner and holder, including pledgees, of the note secured hereby. In this Deed, whenever the context so requires, the masculine gender includes the feminine and/or neuter, and the singular number includes the plural.

(7) Trustee accepts this Trust when this Deed, duly executed and acknowledged, is made a public record as provided by law. Trustee is not obligated to notify any party hereto of pending sale under any other Deed of Trust or of any action or proceeding in which Trustor, Beneficiary or Trustee shall be a party unless brought by Trustee.

(8) The Trusts created hereby are irrevocable by Trustor.

(9) Beneficiary may substitute a successor Trustee from time to time by recording in the office of the Recorder or Recorders of the county where the property is located an instrument stating the election by the Beneficiary to make such substitution, which instrument shall identify the Deed of Trust by recording reference, and by the name of the original Trustor, Trustee and Beneficiary, and shall set forth the name and address of the new Trustee, and which instrument shall be signed by the Beneficiary and duly acknowledged.

The undersigned Trustor request that a copy of any notice of default and any notice of sale hereunder be mailed to him at his address hereinabove set forth.

_____

13

_____

STATE OF _____ } SS.

COUNTY OF _____

On this the _____ day of _____ 19 ____, before me,

the undersigned, a Notary Public in and for said County and State,

personally appeared _____

_____

_____

_____, personally known to me

or proved to me on the basis of satisfactory evidence to be the person ____

whose name____ subscribed to the within instrument and acknowledged

that _____ executed the same.

_____

FOR NOTARY SEAL OR STAMP

— DO NOT RECORD —

FOR RECONVEYANCE OR FORECLOSURE SEND TO THE NEAREST
OFFICE OF SAFECO TITLE INSURANCE COMPANY

REQUEST FOR FULL RECONVEYANCE

To be used only when note has been paid.

Dated _____

To SAFECO TITLE INSURANCE COMPANY, TRUSTEE:

The undersigned is the legal owner and holder of all indebtedness secured by the within Deed of Trust. All sums secured by said Deed of Trust have been fully paid and satisfied; and you are hereby requested and directed, on payment to you of any sums owing to you under the terms of said Deed of Trust, to cancel all evidences of indebtedness, secured by said Deed of Trust, delivered to you herewith together with the said Deed of Trust, and to reconvey, without warranty, to the parties designated by the terms of said Deed of Trust, the estate now held by you under the same.

Mail Reconveyance To:

_____   _____

_____   _____

_____   (By) _____

                            (By) _____

Do not lose or destroy this Deed of Trust OR THE NOTE which it secures. Both
must be delivered to the Trustee for cancellation before reconveyance will be made.

DO NOT RECORD

DEED OF TRUST

WITH POWER OF SALE
(LONG FORM)

**SAFECO TITLE
INSURANCE COMPANY**

AS TRUSTEE

EXHIBIT 8-2

MORTGAGE

THIS MORTGAGE is made and executed as of the _____ day of ____ (1) _____ , 19 ____ , by _____ (2) _____ , hereinafter referred to as "Mortgagor" or "Grantor," and _____ (3) _____ , hereinafter referred to as "Mortgagee" or "Grantee."

WITNESSETH:

WHEREAS, Mortgagor is indebted to Mortgagee in the amount of _____ (4) _____ by virtue of a certain lien (hereinafter referred to as "Lien") made by Mortgagee to Mortgagor pursuant to the terms of that certain Loan Agreement (hereinafter referred to as the "Loan Agreement") evidenced by a promissory note (hereinafter referred to as "Note") heretofore executed by Mortgagor, which Note is dated _____ (5) _____ and is payable to Mortgagee in the original principal amount set forth above and bearing interest as provided therein, and

WHEREAS, Mortgagor desires to secure the payment of the Loan,

NOW THEREFORE, for and in consideration of the sum hereinabove set forth and other good and valuable consideration, the receipt of which is hereby acknowledged, Grantor does hereby grant, bargain, sell, lien, convey, and confirm unto Grantee all that certain tract of land of which Grantor is now seized and in possession situated in _____ (6) _____ and which is more fully described in Exhibit "A" attached hereto and hereby made a part hereof;

TOGETHER with all the estate, right, title, interest, claim, and demand whatsoever of Grantor of, in and to the said real property, and every part and parcel thereof; and

TOGETHER with all buildings, structures, and other improvements now or hereafter located on the said property or any part or parcel thereof, and all Grantor's right, title, and interest in and to all adjacent lands included in enclosures or occupied by buildings located partly on said real property or any part or parcel thereof; and

TOGETHER with all and singular tenements, hereditaments, easements, and appurtenances thereunto or unto any part thereof now or hereafter belonging or in any way appertaining, and all streets, alleys, passages, ways, watercourses, and all leasehold estates, easements, and covenants now existing or hereafter created for the benefit of Grantor or any subsequent owner or tenant of said real property, and all rights to enforce the maintenance thereof, and all other rights, privileges, and liberties of whatsoever kind or character, and the reversions and remainders thereof, and all estate, right, title, interest, property possession, claim, and demand whatsoever, at law or in equity, of Grantor in and to said real property or any part thereof; and

TOGETHER with all Grantor's right, title, and interest in and to all apparatus, chattels, fittings, and fixtures, including all trade, domestic and ornamental fixtures (hereinafter referred to as the "Chattels') now or hereafter actually or constructively attached to said property.

Grantor hereby sells, assigns, sets over, and transfers to Grantee all of the rents,

EXHIBIT 8-2 (cont'd.)

tenant reimbursements, issues, and profits which shall hereafter become due or be paid for the use of the Premises or any part thereof (hereinafter referred to as the "Rents"), reserving to Grantor a license to collect the Rents only so long as there is no Event of Default, as hereinafter defined, which shall have occurred and be continuing, said license to be revocable immediately upon notice to Grantor. Grantor agrees to execute and deliver such other instruments as Grantee may require evidencing the assignment of the Rents.

This Mortgage constitutes a "security agreement" as that term is defined in the Uniform Commercial Code as enacted in the State of _____ (7) _____ (hereinafter referred to as the "UCC") with respect to, among other things, the Chattels and the Rents and any part thereof, and creates a security interest for Grantee in the Chattels and the Rents. At the request of Grantee, a financing statement or statements shall from time to time be executed by Grantee and Grantor or by Grantor alone and filed in the manner required to perfect said security interest under the UCC. Compliance with UCC requirements relating to personal property shall not be construed as altering in any way the rights of Grantee as determined by this instrument under any other statutes or laws of the State of _____ (7) _____ , but is declared to be solely for the protection of Grantee in the event that such compliance is at any time held to be necessary to preserve the priority of Grantee's security interest in the Chattels or Rents against any other claims.

GRANTOR FURTHER COVENANTS AND AGREES WITH GRANTEE AS FOLLOWS:
ARTICLE I
COVENANTS OF GRANTOR

1.01 *Payment of Indebtedness.* Grantor shall pay to Grantee the Indebtedness when due.

1.02 *Taxes and Other Charges.*

(a) Grantor shall pay, on or before the first date on which any part thereof shall become delinquent, all taxes, assessments, water, sewer, and other rents, excises, levies, license fees, permit fees, and all other charges (in each case whether general or special, ordinary or extraordinary, or foreseen or unforeseen) of every character whatsoever (including all penalties and interest thereon) now or hereafter levied, assessed, confirmed, or imposed on, or in respect of, or which may be a lien upon the Premises, or any part thereof, or any estate, right, or interest therein, or upon the Rents or any part thereof, and shall submit to Grantee such evidence of the due and punctual payment of all such taxes, assessments, and other fees and charges as Grantee may require; provided, however, that this Section 1.02(a) shall not require the payment or discharge of any such taxes or any other such charges which are being contested in good faith by appropriate proceedings and for which adequate reserves have been established on the appropriate books.

(b) Grantor shall pay all taxes, assessments, charges, expenses, costs, and fees which may now or hereafter be levied upon, or assessed or charged against, or incurred in connection with the Loan, the Note, the Loan Agreement, the Indebtedness, this Mortgage, or any other instrument now or hereafter evidencing, securing, or otherwise relating to the Indebtedness.

(c) Grantor shall pay, on or before the due date thereof, all premiums on policies of insurance covering, affecting, or relating to the Premises, as required

EXHIBIT 8-2 (cont'd.)

pursuant to Paragraph 1.03 below and all ground rentals, other lease rentals, and other sums, if any, becoming due under any lease or rental contract affecting the Premises. Grantor shall submit to Grantee such evidence of the due and punctual payment of all such premiums, rentals, and other sums as Grantee may require.

1.03 *Insurance.* Grantor shall keep the Premises and the interests and liabilities incident to the ownership, possession, and operation thereof insured for the benefit of Grantee against loss or damage by fire, lightning, windstorm, hail, explosion, riot, riot attending a strike, civil commotion, aircraft, vehicles, and smoke, and against all other such risks and perils as may be customary for similar properties and businesses. All such insurance shall be in such amounts, shall be evidenced by such policies, shall be governed by such terms and conditions (including without limitation provisions prohibiting the cancellation or material modification thereof without providing Grantee at least ten (10) days' prior written notice), and shall be issued by such companies as may be customary for similar properties and businesses; provided, however, the amount of such insurance shall not be less than an amount equal to the full replacement cost of the Premises. All insurance policies shall, to the extent of its interests, be for the benefit of and first payable in the case of loss, without contribution, to Grantee pursuant to a mortgagee clause satisfactory to Grantee and shall contain a standard waiver of subrogation clause for the benefit of Grantee. Grantor shall provide Grantee copies of all such policies and written evidence of the timely payment of all premiums for such policies. Grantor shall deliver to Grantee a copy of a new policy, together with written evidence of the payment of the premium therefor, as a replacement for any expiring policy at least ten (10) days before the date of such expiration. Grantor does hereby transfer and assign to Grantee all such insurance policies, and the proceeds thereof, and in the event of a loss, the proceeds collected may, at the option of Grantee, be used in any one or more of the following ways: (i) apply the same or any part thereof upon the Indebtedness, whether the Indebtedness or any part thereof be then matured or unmatured; (ii) use the same or any part thereof to fulfill any of the convenants and agreements of Grantor hereunder as Grantee may determine; (iii) pay the same or any part thereof to Grantor for the purpose of replacing, restoring, or altering the Premises to a condition satisfactory to Grantee; or (iv) release the same to Grantor. Grantee is hereby irrevocably appointed by Grantor as attorney in fact of Grantor to assign any such policy, without payment to Grantor for any unearned premium thereon, in the event of the foreclosure of this Mortgage or a conveyance in lieu of any foreclosure.

1.04 *Care of Premises.*

(a) Notwithstanding any other provision of the Mortgage, Grantor shall keep the Premises protected and in good order, repair, and condition at all times, promptly replacing, repairing, or restoring any part thereof which may become damaged, destroyed, lost, or unsuitable for use and which is material to the value of the Premises as security for the Indebtedness. In the event the Premises or any part thereof is damaged or destroyed by fire or other casualty, Grantor shall immediately notify Grantee, in writing, of such damage or destruction.

(b) Grantor shall not remove, demolish, destroy, or alter the Premises, or any portion thereof which is material to the value of the Premises as security for the Indebtedness, without the prior written consent of the Grantee.

EXHIBIT 8-2 (cont'd.)

(c) Grantor shall promptly comply with all present and future laws, ordinances, rules, and regulations of any governmental authority affecting the Premises or any part thereof and with which noncompliance would have a materially adverse effect on Grantor, Grantor's business, or the value of thePremises as security for the Indebtedness.

(d) Grantor shall not cause or permit anything to be done which would or could increase to any material extent the risk of fire or other hazard to the Premises, or any part thereof, or which would result in the cancellation of any insurance policy carried with respect to the Premises.

(e) Grantor shall in a timely manner keep and perform all agreements and covenants required to be kept and performed in order to continue in effect any and all leases and other instruments creating Grantor's interest in or defining Grantor's rights with respect to the Premises or any part thereof.

1.05 *Performance by Grantee.* In the event that Grantor fails to observe or perform any of Grantor's obligations or covenants set forth in this Mortgage, in the Loan Agreement or in any other instrument now or hereafter evidencing, securing, or otherwise relating to the Indebtedness, then Grantee, at its option, may endeavor to perform and observe the same, without notice to or demand upon Grantor and without releasing Grantor from any of its obligations or convenants hereunder, and all payments made and costs incurred by Grantee in connection therewith, including but not limited to reasonable attorney fees and expenses, shall be secured by this Mortgage and, upon demand, shall be repaid by Grantor to Grantee, with interest at the rate of _____ (8) _____ % over the rate publicly announced from time to time by _____ (9) _____ as its "prime rate" as in effect from time to time, adjusted automatically as of the opening of business on the effective date of each change in such rate. Grantee is hereby empowered to enter upon and authorize others to enter upon the Premises, or any part thereof, for the purpose of performing or observing any such defaulted covenant or obligation, without thereby becoming liable to Grantor or any person in possession holding under Grantor.

1.06 *Condemnation.* Grantor hereby assigns to Grantee all awards hereafter made by virtue of any exercise of the right of condemnation or eminent domain by any authority, including any award for damage to or taking of title to the Premises, or any part thereof, or the possession thereof, or any right or easement affecting the Premises or appurtenant thereto (including any award for any change of grade of streets), and the proceeds of all sales in lieu of condemnation. Grantee, at its option, is hereby authorized to collect and receive all such awards and the proceeds of all such sales and to give proper receipts and acquittances therefor, and Grantee, at its election, may use such awards and proceeds in any one or more of the following ways: (i) apply the same or any part thereof upon the Indebtedness, whether the Indebtedness, or any part thereof, be then matured or unmatured, (ii) use the same or any part thereof to fulfill any of the covenants and agreements of Grantor hereunder or under the Loan Agreements as Grantee may determine, (iii) pay the same or any part thereof to Grantor for the purpose of replacing, restoring, or altering the Premises to a condition satisfactory to Grantee, or (iv) release the same to Grantor. Grantee shall be under no obligation to question the amount of any such award or proceeds and may accept the same in the amount in which the same shall be paid.

EXHIBIT 8-2 (cont'd.)

Grantor agrees to execute and deliver such other instruments as Grantee may require evidencing the assignment of all such awards and proceeds to Grantee. If, prior to the receipt by Grantee of such award or proceeds, the Premises shall have been sold on foreclosure of this Mortgage, Grantee shall have the right to receive such award or proceeds to the extent of any unpaid Indebtedness following such a sale, with legal interest thereon, whether or not a deficiency judgment on the Mortgage shall have been sought or recovered, and of reasonable attorney fees, costs, including costs of litigation, and disbursements incurred by Grantee in connection of such award or proceeds.

   1.07 *Leases, Tenant Contracts, Etc.*

   (a) As additional collateral and further security for the Indebtedness, Grantor does hereby assign to Grantee Grantor's interest in any and all Contracts; and Grantor hereby warrants and represents that all such Contracts are in full force and effect. Grantor agrees to execute and deliver to Grantee such additional instruments, in form and substance and with such warranties satisfactory to Grantee, as may hereafter from time to time be requested by Grantee further to evidence and confirm said assignment; provided, however, that acceptance of any such assignment shall not be construed as a consent by Grantee to any of the Contracts, or to impose upon Grantee any obligation with respect thereto. Without first obtaining on each occasion the written approval of Grantee, Grantor shall not cancel any of the Contracts or terminate, modify, or accept a surrender thereof or reduce the payment of the rental or fees thereunder or accept, or permit to be made, any prepayment of rent or fees thereunder (except the usual prepayment of rent which results from the acceptance by a landlord on or about the first day of each month of the rent for the ensuing month) other than in the ordinary course of business. Grantor shall faithfully keep and perform, or cause to be kept and performed, all of the material covenants, conditions, and agreements contained in each of the Contracts on the part of Grantor to be kept and performed and shall at all times do all things necessary to compel performance by each other party to said instruments of all material obligations, covenants, and agreements by such other party to be performed thereunder. If an Event of Default, as hereinafter defined, shall occur, Grantor shall immediately pay over to Grantee an amount equal to all unrefunded deposits (hereinafter referred to as the "Deposits") paid by anyone in connection with the occupancy of the Premises or any part thereof.

   (b) Grantor shall not execute an assignment of the Contracts or the Rents or any part thereof unless Grantee shall first consent to such assignment, which consent may be withheld for any reason or for no reason, and unless such assignment shall provide that it is subordinate to the assignment contained in this Mortgage and any assignment then existing or thereafter executed pursuant hereto.

   1.08 *Legal Actions.* In the event that Grantee is made a party to or appears, either voluntary or involuntarily, in any action or proceeding affecting or relating to the Premises, the Loan, the Note, the Indebtedness, the Loan Agreement, or the validity or priority of this Mortgage, then Grantor shall, upon demand, reimburse Grantee for all costs, expenses, and liabilities incurred by Grantee by reason of any such action or proceeding, including, without limitation, reasonable attorney fees and costs and expenses of litigation, and the same shall be secured by this Mortgage. Grantor hereby agrees to indemnify, defend, and hold Grantee harmless from and against any

EXHIBIT 8-2 (cont'd.)

liability, loss, damage, claim, judgment, cost, or expense, including without limitation attorney fees and costs and expenses of litigation, which Grantee may incur, suffer, or be threatened with on account of any claim for fee, commission, or similar compensation by any broker, agent, or finder, whether or not meritorious, in connection with the negotiation or execution of the Loan Agreement or any of the transactions contemplated thereby.

1.09 *Transfer or Encumbrance of Premises.* Grantor shall not transfer, sell, lease, encumber, assign, or convey or place restrictive convenants upon, or grant or create any legal or equitable interest in, the Premises, or any interest therein or any part thereof, whether as security or otherwise, except as may be expressly permitted by the Loan Agreement.

1.10 *Acquisition of Chattels.* Grantor shall not acquire any portion of the Chattels subject to any security interest, conditional sales contract, title retention arrangement, or other charge or lien taking precedence over the security title and lien of this Mortgage, except as permitted by the Loan Agreement.

ARTICLE II
DEFAULT AND REMEDIES

2.01 *Event of Default.* The occurrence of any one of the following events shall constitute an Event of Default hereunder:

(a) Failure to pay the Loan or Note according to the terms or for the breach of any of the terms or conditions of this Mortgage;

(b) The Premises are subjected to actual or threatened waste (other than actions taken by Grantor in the ordinary course of its business operations), or all or any part thereof which is material to the value of the Premises as security for the Indebtedness is removed, demolished, or altered without the prior written consent of Grantee, which consent may be withheld for any reason or for no reason;

(c) Grantor fails to remove within thirty (30) days from the date of filing any lien or claim of lien filed of record against Grantor or the Premises;

(d) Any claim of priority to this Mortgage by title, lien, or otherwise is asserted by Grantor, or is asserted and finally established as valid by any third party, in any legal or equitable proceeding, whether as a claim, counterclaim, defense, or otherwise, except as shown on Exhibit "B." (10)

2.02 *Rights of Grantee Upon Default.* Upon the occurrence of an Event of Default, Grantee, at its option, may do any one or more of the following:

(a) Declare the Indebtedness to be due and payable forthwith, without notice to or demand upon Grantor, and may proceed to protect and enforce all rights by any action at law, suit in equity, or other appropriate proceeding, whether for the specific performance of any agreement contained herein, or for an injunction against the violation of any of the terms hereof, or in aid of the exercise of power granted hereby or by law;

(b) Enter upon and take possession of the Premises without the appointment of a receiver, or an application therefor, and collect and receive the rents, incomes, issues, and profits of and from the Premises, and Grantee is hereby constituted and appointed as the attorney in fact of Grantor to manage and operate the Premises and to collect all such sums. After deducting from the sums so collected all expenses of taking, holding, managing, and operating the Premises (including com-

EXHIBIT 8-2 (cont'd.)

pensation for the services of all persons employed for any such purpose), the net amount so collected shall be applied toward the Indebtedness; provided that nothing herein contained shall be construed to obligate Grantee to discharge or perform the duties of a landlord to any tenant or to impose any liability upon Grantee as the result of any exercise by Grantee of its rights under this Mortgage, and Grantee shall be liable to account only for the rents, incomes, issues, and profits actually received by Grantee;

(c) Apply for the appointment of a receiver of the rents, incomes, issues, and profits of and from the Premises, without notice to Grantor. Grantee shall be entitled to the appointment of such receiver as a matter of right, without regard to the value of the Premises as security for the Indebtedness or the solvency of Grantor or any person or legal entity, if any, which may be liable for the payment of all or any part of the Indebtedness;

(d) May at any time, at Grantee's election, proceed at law or in equity or otherwise to foreclose the lien of this Mortgage as against all or any part of the Premises, subject to such leases, tenant contracts, and rental agreements as Grantee shall at its option designate.

2.03 *Purchase of Premises by Grantee.* Grantee, its agents, representatives, successors, or assigns, may be a purchaser of the Premises or any part thereof or of any interest therein at any sale thereof, whether pursuant to foreclosure or otherwise hereunder, and may apply upon the purchase price the Indebtedness owing to such purchaser, to the extent of such purchaser's distributive share of the purchase price. Any such purchaser shall, upon any such purchase, acquire good title to the properties so purchased, and to the abstracts of title covering the Premises or any part thereof.

2.04 *Receipt a Sufficient Discharge to Purchaser.* Upon any sale of the Premises or any part thereof or any interest therein, whether pursuant to foreclosure or otherwise hereunder, the receipt of the officer making the sale under judicial proceedings or of Grantee shall be sufficient discharge to the purchaser for the purchase money, and such purchaser shall not be obliged to see to the application thereof.

2.05 *Separate Sales.* To the extent permitted by _____ (7) _____ law, in the event of any sale under this Mortgage pursuant to any order in any judicial proceeding or otherwise, the Premises may be sold as an entirety or in separate parcels in such manner or order as Grantee in its sole discretion may elect; and if Grantee so elects it may sell or cause to be sold the Chattels at one or more separate sales in any manner permitted by the UCC; and one or more exercises of the powers herein granted shall not extinguish or exhaust such powers, until the entire Premises are sold or the Indebtedness is paid in full. If the Indebtedness is now or hereafter further secured by any chattel mortgages, pledges, contracts of guaranty, assignments of lease, or other security, Grantee may at its option exhaust the remedies granted under any of said security, either concurrently or independently, and in such order as it may determine.

2.06 *Waiver of Appraisement and Valuation.* Grantor hereby waives, to the full extent it may lawfully do so, the benefit of all appraisement, valuation, stay, extension, moratorium, inventory, and redemption laws now or hereafter in force with

EXHIBIT 8-2 (cont'd.)

respect to any amount secured hereby, all rights of marshalling in the event of any sale of the Premises or any part thereof, or any interest therein upon foreclosure as provided in this Mortgage, and any right Grantor may have to require Grantee to obtain any bond.

2.07 *Application of Proceeds of Sale and Income from Management.* The proceeds of any sale of the Premises or any part thereof or any interest therein, whether pursuant to foreclosure or otherwise hereunder, and all amounts received by Grantee by reason of any holding, operation, or management of the Premises or any part thereof pursuant to Paragraph 2.02 hereof, together with any other monies at the time held by Grantee as part of the Premises, shall be applied as Grantee may determine to pay:

(a) All costs and expenses of the sale of the Premises or any part thereof or any interest in connection therewith, including without limitation such attorney's fees as a court may determine to be reasonable and just and costs of abstracts of title and all costs and expenses of entering upon, taking possession of, removal from, holding, operating, and managing the Premises or any part thereof, as the case may be, together with any taxes, assessments, or other charges which Grantee may consider it necessary or desirable to pay;

(b)The payments, costs, and expenses, if any, referred to in Paragraph 1.05 hereof;

(c) All amounts of principal, premiums, if any, and interest at the time due and payable on the Note or under the Loan Agreement or either of them (whether at maturity or on a date fixed for any installment payment or any prepayment or by declaration or otherwise); and

(d) any other portion of the Indebtedness.

The balance, if any, of such proceeds, amounts and monies shall be paid over to Grantor or as it may direct or as may be required by law.

2.08 *Separate Suits.* Subject to such provisions limiting the liability of Grantor as may hereinafter be set forth, Grantee shall have the right, at any time and from time to time, to sue for any sums required to be paid under this Mortgage, the Loan Agreement, the Note, or any other instrument now or hereafter evidencing, securing, or otherwise relating to the Indebtedness, as the same become due and payable, without regard to whether or not the entire Indebtedness shall be due, and without prejudice to the right of Grantee thereafter to enforce any appropriate remedy against Grantor, including an action of foreclosure or any other action for a default or defaults by Grantor existing at the time such earlier action was commenced.

2.09 *Restoration of Parties.* In the event Grantee shall have proceeded to enforce any right or remedy under this Mortgage, and such proceedings are discontinued or abandoned for any reason, then Grantor and Grantee shall immediately be restored to their former positions and rights hereunder, and all rights, powers, and remedies of Grantee shall continue as if no such proceeding had taken place.

2.10 *Subrogation.* To the full extent of the Indebtedness, Grantee is hereby subrogated to the liens, claims, and demands, and to the rights of the owners and holders of each and every lien, claim, demand, and other encumbrance on the Premises which is paid or satisfied, in whole or in part, out of the proceeds of the Indebtedness, and the respective liens, claims, demands, and other encumbrances

EXHIBIT 8-2 (cont'd.)

shall be, and each of them is hereby preserved and shall pass to and be held by Grantee as additional collateral and further security for the Indebtedness, to the same extent they would have been preserved and would have passed to and been held by Grantee had they been duly and legally assigned, transferred, set over, and delivered unto Grantee by assignment, notwithstanding the fact that the same may be satisfied and cancelled of record.

2.11 *Remedies Cumulative.* Each of the rights of Grantee under this Mortgage, the Loan Agreement, and the Note is separate and distinct from and cumulative to all other rights herein and therein granted, and all other rights which Grantee may have in law or equity, and no such right shall be in exclusion of any other.

2.12 *No Waiver.* No modification or waiver by Grantee of any right or remedy under this Mortgage shall be effective unless made in writing. No delay by Grantee in exercising any right or remedy hereunder, or otherwise afforded by law, shall operate as a waiver thereof or preclude the exercises thereof upon the occurrence of an Event of Default. No failure by Grantee to insist upon the strict performance by Grantor of each and every covenant and agreement of Grantor under the Note, this Mortgage or the Loan Agreement or either of them shall constitute a waiver of any such covenant or agreement, and no waiver by Grantee of any Event of Default shall constitute a waiver of or consent to any subsequent Event of Default. No failure of Grantee to exercise its option to accelerate the maturity of the Indebtedness, nor any forebearance by Grantee before or after the exercise of such option, nor any withdrawal or abandonment by Grantee of any action of or sale upon foreclosure hereunder or any of its rights under such action or sale, shall be construed as a waiver of any option, power, or right of Grantee hereunder.

ARTICLE III
GENERAL PROVISIONS

3.01 *Further Assurances.* Grantor will, at the expense of Grantor, and without expense to Grantee, do, execute, acknowledge, and deliver all such further acts, deeds, conveyances, mortgages, assignments, security agreements, notices of assignment, transfers, and assurances as Grantee shall from time to time require, for the better assuring, conveying, mortgaging, assigning, transferring, and confirming unto Grantee the Premises and rights hereby conveyed or assigned or intended now or hereafter to be conveyed or assigned, or which Grantor may be or may hereafter become bound to convey or assign to Grantee, or for carrying out the intention or facilitating the performance of the terms of this Mortgage, or for correcting this Mortgage, or for filing, registering, or recording this Mortgage and, on demand, will execute and deliver, and hereby authorizes Grantee to execute in the name of Grantor to the extent it may lawfully do so, one or more financing statements, chattel mortgages, or comparable security instruments, to evidence more effectively the security interest and lien hereof upon the Chattels. Grantor forthwith upon the execution and delivery of this Mortgage, and thereafter from time to time, will cause this Mortgage and any security instrument creating a security interest in the Chattels and each instrument of further assurance to be filed, registered, or recorded in such manner and in such places as may be required by any present or future law in order to publish notice of and to protect fully the security interest and lien hereof upon and the interest of Grantee in the Chattels.

EXHIBIT 8-2 (cont'd.)

3.02 *Grantor as Tenant Holding Over.* So long as the Indebtedness, or any part thereof, remains unpaid, Grantor agrees that possession of the Premises by Grantor, or any person claiming under Grantor, shall be as tenant under Grantee, and, in case of a sale upon foreclosure as provided in this Mortgage, Grantor and any person in possession under Grantor, as to whose interest such sale was not made subject, shall, at the option of the purchaser at such sale, then become and be tenants holding over, and shall forthwith deliver possession to such purchaser, or be summarily dispossessed in accordance with the laws applicable to tenants holding over.

3.03 *Greater Estate.* In the event that Grantor is the owner of a leasehold estate with respect to any portion of the Premises, and, prior to the satisfaction of the Indebtedness and the cancellation of this Mortgage of record, Grantor obtains a fee estate in such portion of the Premises, then such fee estate shall automatically, and without further action of any kind on the part of Grantor, be and become subject to the lien of this Mortgage; provided that there shall be no merger of such leasehold estate with such fee estate without Grantee's prior written consent, and all instruments by which Grantor acquires such fee estate shall so provide.

3.04 *Interest Not to Exceed Maximum Allowed by Law.* Anything in the Note, the Loan Agreement, or this Mortgage to the contrary notwithstanding, it is understood and agreed by the parties that if by reason of acceleration or otherwise, interest paid or contracted to be paid by Grantor on the Indebtedness or any part thereof shall exceed the maximum amount permitted by applicable law, the excess shall be credited on interest accrued or principal or both at the time of acceleration so that such interest shall not exceed the maximum amount permitted by such law, provided that this Paragraph 3.04 shall not operate if there is no applicable law regulating the amount of interest which can be paid on the Indebtedness or if no usury defense is available to Grantor.

3.05 *Severability.* If any provision, paragraph, sentence, clause, phrase, or word of the Mortgage, or the application thereof in any circumstance, is held invalid or unenforceable, the validity and enforceability of the remainder of this Mortgage, and of the application of any such provision, paragraph, sentence, clause, phrase, or word in any other circumstance, shall not be affected thereby, it being intended that all rights, powers, and privileges of Grantee hereunder shall be enforceable to the fullest extent permitted by law.

3.06 *Assignment.* This Mortgage is assignable by Grantee, and any assignment hereof by Grantee shall operate to vest in such assignee the lien hereof upon and to the Premises and all rights and powers herein conferred.

3.07 *Time of the Essence.* Time is of the essence with respect to each and every covenant, agreement, and obligation of Grantor under this Mortgage, the Note, the Loan Agreement, and any and all other instruments now or hereafter evidencing, securing, or otherwise relating to the Indebtedness.

3.08 *Power of Grantee to Reconvey or Consent.* Without affecting the liability of Grantor or any other person for the payment of the Indebtedness or any part thereof, including such of the Indebtedness as may be due at the time of or after any reconveyance of the Premises to Grantor, or the lien of this Mortgage upon any remainder of the Premises which has not been so reconveyed for the full amount of the Indebtedness then or thereafter secured hereby, or the rights and powers of Grantee with respect to such remainder of the Premises, Grantee may, at its option,

EXHIBIT 8-2 (cont'd.)

do any one or more of the following: (i) release all or any part of the Indebtedness; (ii) extend the time or otherwise alter the terms of payment of all or any part of the Indebtedness; (iii) accept additional or substitute security hereunder; (iv) substitute for or release all or any part of the Premises as security hereunder; (v) reconvey to Grantor all or any part of the Premises; (vi) consent to the making of any map or plat of all or any part of the Premises; (vii) join in the granting of any easement upon all or any part of the premises; or (viii) join in any extension agreement or any agreement subordinating or otherwise affecting the lien or charge hereof or the priority thereof.

3.09 *Successors and Assigns.* Each and every covenant, warranty, and agreement of Grantor herein, if Grantor be more than one, shall be jointly and severally binding upon and enforceable against Grantor, and each of them. As used herein the terms "Grantor" and "Grantee" shall include the named Grantor and the named Grantee and their respective heirs, executors, administrators, legal representatives, successors, successors in title, and assigns. The provisions of this paragraph are subject to the provisions of Paragraph 1.09 above.

3.10 *Notices.* Any and all notices, elections, or demands permitted or required to be made under this Mortgage shall be in writing and shall be delivered personally, or sent by registered or certified mail, to the other party at the address set forth below, or at such other address as may be supplied in writing. The date of personal delivery or the third day after the date of mailing, as the case may be, shall be the date of such notice, election, or demand. For the purpose of this Mortgage,

The address of the Grantor is:

(11)

The address of the Grantee is:

(12)

or such other address as any party hereto may give the other pursuant to the provisions hereof. In the event that Grantee is required or permitted to give any notice to Grantor under the UCC, ten (10) days' notice hereunder shall be deemed to be sufficient. Nothing contained in this paragraph shall be construed to require any notice from Grantee to Grantor not otherwise specifically provided for in this Mortgage.

3.11 *Captions.* Titles or captions of articles and paragraphs contained in this Mortgage are inserted only as a matter of convenience and for reference, and in no way define, limit, extend, or describe the scope of this Deed or the intent of any provision hereof.

3.12 *Number and Gender.* Whenever required by the context the singular number shall include the plural, and the gender of any pronoun shall include the other genders.

3.13 *Applicable Law.* This Mortgage shall be governed by and interpreted and construed in accordance with the laws of the State of _____ (7) _____ .

IN WITNESS WHEREOF, this Mortgage and Assignment of Leases and Rents has been duly executed, delivered, and sealed by Grantor the day and year first above written.

_____

(13)

_____

8. The penalty rate of interest for violation of this clause.

9. The bank to be used as a benchmark for determining the penalty rate of interest.

10. Attach a list of approved lienholders as Exhibit B, if applicable.

11. The address of the borrower (the mortgagor) to which notices should be sent.

12. The address of the lender (the mortgagee) to which notices should be sent.

13. Type in a signature block for the mortgagor, with lines for the parties who will sign.

As with the trust deed the mortgage should be notarized and recorded.

Using Deeds of Trust and Mortgages with Leasehold Interests

A special case arises when the property being financed sits on leased land. In this instance the lender's loan is secured by a leasehold deed of trust or mortgage, dealing only with the property owned in fee. The same trust deed or mortgage instrument can be used to perfect the lender's interest. Language should be included to incorporate performance on the underlying ground lease as part of the borrower's responsibilities, and default on lease payments as another incidence of default on the leasehold trust deed or mortgage.

Modifying a Trust Deed or Mortgage

Once the document is recorded and the loan funded, there are usually no changes to the basic agreements initially put in place. A special instance involves construction loans where the deed of trust specifically allows periodic advances.

But sometimes a change in loan terms is necessary and agreed to by the parties involved. In such a case a Modification Agreement can be used. Exhibit 8-3 shows such a document. Complete it as follows:

1. The name and address of the party to whom the document should be returned once it is recorded. This is usually the lender.

2. The date of the agreement.

3. The name of the lender, the beneficiary under the deed of trust.

4. The name of the borrower, the trustor under the deed of trust.

5. The recitals may vary depending on the circumstances to be reviewed in this modification document. In the example, the original deed of trust is recited as well as an assignment of the deed of trust from a mortgage company to the lender.

6. The terms of the agreement will vary depending on what modifications are being granted. In the example the payments are being altered.

7. Type in a signature block for the lender and the borrower.

As with all documents that are to be recorded the modification agreement should be notarized. A legal description should be attached defining the property, most likely the same one used when the deed of trust was originally recorded.

Amending a Trust Deed to Provide for Additional Advances

A Trust Deed can be amended to specifically provide for an additional advance of funds. Title should be checked to make sure that no intervening liens have upset the

EXHIBIT 8-3

Recording Requested by and
When Recorded Return To:

(1)

MODIFICATION OF DEED OF TRUST

This Modification is made this _____ day of _____ (2) _____ , 19 ___ , by and between _____ (3) _____ (hereinafter referred to as "Lender,") and _____ (4) _____ (hereinafter referred to as "Borrower").

RECITALS
(5)

WHEREAS on or about _____ , Borrower executed a promissory note in the original principal sum of $_____ (the "Note") in favor of _____ Mortgage Corporation, which Note is secured by a Deed of Trust and Security Agreement of the same date covering that certain real property located in _____ more particularly described in the attached Exhibit "A." The Deed of Trust was recorded in the official records of _____ County, State of _____ on the _____ day of _____ , 19 ___ as File No. _____ (the "Deed of Trust").

WHEREAS, the beneficial interest in the Deed of Trust was duly assigned by _____ Mortgage Corporation to Lender by the certain Assignment of Deed of Trust recorded on the _____ day of _____ , 19 ___ , in the official records of _____ County, State of _____ , as File No. _____ .

NOW THEREFORE Borrower and Lender agree to supplement the Deed of Trust by the following agreement:

AGREEMENT (6)

1. Borrower and Lender have agreed to a reduction in the payments due on the Note on the first of each month from _____ , 19 ___ to and including _____ , 19 ___ , with the difference between the payments owing on the Note and the amount paid accruing, and charged with interest on a monthly basis, which will result in an increase in the indebtedness outstanding.

2. Borrower and Lender hereby agree to execute this Modification of Deed of Trust. Pursuant to the Deed of Trust the Note shall continue to be secured by the Deed of Trust as provided in the Note, and the foregoing Modification shall in no way affect the enforceability or validity of the Deed of Trust, or the priority of the lien of the Deed of Trust on the real property described in the Deed of Trust.

IN WITNESS WHEREOF, the parties hereto have executed this Modification of Deed of Trust on the day first written above.

BORROWER:

_____ (7) _____

_____

LENDER:

_____ (7) _____

_____

lender's priority. If there are such liens, this form should not be used without first obtaining subordinations from the lienholders.

Exhibit 8-4 shows a Modification Agreement to allow an additional advance under an already recorded Deed of Trust. Fill it in as follows:

1. The name and address of the entity to whom the recorded instrument should be returned, usually the lender.
2. The date of the agreement.
3. The name of the borrower.
4. The name of the lender.
5. The date of the original promissory note.
6. The amount of the original loan, as set forth in the promissory note.
7. The name of the trustee, usually a title company.
8. The location within the official records of the recorded Deed of Trust.
9. The county and state in which the document was recorded.
10. The county and state in which the property secured by the Deed of Trust is located.
11. The legal description of the secured property. If the space is not large enough for the entire description, attach a separate sheet headed Exhibit A and make reference to it in this section as: "See Exhibit A attached hereto and by this reference made a part hereof" or similar phrasing.
12. The amount of the outstanding principal balance on the original loan.
13. The amount of the additional advance currently being made.
14. The recording information of the original Deed of Trust.
15. The total amount of loan currently outstanding.
16. The date of the original promissory note.
17. The amount of the additional loan.
18. The date of the new note.
19. The signature of the lender's authorized representative.
20. The signature of the borrower.

Substitution of Trustee

This document is used to change the trustee identified in the original Deed of Trust. Circumstances can arise, relationships change, where such an amendment is desirable. Exhibit 8-5 shows such a document, which should be completed in the following manner:

1. The name and address of the party to whom the recorded document should be returned, usually the lender.
2. The name of the original trustor.
3. The name of the original trustee.
4. The name of the original beneficiary.
5. The date of the recorded Deed of Trust.
6. The date the Deed of Trust was recorded.
7. The recording information pertaining to the Deed of Trust.
8. The county and state in which the Deed of Trust was recorded.
9. The name of the new trustee being substituted.

EXHIBIT 8-4

WHEN RECORDED MAIL TO:

1

Attn:

SPACE ABOVE FOR RECORDER'S USE

AGREEMENT

THIS AGREEMENT, made this ____2/3____ day of _____ by and between _____ hereinafter called "Borrower", and ____4____ hereinafter called "Lender".

WHEREAS, Lender is the owner and holder of a promissory note dated _____5_____ for $ _____6_____ executed by Borrower in favor of Lender, and of the Deed of Trust securing it to _____7_____ as Trustee, recorded _____ in book ____8____ Page _____ Official Records of _____9_____ County, _____ , affecting the following described property located in the county of ____10____ , State of

11

WHEREAS, Borrower is now the owner of the premises affected by said Deed of Trust; and

WHEREAS, there is now due and owing on the aforesaid note the principal sum of $ ____12____ and it is desired to make an additional loan from Lender to Borrower of $ ____13____ to be secured by said Deed of Trust, and to amend said Deed of Trust to provide that the same secures not only payment of the indebtedness evidenced by the note referred to therein, but also a further and additional loan which Lender is making to Borrower.

IT IS HEREBY AGREED by and between the parties hereto, that said Deed of Trust recorded _____ in Book _____ Page ____14____ Official Records of _____ _____ be and it is hereby amended so that the paragraph immediately preceding paragraph numbered "1" on the first page of said Deed of Trust shall read as follows:

"For the purpose of securing (1) performance of each agreement of Trustor herein contained, (2) payment of the balance due with interest thereon according to the terms of a promissory note for $ ____15____ dated ____16____ , payable to Beneficiary or order and made by Trustor, and (3) payment of any additional loan or loans to be made by Beneficiary to Trustor evidenced by promissory note or notes of Trustor to Beneficiary and stated to be secured by this Deed of Trust,"

and that said Deed of Trust is further amended by adding thereto a new paragraph numbered "15" providing as follows:

"15.   Wherever the word 'note' appears therein, it shall be construed to mean 'notes'; wherever the singular appears herein, it shall also mean the plural, and the term 'Trustor' shall also mean his or its successor in interest."

IT IS FURTHER UNDERSTOOD AND AGREED that concurrently with the execution of this Agreement, Lender is making an additional loan of $ ____17____ to Borrower and evidenced by Borrower's note to Lender for $ ____17____ dated ____18____ , and stating that it is secured by said Deed of Trust, and that said note dated ____18____ evidences an additional loan made under the terms of the Deed of Trust as hereby amended.

IN WITNESS WHEREOF, this Agreement has been duly executed by the parties hereto.

By ____20____   ____19____

By _____   _____

EXHIBIT 8-5

SUBSTITUTION OF TRUSTEE

WHEREAS, _____ (2) _____
was the original Trustor, _____ (3) _____
_____ was the original Trustee, and _____
_____ (4) _____ , is/are the present Beneficiary under that certain Deed of Trust, executed on _____ (5) _____ and recorded _____
(6) _____ as document number _____ (7) _____ , in Book _____
(7) _____ , Page _____ (7) _____ of Official Records of _____
(8) _____ County, State of _____ (8) _____ ; and

WHEREAS, the undersigned desires to substitute a new Trustee under said Deed of Trust in the place and stead of _____ (3) _____

NOW THEREFORE, the undersigned being all of the present Beneficiaries under said Deed of Trust hereby substitutes _____ (9) _____ ,
_____ (10) _____ as Trustee under said Deed of Trust.

Dated this _____ day of _____ (11) _____ , 19 ___ .

_____ (12) _____
Beneficiary

_____
Beneficiary

10. The address of the new trustee.
11. The date of the substitution document.
12. The signature of the beneficiary under the original Deed of Trust.

The Notary Acknowledgment should be completed and signed by a Notary prior to recording the document.

How to Prepare an Assignment of Trust Deed or Mortgage

The Assignment of Trust Deed is used when one lender transfers an interest in a trust deed to another lender. Frequently this will happen if a mortgage company originates the loan, then sells it either to a parent company or to an outside lender. Like other documents that have to do with the lien of record, the assignment should be notarized and recorded with the appropriate county recorder's office.

EXHIBIT 8-6

RECORDING REQUESTED BY AND
WHEN RECORDED RETURN TO:

   (1)

ASSIGNMENT OF DEED OF TRUST

For value received, the undersigned hereby grants, assigns, and transfers to
_____ (2) _____ _____ all beneficial interest under
that certain Deed of Trust dated _____ (3) _____ executed
by _____ (4) _____ , Trustor, to _____
(5) _____ , Trustee, and recorded as Instrument
No. _____ (6) _____ on _____ (6) _____ , in
Book _____ (6) _____ Page _____ (6) _____ , of Official Records in the
County Recorder's office of _____ (7) _____ County, State of _____ ,
describing land therein as:

               (8)

Together with the note or notes therein described or referred to, the money due and
to become due thereon with interest, and all rights accrued or to accrue under said
Deed of Trust.

Dated _____ (9) _____
_____ (10) _____   _____
_____   _____

Assignment of Deed of Trust

Exhibit 8-6 is a sample Assignment of Deed of Trust. Complete the document in
the following manner:

1. The name and address of the party to whom the recorded document should be
returned, usually the lender.

2. The name of the new lender, the new beneficiary under the Deed of Trust.

3. The date of the original Deed of Trust.

4. The name of the trustor, the borrower.

5. The name of the trustee, usually a title company.

6. The recording information for the existing Deed of Trust.

7. The county in which the Deed of Trust is recorded.

8. The legal description of the property secured by the Deed of Trust. If the legal
description is too long, attach a separate sheet headed Exhibit A with the legal
description and type in the blank: "See Exhibit A attached hereto and by this reference
made a part hereof" or similar phrasing.

9. The date on which the assignment is executed.

10. Signatures of the current lender (beneficiary), the one who is assigning the
interest in the Deed of Trust.

EXHIBIT 8-7

WHEN RECORDED MAIL TO

(1)

ASSIGNMENT OF MORTGAGE

This assignment of mortgage made as of this ___ (2) _____ day of _____ , 19 ___ , by _____ (3) _____ , a Delaware corporation ("Assignor"), to _____ (4) _____ Bank ("Assignee"), a national banking association,

WITNESSETH:

Whereas, _____ (5) _____ , a Vermont corporation ("Borrower"), has executed that certain Mortgage (the "Mortgage") dated _____ (6) _____ , and recorded on _____ (7) _____ as Instrument No. ___ (8) _____ Official Records of _____ (9) _____ to _____ (10) _____ Bank, to secure payment of indebtedness evidenced by that certain promissory note made by Borrower in the principal amount of $ _____ (11) _____ ; and

Whereas, the Mortgage encumbers the real property described on Exhibit A attached hereto and by this reference made a part hereof; and

Whereas, to secure payment of indebtedness arising under the Loan Agreement, by Security Agreement, Assignment and Pledge Agreement of even date herewith (the "Security Agreement") Assignor has pledged to Assignee the promissory note secured by the Mortgage and has assigned to Assignee the interest of Assignor under the Mortgage; and

Whereas, Assignor and Assignee now wish to give notice of such Assignment;

Now therefore, by this Assignment of Mortgage and by the Security Agreement, Assignor has assigned and does hereby assign to Assignee all right, title, estate, and interest of Assignor under the Mortgage upon the terms and conditions of the Security Agreement.

In Witness Whereof, Assignor has executed this Assignment of Mortgage as of the date and year first set forth hereinabove.

By: _____ (12) _____
By: _____ (12) _____

Assignment of Mortgage

Mortgages can also be assigned, by documents very similar to the one discussed above. Exhibit 8-7 is an Assignment of Mortgage document. Fill it in with the following information:

1. The name and address of the party to whom the document should be returned after recording.

2. The date of the Assignment document.

3. The name of the Assignor, the current beneficiary who is pledging over his or her interest in the Mortgage.

4. The name of the Assignee, the party who will now have the beneficial interest under the Mortgage.

5. The name of the borrower, the Mortgagor on the Mortgage document.

6. The date of the Mortgage instrument.

7. The date the Mortgage was recorded.

8. The instrument number assigned to the Mortgage document when it was recorded.

9. The county and state in which the Mortgage document was recorded.

10. The name of the Mortgagee, the lender on the Mortgage document.

11. The amount of the Note secured by the Mortgage.

12. The signature of the Assignor, the lender giving up the beneficial interest in the Mortgage instrument.

Preparing Quitclaim Deeds

Quitclaim Deeds are used when one party is giving up all right, title, and interest in a piece of property to another party. In commercial real estate transactions they can be used to insure clear title, as a means of making sure that a party has no interest in the real property to be used as collateral for a loan.

Exhibit 8-8 is a Quitclaim Deed. Fill it out as follows:

1. The name and address of the party to whom the recorded instrument should be sent.

2. The date of the Quitclaim Deed.

3. The name of the Assignor, the party who is releasing all interest in the property.

4. The name of the Assignee, the party who is going to receive the Quitclaim; that is, receive clear title to the real estate.

5. The agreement under which the Quitclaim is issued or granted should be referenced.

6. The date of the agreement relative to the Quitclaim.

7. The state and county in which the property in question is located.

8. The legal description of the property for which the Quitclaim is issued. If the space is not large enough for the entire description, attach a separate sheet headed Exhibit A and make reference to it in this section with "See Exhibit A attached hereto and by this reference made a part hereof" or similar phrasing.

9. The signature of the party quitclaiming interest in the real estate.

The Quitclaim Deed should be notarized and recorded in the office of the recorder of documents in the county in which the real estate is located.

Preparing Security Agreements and UCC Certificates

Security Agreements are used by lenders to gain an interest in property other than real estate. Use of such instruments in commercial real estate lending transactions is limited, since most lenders are not that concerned with the personal property.

Taking a Security Agreement has value in situations involving special-purpose

EXHIBIT 8-8

WHEN RECORDED MAIL TO:

(1)

QUITCLAIM

QUITCLAIM dated _____ (2) _____ by _____ (3) _____ ("Assignor") to _____ (4) _____ ("Assignee").

For valuable consideration, receipt of which is hereby acknowledged, Assignor hereby remises, releases, and quitclaims to Assignee, its successors, and assigns, all of Assignor's right, title, and interest under the agreement set forth _____ (5) _____ dated _____ (6) _____ from Assignor to Assignee, a copy of which is attached hereto and incorporated herein by reference, to the real property located in the state of _____ (7) _____ , county of _____ (7) _____ and more fully described as:

(8)

Assignor hereby warrants and represents that it has not conveyed or surrendered any rights pursuant to said agreement to any person other than Assignee.

By: _____ (9) _____

real estate, where the personal property is integral to the operation of the business venture that gives the property value. Restaurants or hospitals are examples of such special-purpose property. The facility would lose value or be unable to operate at all if the personal property were removed.

Commercial real estate lenders do not take a prior interest in such property. That is reserved for the purchase money lenders, the equipment and furniture suppliers, and lenders who finance such assets. Real estate lenders are only interested in making sure that the assets are not liquidated without their knowledge.

How to Use the Security Agreement

A Security Agreement is the instrument that grants the lender an interest in the property listed. The financing statement, or UCC certificate, is the vehicle by which this interest is recorded, or made a part of the public record. Security Agreements and UCC Certificates may vary slightly in form by state, but their use is uniform.

Exhibit 8-9 is a Security Agreement to be used when the bank is not to be in possession of the asset in which it is taking an interest. Such an agreement would cover assets located at the subject property. It is the form most typically used in a real estate transaction. Sometimes a lender may take a specific form of collateral, like a Certificate of Deposit or Letter of Credit. In such a case the form is essentially the same, but provides for the bank not to be in possession of the collateral.

EXHIBIT 8-9

SECURITY AGREEMENT
(BANK **NOT** TO BE IN POSSESSION)

GOODS—Consumer Goods, Equipment, Farm Products and Timber under Contract to be Cut and Removed.

In consideration of the covenants and agreements contained herein, and financial accommodations given, to be given or continued, the undersigned Borrower hereby, pursuant to the California Uniform Commercial Code, grants to the Secured Party (Bank) a security interest in all of the Collateral described in paragraph 3 and indicated in paragraph 4 herein. The security interest created by this Agreement attaches immediately upon execution hereof or as soon as Borrower acquires rights to the Collateral and secures payment of any and all of Borrower's Indebtedness (including all debts, obligations, or liabilities now or hereafter existing, absolute or contingent, and future advances) to Bank.

1. BORROWER(S)

a. _____ (1) _____ (2) _____

   Name   Social Security or Employer Number

b. _____ (3) _____

   Trade Name (if any)

c. _____ (4) _____

   Mailing Address   City   State   Zip

d. _____ (5) _____

   Chief Place of Business (6)   City   State   Zip

e. _____

   Residence (individuals) City   State   Zip

2. SECURED PARTY—Name and Mailing Address (Transit and A.B.A. No.)

   (7)

3. COLLATERAL DESCRIPTION (AND LOCATION):

   (8)

4. COLLATERAL (OTHER): Indicated by Borrower's initials:

   a. EQUIPMENT:

   _____ All other equipment now owned by Borrower.

   _____ All after acquired equipment.

   _____ All accessions to equipment.

   b. CROPS AND TIMBER UNDER CONTRACT TO BE CUT AND REMOVED:

   _____ All products (in unmanufactured state) of crops and timber.

   _____ All proceeds from crops and timber and products thereof.

   c. LIVESTOCK:

   _____ All other livestock now owned by Borrower.

   _____ All after acquired livestock.

   _____ All increases of livestock.

   _____ All products (in unmanufactured state) of livestock.

   _____ All proceeds from livestock and products thereof.

   d. FARM SUPPLIES:

   _____ All other farm supplies now owned by Borrower.

   _____ All after acquired farm supplies.

5. PURCHASE MONEY SECURITY INTEREST:

   _____ If indicated by Borrower's initials, Bank is giving value to enable Borrower to acquire rights in, or the use of, Collateral.

6. INCORPORATION OF PROVISIONS ON REVERSE: All provisions on the reverse side are incorporated herein as if set forth fully at this point.

Dated _____ (9) _____, 19____

_____ (10) _____

By _____

Title _____

SIGNATURE OF BORROWER(S)

EXHIBIT 8-9 (cont'd.)
SECURITY AGREEMENT
(BANK NOT TO BE IN POSSESSION)

I. WARRANTIES AND REPRESENTATIONS. Borrower warrants and represents that:

1. Borrower's Title—Except as specified herein, Borrower has, or upon acquisition will have, title to all Collateral and no other person, entity, agency, or government has or purports to have, or upon acquisition will have, any right, title, lien, encumbrance, adverse claim, or interest in any Collateral.
2. Borrower's Authority—Borrower has authority to enter into the Agreement and any person signing it on Borrower's behalf has been duly authorized to execute the Agreement for Borrower.
3. Information—Any and all information now or hereafter supplied to Bank by Borrower, or at Borrower's request or instruction is correct.

II. COVENANTS AND AGREEMENTS: Borrower covenants and agrees that:

1. Payment—Borrower will pay any of Borrower's Indebtedness to Bank promptly when due and Borrower will repay immediately and without demand, all expenses (including reasonable attorneys' fees, legal expenses and costs) incurred by Bank under the Agreement with interest at the legal rate from the date of expenditure.
2. Financial Condition—Borrower will not commence nor permit to continue any proceeding in bankruptcy, receivership, or similar proceedings concerned with involuntary liquidation, reorganization or dissolution or arrangements with creditors, nor will it commit any act of bankruptcy, nor make an assignment for creditors, or become insolvent.
3. Additional Information—Borrower will, upon Bank's demand, establish the correctness of any information supplied to Bank and will promptly notify Bank of any adverse changes in any information supplied to Bank and of any change in Borrower's residence, chief place of business or mailing address, and of any change of address to which notices should be sent.
4. Additional Documents—Borrower will execute any additional agreements, assignments or documents that may be deemed necessary or advisable by Bank to effectuate the purpose of the Agreement.
5. Location and Identification—Borrower will keep the Collateral separate and identifiable and at the location described herein and will not remove the Collateral from that location without the Bank's written consent.
6. Sale, Lease, or Disposition—Except as specified herein, Borrower will not, without written consent of Bank, sell, encumber or otherwise dispose of or transfer any Collateral or interest therein or permit or suffer any such disposition or transfer until the Indebtedness to Bank has been completely discharged.
7. Maintenance, Repair, Use and Inspection—Borrower will maintain and repair the Collateral; will use the Collateral lawfully and only within Insurance coverage; will not use the Collateral so as to cause or result in any waste, unreasonable deterioration or depreciation; and will permit Bank to enter on Borrower's property and to inspect the Collateral at any reasonable time.
8. Cultivation and Animal Husbandry—If the Collateral is timber, crops or livestock, Borrower will protect and cultivate, or husband the Collateral using methods of cultivation and animal husbandry acceptable to Bank.
9. Insurance—Borrower will insure the Collateral, with Bank as Loss Payee, in form and amounts, with companies, and against risks and liability satisfactory to Bank and hereby assigns the policies to Bank, agrees to deliver them to Bank at Bank's request, and authorizes Bank to make any claim thereunder, to cancel the insurance upon default, and to receive payment of and endorse any instrument in payment of loss or return premium or other refund or return.
10. Decrease in Value of Collateral—Borrower will, if in the Bank's judgment the Collateral has materially decreased in value, either provide enough additional collateral to satisfy the Bank or reduce the total indebtedness by an amount sufficient to satisfy the Bank.
11. Taxes-Assessments-Charges-Liens-Encumbrances—Borrower will pay when due all taxes, assessments, charges, liens or encumbrances now or hereafter affecting the Collateral, and, if the Collateral is on or attached to realty owned by Borrower, the realty on which the Collateral is located.
12. Defense of Title—Borrower at its own cost and expense will appear in and defend any action or proceeding which may affect the Bank's security interest in or Borrower's title to any Collateral.
13. Appointment of Bank as Attorney in Fact; Reimbursement—Borrower will and hereby does appoint Bank as Borrower's Attorney in Fact to do any act which Borrower is obligated by the Agreement to do, to exercise such rights as Borrower might exercise, to use such equipment as Borrower might use, and to collect such proceeds as Borrower might collect, all to protect and preserve Bank's rights hereunder and the Collateral. Borrower will immediately reimburse Bank for any expenses Bank may incur while acting as Borrower's Attorney in Fact.
14. Endorser-Surety-Guarantor—Borrower will, if any present endorser, surety, or guarantor, dies or does any act described in covenant 2, either, at Bank's option, pay all of Borrower's Indebtedness or substitute an endorser, surety, or guarantor acceptable to Bank.
15. Purchase Money—Borrower will, if Bank, as indicated herein, gives value to enable Borrower to acquire rights in or the use of Collateral, use such value for such purpose.

III. REMEDIES: Borrower understands and agrees that in the event that: (a) Any warranty or representation is false or is believed in good faith by Bank to be false; (b) any covenant or agreement is violated; or (c) Bank in good faith deems itself insecure (because the prospect of payment is impaired; the prospect of performance of any covenant or agreement is impaired; or the value or priority of the security interest is impaired), Bank, in addition to any other rights or remedies provided by law or the Agreement, and to the extent permitted by law, may at its option:

1. Expenses—incur expenses (including reasonable attorney's fees, legal expenses and costs) in exercising any right or power under the Agreement.
2. Require Additional Collateral—demand that Borrower provide enough additional Collateral to satisfy the Bank.
3. Performance of Borrower's Obligations by Bank—perform any obligation of Borrower, and may make payments, purchase, contest or compromise any encumbrance, charge or lien, and pay taxes and expenses.
4. Set-Off—exercise all rights of set-off and Banker's lien to the same effect and in the same manner as if no Collateral had been given.
5. Default—declare, without notice to the Borrower, that a default has occurred.
6. Acceleration—declare, without notice to the Borrower, that the entire Indebtedness is immediately due and payable.
7. Possession—if not then in possession of the Collateral, take possession of and protect the Collateral; require the Borrower or other person in possession to assemble the Collateral and make it available to Bank at a reasonably convenient place to be designated by Bank; render the Collateral unusable without removing it; and enter upon such lands and properties where the Collateral might be located.
8. Notice—notify other interested persons or entities of the default, acceleration and other actions of the Bank.
9. Suit, Retention or Disposition of Collateral, Application of Proceeds—sue the Borrower or any other person or entity liable for the Indebtedness; retain the Collateral in satisfaction of the obligation and Indebtedness; dispose of the Collateral; and apply the proceeds of disposition, including provision for reasonable attorneys' fees and legal expenses incurred by Bank; all as provided by law.

IV. RULES TO CONSTRUE AGREEMENT: Borrower understands and agrees that:

1. Time of Essence—Time is of the essence of the Agreement.
2. Waiver—Bank's acceptance of partial or delinquent payments or failure of Bank to exercise any right or remedy shall not be a waiver of any obligation of Borrower or right of Bank nor constitute a modification of the Agreement, nor constitute a waiver of any other similar default subsequently occurring.
3. Entire Agreement—The Agreement contains the entire security agreement between Bank and Borrower.
4. Assignments, etc.—The provisions of the Agreement are hereby made applicable to and shall inure to the benefit of Bank's successors and assigns and bind Borrower's heirs, legatees, devisees, administrators, executors, successors and assigns.
5. Law Governing—Subject to the terms hereof, this Agreement shall be construed and governed by the laws of the State of California.
6. Multiple Borrowers—When more than one Borrower signs the Agreement all agree:
   a. Construction—that whenever "Borrower" appears in the Agreement it shall be "each Borrower."
   b. Breach—that breach of any covenant or warranty by any Borrower may, at the Bank's option, be treated as a breach by all Borrowers.
   c. Liability—that the liability of each Borrower is joint and several and the discharge of any Borrower, for any reason other than full payment, or any extension, forbearance, change of rate of interest, or acceptance, release or substitution of security or any impairment or suspension of Bank's remedies or rights against one Borrower, shall not affect the liability of any other Borrower.
   d. Waiver—all Borrowers waive the right to require the Bank to proceed against one Borrower before any other or to pursue any other remedy in Bank's power.

Fill in the following information:

1. The name of the borrower, the party who is pledging the asset taken as collateral.

2. The identifying number, either social security number (if an individual) or tax identification number (corporation or partnership).

3. The trade name used by the borrowing entity if different from the real name. This would apply to an individual who is using a "DBA,"; that is, a "doing business as" name.

4. The mailing address of the entity giving a security interest.

5. The chief place of business of the entity; that is, the place where they conduct their business.

6. The residence address of the individuals involved.

7. The secured party, your bank.

8. A complete description of the collateral involved and on which the lien is being taken. For example, one might describe the collateral as: "All articles of personal property, fixtures, goods, substitutions or changes in or replacement of the whole or any part thereof, now or at any time hereafter, affixed to, attached to, placed upon, or used in any way in connection with the use, enjoyment, occupancy, or operation of the real property located at 123 Main Street, Santa Fe, New Mexico or any portion thereof and owned by the undersigned or in which the undersigned has now or hereafter acquires an interest and all building materials and equipment now or hereafter delivered to said premises together with the proceeds, including insurance proceeds, thereof."

9. The date of the document.

10. The name and signature of the borrowing entity.

Using the UCC Certificate

A UCC Certificate and filing goes along with the Security Agreement discussed above. The UCC filing covers personal property taken as collateral along with the real estate and is recorded with the Secretary of State of the state in which the collateral is located. A UCC certificate, when recorded, grants the real estate lender a lien on the assets in question.

A typical format that is used by the State of California is shown as Exhibit 8-10. Use this form to perfect an interest in the collateral covered by the Security Agreement. The form should be completed with the following information:

1. The name of the debtor, your borrower.

2. The identification number of the borrower, either a Tax ID Number or Social Security Number.

3. The mailing address of the borrower.

4. The name, ID number, and mailing address of any additional debtor or debtors, if applicable to the current loan. If there are more than one additional debtor, others can be listed on an attached form, with the same information called for on the UCC certificate. The certificate can reference attached Exhibit A.

5. The debtor's trade name, if any, and federal tax number. This would be needed if an individual is "doing business as" a company name different than his name.

EXHIBIT 8-10

This FINANCING STATEMENT is presented for filing pursuant to the California Uniform Commercial Code.

1. DEBTOR (LAST NAME FIRST—IF AN INDIVIDUAL) (1)		1A. SOCIAL SECURITY OR FEDERAL TAX NO. (2)	
1B. MAILING ADDRESS (3)	1C. CITY, STATE	1D. ZIP CODE	
2. ADDITIONAL DEBTOR (IF ANY) (LAST NAME FIRST—IF AN INDIVIDUAL) (4)		2A. SOCIAL SECURITY OR FEDERAL TAX NO.	
2B. MAILING ADDRESS (4)	2C. CITY, STATE	2D. ZIP CODE	
3. DEBTOR'S TRADE NAMES OR STYLES (IF ANY) (5)		3A. FEDERAL TAX NUMBER	

4. SECURED PARTY

NAME (6)
MAILING ADDRESS
CITY   STATE   ZIP CODE

4A. SOCIAL SECURITY NO., FEDERAL TAX NO. OR BANK TRANSIT AND A.B.A. NO. (7)

5. ASSIGNEE OF SECURED PARTY (IF ANY)

NAME
MAILING ADDRESS (8)
CITY   STATE   ZIP CODE

5A. SOCIAL SECURITY NO., FEDERAL TAX NO. OR BANK TRANSIT AND A.B.A. NO.

6. This FINANCING STATEMENT covers the following types or items of property **(include description of real property on which located and owner of record when required by instruction 4).**

(9)

7. CHECK IF APPLICABLE ☒	7A. ☐ PRODUCTS OF COLLATERAL ARE ALSO COVERED	7B. DEBTOR(S) SIGNATURE NOT REQUIRED IN ACCORDANCE WITH INSTRUCTION 5(a) ITEM: ☐ (1) ☐ (2) ☐ (3) ☐ (4)
8. CHECK IF APPLICABLE ☒	☐ DEBTOR IS A "TRANSMITTING UTILITY" IN ACCORDANCE WITH UCC § 9105 (1) (n)	

9.

► (10)

SIGNATURE(S) OF DEBTOR(S)   DATE:

(11)

TYPE OR PRINT NAME(S) OF DEBTOR(S)

► (12)

SIGNATURE(S) OF SECURED PARTY(IES)

(13)

TYPE OR PRINT NAME(S) OF SECURED PARTY(IES)

11. *Return copy to:*

NAME
ADDRESS (14)
CITY
STATE
ZIP CODE

CODE
1
2
3
4
5
6
7
8
9
O

10. THIS SPACE FOR USE OF FILING OFFICER (DATE, TIME, FILE NUMBER AND FILING OFFICER)

(1) FILING OFFICER COPY

FORM UCC-1—FILING FEE $3.00
Approved by the Secretary of State

6. The name and mailing address of the secured party, your bank.

7. Your bank's transit and ABA numbers.

8. The name and address, and ABA number, of any assignee bank, an entity to whom you are assigning your interest in the loan, and the underlying collateral.

9. A description of the property taken as collateral. Language that can be used includes:

a. "All fixtures now or hereafter located on the premises described on Schedule A attached hereto to and made a part hereof." Schedule A would then be an itemization of all the assets taken as collateral.

b. "All right, title, and interest of Debtor in, to, and under that certain Construction Account to be maintained by Debtor with Secured Party at Secured Party's office at 123 Main Street, Santa Fe, New Mexico.

c. "All articles of personal property, fixtures, goods, or substitutions for changes in, or replacement of the whole or any part thereof, now or at any time hereafter, affixed to, attached to, placed upon, or used in any way in connection with the use, enjoyment, occupancy, or operation of the real property located at 123 Main Street, Santa Fe, New Mexico or any portion thereof and owned by the undersigned or in which the undersigned has now or hereafter acquires an interest and all building materials and equipment now or hereafter delivered to said premises together with the proceeds, including insurance proceeds, thereof."

10. The signature of the borrower or borrowers, and the date of the signature.

11. The typed name of the borrower or borrowers.

12. The signature of the secured party, your bank.

13. The typed name of the secured party.

14. The name and address of the entity to whom the recorded copy is to be returned when filed.

How to Request Information Regarding Liens on Collateral Taken

One other certificate deserves mention, although its use in real estate transactions is questionable. The UCC-3 is used to request from the recording office any information as to liens on the collateral taken. Such a request will usually turn up all of the purchase money financing used to acquire the equipment or fixtures.

As we have discussed, the real estate lender is usually not concerned with a first lien on chattels. First position is reserved for the companies from whom the item was acquired and who are usually equipped to provide chattel financing. The real estate lender is only concerned with putting a cloud on title to prevent any effort to sell off the equipment or transfer title to it without his consent. A UCC filing is used only for those properties where a lender is concerned that a removal of the equipment or fixtures would seriously affect the value of viability of the real estate that supports his loan.

When to Use an Assignment of Rents

An Assignment of Rents is basic to financing transactions involving income-producing real estate. Cash flow repays debt, cash flow that is derived from leasing or renting the real estate. Insuring the availability of the income stream in the event of a default is the purpose of an Assignment.

The Assignment gives a lender the right to step into the role of landlord and directly collect the rents from the property, bypassing the owner. The Assignment would only be exercised in the event of a default under the loan. It allows the lender to control the cash flow and insure that income generated will not be diverted from the subject property to other uses.

Typically a blanket Assignment of Rents clause is contained as part of the Trust Deed or Mortgage instrument. For example, in the trust deed discussed earlier in this chapter, there is the clause "Trustor also assigns to Beneficiary all rents, issues, and profits of said realty reserving the right to collect and use the same except during continuance of default hereunder and during continuance of such default authorizing Beneficiary to collect and enforce the same by any lawful means in the name of any party hereto." Such a clause inserted into the Trust Deed or Mortgage is sufficient to give the lender the right to collect rents from the property.

An Assignment of Rents is used for properties that have month-to-month occupancy; for example, apartments or retirement hotels, where a lease agreement is not usually taken. Such properties use ongoing rental agreements that call for the payment of a monthly sum as long as there is occupancy.

Preparing an Assignment of Lease

An Assignment of Lease is a more specific document. It is used when there are lease agreements between the owner and lessees, agreements that call for the occupancy of the property for certain specified periods of time. A lessee will occupy the premises for a year, or five years, or 20 years. The basic agreement, clauses, and conditions do not generally change.

An Assignment of Lease gives the lender the same basic powers as an Assignment of Rent. The lender can step into the role of owner and receive the rents due under the lease. The lender must also take on the liabilities of the owner, as well, including maintenance of the property in a useable condition.

Exhibit 8-11 is an Assignment of Lease form. Fill it in with the following information:

1. The name and address of the entity to whom the recorded document is to be returned, usually your bank's address.

2. The date of the agreement.

3. The name of the Assignor, the one who is giving up an interest in the lease agreements.

4. The name of the Assignee, the one who is to receive the benefit of the Assignment, your bank.

5. The county and state in which the land is located.

6. The amount of the loan to be secured by the assignment.

7. The name of the title company to be used as trustee under the Deed of Trust (if mortgage there would be no such title company).

EXHIBIT 8-11

WHEN RECORDED RETURN TO:

(1)

ASSIGNMENT OF LESSOR'S INTEREST IN LEASES

This Assignment, made this _____ day of _____ (2) _____ 19__, by _____ (3) _____, a Delaware corporation, hereinafter "Borrower," or "Assignor," to _____ (4) _____Bank, a national banking association, hereinafter "Lender" or "Assignee,"

WITNESSETH:

Whereas, Assignor is the owner of certain land situated in the County of ____ (5) ____, State of ____ (5) ____ described more fully in Exhibit A attached hereto and by reference made a part hereof (the "Property"); and

Whereas, the Lender has agreed to make a loan to the Borrower in the amount of _____ (6) _____ pursuant to the terms and conditions of that certain Loan Agreement of an even date herewith by and between the Borrower and Lender; and

Whereas, the obligation of Borrower to repay the loan is evidenced by a promissory note in the amount of _____ (6) _____payable to the Lender; and

Whereas, payment of the indebtedness evidenced by the Note is secured by a Deed of Trust encumbering the Property of an even date herewith made by Borrower to _____ (7) _____, Trustee, for the benefit of Assignee, to be recorded immediately prior to this Assignment; and

Whereas the Property is subject to that certain Lease Agreement dated _____ (8) _____ by and between _____ (9) _____, as Landlord, and _____ (10) _____, as Lessee, hereinafter referred to as "Lease;"

Now, therefore, for Value Received, Assignor hereby absolutely and unconditionally grants, transfers, and assigns to Assignee, its successors, and assigns, all interest of Assignor as landlord under the lease, and Borrower hereby absolutely and unconditionally grants, transfers, and assigns to Assignee, its successors and assigns:

A. all rents, issues, and profits from the Property; and

B. all of the other right, title, and interest of Assignor in and to:

(i) any and all leases of space now or hereafter affecting the Property; and

(ii) any extensions, renewals, or modifications of said Lease or Leases and any guaranties of the obligations owed Assignor thereunder,

provided, however, that so long as no event of default (as defined in the Loan Agreement) shall have occurred or be continuing, Assignor shall have the right to collect, but not more than one month prior to accrual, all rents, issues, and profits from the Property and to retain, use, and enjoy the same;

Assignor Agrees with Respect to Each Lease That:

1. Assignor shall fulfill or perform each and every condition and covenant of each Lease by Assignor to be fulfilled or performed, give prompt notice to Assignee to any notice received by Assignor of default under any Lease, together with a

EXHIBIT 8-11 (cont'd.)

complete copy of any such notice; at the sole cost and expense of Assignor, enforce, short of termination of any Lease, the performance or observance of each and every covenant and condition of such Lease to be performed or observed by the other parties thereto; not modify the terms of any of the Leases in any manner which materially adversely affects the rights of the Lessor thereunder; not terminate the term of any Lease nor accept a surrender thereof without the consent of Assignee, unless such surrender is required by the terms of such Lease; not anticipate the rents payable to Assignor thereunder for more than one month prior to accrual; not consent to any assignment by a tenant of its interest in any Lease; not waive or release the other parties thereto from any material obligations or conditions by them to be performed; and not make any assignment of any Lease to any person, without the prior written consent of Assignee.

2. Except as provided in Section 1 of this Assignment, the rights assigned hereunder include all Assignor's right and power to modify the Leases or to terminate the term or to accept a surrender or termination thereof or to waive, or release the other parties from, the performance or observance by them of any obligation or condition thereof or to anticipate rents payable to Assignor thereunder for more than one month prior to accrual; provided, that Assignee may not exercise such rights and powers so long as no event of default (as defined in the Loan Agreement) shall have occurred and be continuing.

3. At its sole cost and expense, Assignor will appear in and prosecute its claims and defend its rights in any action growing out of or in any manner connected with the Lease or the obligations or liabilities of Assignor, other parties, or any guarantor thereunder, and Assignee, if made a party to any such action, may engage counsel and incur and pay costs and expenses and attorneys' fees, and all such sums, with interest thereon from the date of each such expenditure at the rate provided in the Loan Agreement, shall be due from Borrower upon demand and secured hereby and by the Deed of Trust.

4. Should Assignor fail to make any payment or do any action as herein provided, then Assignee, without obligation so to do and without notice to or demand from Assignor and without releasing Assignor from any obligation herein, may make or do the same, including specifically, without limiting its general powers, appearing in and defending an action purporting to affect the security hereof or the rights or powers of Assignee and performing any obligation of Assignor in the Leases contained, and, exercising any such powers, paying necessary costs and expenses, employing counsel, and incurring and paying attorneys' fees and expenses; and Borrower will pay immediately upon demand all sums expended by Assignee under the authority hereof, together with interest thereon from the date of each such expenditure at the rate provided in the Loan Agreement and payment of the same shall be secured hereby and by the other Security Documents, as defined in the Loan Agreement.

5. Upon the occurrence of any event of default, Assignee, at its option, without notice, and without regard to the adequacy of security for the indebtedness hereby secured, either in person or by agent with or without bringing any action or proceeding, or by a receiver to be appointed by a court, may: enter upon, take possession of, and operate the Property; make, enforce, modify, and accept any surrender of any

EXHIBIT 8-11 (cont'd.)

Lease; obtain and evict operators, concessionaires, and licensees; fix or modify rents; and do any acts which Assignee deems proper to protect the security thereof until all indebtedness secured hereby is paid in full, and either with or without taking possession of the Property, in its own name, sue for or otherwise collect and receive all rents, issues, and profits, including those past due and unpaid, and apply the same, less costs and expenses of operation and collection, including reasonable attorneys' fees and expenses, upon any indebtedness secured hereby in such order as Assignee may determine. The entering upon and taking possession of the Property, the collection of such rents, issues, and profits, and the application thereof as aforesaid, shall not cure or waive any default or waive, modify, and affect any event of default under the Loan Agreement or invalidate any act done pursuant to such notice.

6. Assignee and the purchaser at any foreclosure sale shall have the right, but not the obligation, following foreclosure of the lien of the Deed of Trust to preserve any Lease and the rights of the landlord thereunder. Any lease hereafter entered into shall provide for such right of preservation and shall contain a covenant by the other parties thereto to attorn to or perform for the benefit of any such purchaser.

7. Assignee shall not be obligated to perform or discharge any obligation under a Lease, or under or by reason of this Assignment, and Assignor hereby agrees to indemnify Assignee against and hold it harmless from any and all liability, loss, cost, claims, or damage which it may or might incur under any Lease or under or by reason of this Agreement and of and from any and all claims and demands whatsoever which may be asserted against it by reason of any alleged obligation or undertaking on its part to perform or discharge any of the terms of any Lease; should Assignee incur any such liability, loss, cost, claims, or damage under any Lease or under or by reason of this Assignment, or in defending against any such claims or demands, the amount thereof, including costs, expenses, and attorneys' fees, together with interest thereon provided for in the Loan Agreement, shall be secured hereby and by the other Security Documents, and Assignor shall reimburse Assignee therefor immediately upon demand.

8. This Assignment shall inure to the benefit of the successors and assigns of Assignee and shall bind the Assignor's legal representatives, successors, and assigns.

9. Upon the payment in full of all indebtedness secured hereby, as evidenced by the recording of an instrument of reconveyance or satisfaction or release of the Deed of Trust without the recording of another Deed of Trust in favor of or for the benefit of Assignee encumbering the Property, the Assignment shall become null and be void and of no effect.

10. This Assignment shall be governed by and construed and interpreted in accordance with the laws of the State of _____ (11) _____.

11. This Assignment is delivered in satisfaction of conditions specified in the Loan Agreement and is entitled to the benefits of the Loan Agreement. Terms used in this Assignment which are defined in the Loan Agreement shall have the meanings specified therein.

IN WITNESS WHEREOF, Assignor has duly executed this Assignment the day and year first written above.

(12)

8. The date of the Lease Agreement.

9. The name of the Landlord, the owner of the property, your borrower.

10. The name of the Lessee, the tenant occupying the property.

11. The state whose laws will be used to govern the Assignment.

12. Type a signature block and a place for the borrower, the Assignor, to sign.

Using Subordination Agreements

Subordination Agreements are used to change the priority of liens against the property. There are two kinds of subordinations with which the real estate lender will be involved, one for trust deeds/mortgages and the other for leases.

Subordination of a Trust Deed or Mortgage

A subordination of a trust deed or mortgage changes the priority of an existing lien of record by making it subordinate to a later lien. In essence it takes a first and makes it a second. A subordination is frequently used in a transaction where property is purchased with financing carried back by the seller. Later, the owner may want to build on the land, and obtains construction financing from a lending institution for that purpose. The holder of the first, the original seller, elects to subordinate his land loan to the construction lender's loan. The new owner does not have to come up with as much cash as he would if the loan had to be paid in order to give the new lender first position. An agreement to subordinate can be worked out when the property is originally sold. A condition is written into the sale agreement that the seller will subordinate his interest to that of a later construction lender. Sometimes agreement to subordinate can be reached later because the holder of the first sees that an improvement of the property is to his advantage, as well.

Subordinating Building and Ground Leases

The other type of subordination agreement involves subordinating leases, either building or ground leases, to the interest of the lender making the mortgage loan. Whether or not such a subordination is warranted depends on the nature of the deal and the policies of the lender. In the event that building leases are subordinated, the effect is to give the lender the right, if he acquires title to the property through a default and foreclosure action, to remove the tenants and release the property to tenants of his own choosing. With ground leases, a subordination allows the leasehold lender, if title to the improvements is taken through foreclosure, to acquire fee interest in the land at the same time.

Exhibit 8-12 reflects a form to use in subordinating an existing trust deed. It can be completed as follows:

1. The name and address of the entity to whom the recorded document should be returned.

2. The date of the Agreement.

3. The owner of the land, typically your borrower.

EXHIBIT 8-12

SUBORDINATION AGREEMENT

NOTICE: THIS SUBORDINATION AGREEMENT RESULTS IN YOUR SECURITY INTEREST IN THE PRO-PERTY BECOMING SUBJECT TO AND OF LOWER PRIORITY THAN THE LIEN OF SOME OTHER OR LATER SECURITY INSTRUMENT.

THIS AGREEMENT, made this ..... (2) .... day of ...., 19 ......,
(3)
by ....,
owner of the land hereinafter described and hereinafter referred to as "Owner", and ....
....
(4)
present owner and holder of the deed of trust and note first hereinafter described and hereinafter referred to as "Beneficiary";

WITNESSETH

THAT WHEREAS, ... (5) ....
(6)
did on ...., execute a deed of trust to ....
(7)
...., as trustee, covering:

(8)

to secure a note in the sum of $ .... (9) ......, dated .... (10) ....,
(11)
in favor of ....,
(12)   (13)
which deed of trust was recorded ...., in book .... page ....,
Official Records of said county and is subject and subordinate to the deed of trust next hereinafter described; and

WHEREAS, ... (14) ...., did on ....,
execute a deed of trust to ....,
as trustee, covering said land and securing an indebtedness in the amount of $ .... in favor
of ...., hereinafter referred to as "Lender", which deed of trust was
recorded ...., in book .... page ...., Official Records of said county
and provides among other things that it shall also secure additional loans and advances thereafter made upon the terms and conditions therein set forth; and

WHEREAS, Owner has executed, or is about to execute, a note in the amount of $ .... (15)
(16)
dated ...., in favor of Lender, payable with interest and upon the terms and conditions
described therein, which note evidences an additional loan to be made by Lender to Owner under the terms and provisions of, and secured by, said deed of trust in favor of Lender; and

WHEREAS, it is a condition precedent to obtaining said additional loan that said deed of trust in favor of Lender, securing all obligations recited therein as being secured thereby, including but not limited to said additional loan, shall unconditionally be and remain at all times a lien or charge upon the land hereinbefore described, prior and superior to the lien or charge of the deed of trust first above mentioned; and

-1-

EXHIBIT 8-12 (cont'd.)

WHEREAS, Lender is willing to make said additional loan provided the deed of trust securing the same is a lien or charge upon said land prior and superior to the lien or charge of the deed of trust first above mentioned and provided that Beneficiary will specifically and unconditionally subordinate the lien or charge of the deed of trust first above mentioned to the lien or charge of said deed of trust in favor of Lender; and

WHEREAS, it is to the mutual benefit of the parties hereto that Lender make said additional loan to Owner; and Beneficiary is willing that the deed of trust securing the same shall constitute a lien or charge upon said land which is unconditionally prior and superior to the lien or charge to the deed of trust first above mentioned.

NOW THEREFORE, in consideration of the mutual benefits accruing to the parties hereto and other valuable consideration, the receipt and sufficiency of which consideration is hereby acknowledged, and in order to induce Lender to make the additional loan above referred to, it is hereby declared, understood, and agreed as follows:

(1) That said deed of trust in favor of Lender, as to said additional loan as well as all other obligations recited as being secured thereby, and any renewals or extensions thereof, shall unconditionally be and remain at all times a lien or charge on the property therein described, prior and superior to the lien or charge of the deed of trust first above mentioned.

(2) That Lender would not make its additional loan above described without this subordination agreement.

(3) That this agreement shall be the whole and only agreement with regard to the subordination of the lien or charge of the deed of trust first above mentioned to the lien or charge of the deed of trust in favor of Lender above referred to and shall supersede and cancel, but only insofar as would affect the priority between the deeds of trust hereinbefore specifically described, any prior agreements as to such subordination including, but not limited to, those provisions, if any, contained in the deed of trust first above mentioned, which provide for the subordination of the lien or charge thereof to another deed or deeds of trust or to another mortgage or mortgages.

Beneficiary declares, agrees, and acknowledges that

(a) He consents to and approves (i) all provisions of the note evidencing said additional loan and the deed of trust securing same, and (ii) all agreements, including but not limited to any loan or escrow agreements, between Owner and Lender for the disbursement of the proceeds of Lender's additional loan;

(b) Lender in making disbursements pursuant to any such agreement is under no obligation or duty to, nor has Lender represented that it will, see to the application of such proceeds by the person or persons to whom Lender disburses such proceeds and any application or use of such proceeds for purposes other than those provided for in such agreement or agreements shall not defeat the subordination herein made in whole or in part;

(c) He intentionally and unconditionally waives, relinquishes, and subordinates the lien or charge of the deed of trust first above mentioned in favor of the lien or charge upon said land of the deed of trust in favor of Lender, as to said additional loan as well as all other obligations recited therein as being secured thereby, and understands that in reliance upon and in consideration of this waiver, relinquishment and subordination specific loans and advances are being and will be made and, as part and parcel thereof, specific monetary and other obligations are being and will be entered into which would not be made or entered into but for said reliance upon this waiver, relinquishment and subordination; and

(d) An endorsement has been placed upon the note secured by the deed of trust first above mentioned that said deed of trust has by this instrument been subordinated to the lien or charge of the deed of trust in favor of Lender above referred to.

NOTICE: THIS SUBORDINATION AGREEMENT CONTAINS A PROVISION WHICH ALLOWS THE PERSON OBLIGATED ON YOUR REAL PROPERTY SECURITY TO OBTAIN A LOAN, A PORTION OF WHICH MAY BE EXPENDED FOR OTHER PURPOSES THAN IMPROVEMENT OF THE LAND.

(17)	(18)
Beneficiary	Owner

(All signatures must be acknowledged)

-2-

IT IS RECOMMENDED THAT, PRIOR TO THE EXECUTION OF THIS SUBORDINATION AGREEMENT, THE PARTIES CONSULT WITH THEIR ATTORNEYS WITH RESPECT THERETO.

4. The lender under the existing first trust deed loan secured by the property.

5. The name of the property owner, your borrower.

6. The date of the prior Deed of Trust.

7. The name of the title company acting as trustee under the prior Deed of Trust.

8. A description of the property secured by the Deed of Trust.

9. The amount of the promissory note secured by the Deed of Trust.

10. The date of the promissory note.

11. The name of the lender who made the prior loan.

12. The date the prior Deed of Trust was recorded.

13. The book and page reference in which the recorded document can be found.

14. If there is a second Deed of Trust to be subordinated, this section is filled out as indicated in 6 through 13 above.

15. The amount of your promissory note, the current loan.

16. The date of your promissory note.

17. The signature of the Beneficiary under the first Deed of Trust.

18. The signature of the property owner, your borrower.

As with all documents that are to be recorded, a Notary Public should witness the signatures.

Exercising Care with Non-Disturbance Clauses

If the lender requires a subordination of a building lease, there are times when the tenant will consent, but only if the lender includes an Attornment or Non-Disturbance Clause in the agreement. Such a clause limits the usefulness of the subordination agreement. An attornment clause protects the tenant if the lender forecloses and takes over the property by requiring that the tenant's occupancy not be disturbed so long as rent payments are current and there is compliance with the terms and conditions of the lease. Put another way, if the tenant is current in rent payments and is not in default under the lease, the lender has no right to remove him from the property.

Notary Acknowledgments for Individuals, Partnerships, and Corporations

The Notary Acknowledgment is used to certify the signatures on a document that is to be recorded. Unless this is properly used, the recorder's office will not accept the document for recording. The Notary Public will have these forms and should be aware of the proper format. If not, check with the title company involved. Depending on whether the signers are individuals, partnerships, corporations, or combinations thereof, different notary forms will be needed. These forms are filled out, signed, and stamped by the Notary certifying that they know the signatures of the parties involved to be real.

Exhibit 8-13 shows a notary form to be used for an individual. Fill it out as follows:

1. The state in which the document is to be recorded.

2. The county in which the document is to be recorded.

3. The date on which the document was signed, which is also the date on which the individual(s) appeared before the notary and signed the document.

EXHIBIT 8-13

INDIVIDUAL NOTARY ACKNOWLEDGMENT

State of _____ (1) _____
County of _____ (2) _____
On this _____ (3) _____ day of _____ (3) _____ , 19 ___
before me personally appeared _____ (4) _____ personally
known to me (or proved to me on the basis of satisfactory evidence) to be the person
whose name is subscribed to this instrument as the person who executed the within
instrument.

_____ (5) _____

(6)

4. The name of the individual who signed the document.
5. The signature of the Notary Public.
6. The Notary's Stamp.

Exhibit 8-14 is a Notary Acknowledgment for a Partnership. It can be filled out as follows:

1. The state in which the document is to be recorded.
2. The county in which the document is to be recorded.
3. The date the document was signed before the Notary Public.
4. The name of the party signing the document.
5. The name of the partnership.

EXHIBIT 8-14

NOTARY ACKNOWLEDGMENT FOR PARTNERSHIP

State of _____ (1) _____
County of _____ (2) _____
On this the _____ (3) _____ day of _____ (3) _____ ,
19 ___ , before me, the undersigned, a Notary Public in and for said state, personally
appeared _____ (4) _____ , known to me (or proved to me on
the basis of satisfactory evidence) to be the person who executed the within instrument on behalf of _____ (5) _____ partnership that executed
the within instrument, and acknowledged to me that he executed the same as such
partner and that such partnership executed the same.

Witness my hand and official seal.

_____ (6) _____

(7)

EXHIBIT 8-15

NOTARY ACKNOWLEDGMENT FOR CORPORATION

State of _____ (1) _____
County of _____ (2) _____
On_____ (3) _____ , before me, the undersigned Notary Public in and for said State, personally appeared _____
(4) _____ and _____
(4) _____ , personally known to me (or proved to me on the basis of satisfactory evidence) to be the person(s) who executed the within instrument as the _____ (5) _____ President and as the _____ (6) _____ Secretary on behalf of the corporation therein named and acknowledged to me that such corporation executed the within instrument pursuant to its by-laws or a resolution of its board of directors.

Signature _____ (7) _____

(8)

6. The signature of the Notary Public.
7. The Notary's stamp.

Exhibit 8-15 is a Notary's Acknowledgment to be used in acknowledging corporate signatures. It can be filled out as follows:

1. The state in which the document is to be recorded.
2. The county in which the document is to be recorded.
3. The date the document was signed before the Notary Public.
4. The persons who appeared before the Notary to sign on behalf of the corporation. Typically they would be the corporation President and Secretary, but they could be other officers; for example, a Vice-President or Assistant Secretary. The corporate by-laws set out authorized signatures.
5. If a Vice-President of the corporation signed, type in "Vice-" in this blank.
6. If an Assistant Secretary of the corporation signed, type in "Assistant" in this blank.
7. The signature of the Notary Public.
8. The Notary's stamp.

How to Complete a Beneficiary's Statement

A Beneficiary's Statement would be sent by the lender to request information from the beneficiary of an existing trust deed as to the status of the loan. This would be sent to the mortgage if the instrument involved is a mortgage. The information sought enables the new lender to know exactly how much to pay to the old lender in order to clear all obligations affecting the property and get a reconveyance of the earlier lender's interest.

EXHIBIT 8-16

BENEFICIARY'S STATEMENT

_____ BANK

Escrow No. ____ (1) _____

Date _____ (2) _____

_____

_____ (3) _____

_____

An escrow has been opened with us by _____ (4) _____ cover-ing the sale of _____ (5) _____ Lot ____ (6) _____ Block _____ (6) _____ Tract _____ (6) _____ in _____ (7) _____ County, ____ (7) ____ which property we understand is en-cumbered by a Trust Deed held by you.

At the request of the parties in interest please fill in and sign the original of the beneficiary's statement below and return this entire page, together with any insur-ance policies which you may hold in connection with your loan. Insurance policies which you send us, together with the name and address of the new owner, will be mailed to you at completion of escrow.

_____ Bank

By: _____ (8) _____

BENEFICIARY'S STATEMENT

Escrow No. _____

Date _____

To: _____

I hereby certify as follows: I am the legal holder of that certain promissory note dated _____ executed by _____ in favor of _____ payable at _____ and secured by a Trust Deed _____ recorded in Book _____ Page _____ of Official Records of _____ County, State of _____ , and covering the property described as follows: _____

_____

_____ .

The original principal of said note was $ _____ .

I have made no advances under the terms of said encumbrance except $_____ . The unpaid balance of said note, plus advances, if any, is $_____ . The rate of interest is _____ percent per annum and is fully paid to _____ . The Principal and Interest is payable in installments of

EXHIBIT 8-16 (cont'd.)

$_____ or   more,   on   the _____ day   of each _____ month, _____.

The balance of principal and interest is due and payable on _____

_____

_____ .

No default now exists in the terms of said note or encumbrance, except _____

_____

_____ .

All of the consideration for said note actually passed to the makers thereof.

I make this statement for the benefit of _____ Bank and all parties in interest, including buyer of said real property, and understand that it is being relied upon by all of said parties.

I understand that said property has been sold and that you will furnish me with the new owner's name and address. Upon completion of your escrow any insurance policies deposited by me are to be mailed to me at the address shown below.

_____	_____
(Address)	(Signature)
_____	_____
(Telephone)	(Signature)

Exhibit 8-16 is a typical Beneficiary's Statement. Since we're dealing with new loans that you as a lender will be making, you will fill in the top portion of the form. The existing lender will fill out the bottom portion and return the form to you. The form should be completed with the following information:

1. The escrow number to which the loan applies, if applicable.
2. The date of the form.
3. The name and address of the existing lender, to whom the form is being addressed.
4. The name of the borrower.
5. The address of the property.
6. The lot number, block number, and tract number of the subject property, along with other legal description.
7. The county and state in which the property is located.
8. The signature of an appropriate party within your bank.

Completing an Approval-to-Pay Demand

An Approval-to-Pay Demand form (Exhibit 8-17) is used to secure the borrower's approval of the demand figures that the existing lender is submitting. As mentioned the beneficiary's statement is an accounting by the lender of all the sums due before he will release his interest in the property. The approval-to-pay demand says that the

EXHIBIT 8-17

APPROVAL-TO-PAY DEMAND

We hereby give approval to pay the attached demand of _____ (1) _____ , dated _____ (2) _____ from the proceeds of the loan which you will be funding in the amount of $ _____ (3) _____ .

Borrower understands that the lender will fund his loan only at such time as the Loan Documents have been signed and recorded as a first lien on the property located at _____ (4) _____ .

Approval given by:

_____ (5) _____

By: _____ (6) _____

By: _____ (6) _____

borrower agrees with the figures and authorizes the new lender to pay those funds. If your borrower does not agree, then you should have him work out his differences with the existing lender. This form should be completed as follows:

1. The name of the existing lender, the one who is providing the demand.
2. The date of the demand.

EXHIBIT 8-18

CHECKLIST

	Needed	Prepared	Signed	Recorded
Trust Deed/Mortgage	____	____	____	____
Quitclaim Deed	____	____	____	____
Security Agreement	____	____	____	N/A
UCC Filing	____	____	____	____
Assignment of Rents	____	____	____	____
Assignment of Lease(s)	____	____	____	____
Subordination Agreement				
Of Trust Deed	____	____	____	____
Of Lease(s)	____	____	____	____

Beneficiary's Statement:

    Sent _____

    To _____

    Received _____

Approval to Pay Demand:

    Signed _____

    By _____

3. The amount of the demand.
4. The address of the property covered by the existing lender's lien.
5. The name of the borrowing entity.
6. The signature(s) of the borrower.

End Note

This has of necessity been a lengthy chapter. The documenting of the lien the lender is taking is crucial. After all, the property forms the basis for the whole loan when doing a real estate deal. The lender must properly document his interest otherwise the loan he has is different from the loan he thought he was going to get. It would not be inappropriate to consult with legal counsel on questions of proper documentation relative to the security interest for your loan. Rules vary sometimes by state and even city, so being mindful of local differences is important.

The final exhibit (Exhibit 8-18) in this chapter is a checklist to use in making sure that you've considered all aspects of documenting the security interest. This chapter has dealt with how to make sure that your security is properly tied up. The next chapter will look at issues of property rights, making sure that the property ownership and use is correct.

9

How to Document Property Rights

The property rights held by the borrower and the manner in which title to real estate is held are important issues to the lender. Loan documents should mirror the vesting unless a third party is pledging the real estate collateral.

The lender needs to consider the ways in which rights to the property can be granted to others, thereby limiting the owner's right to use his property. If limits exist, then they may impact the loan decision because of their influence on the owner's ability to service the loan being requested.

Provisions of Typical Building Leases

The most common way in which property rights are limited is through building leases. With such a document the owner grants to someone else the right to use some or all of the real estate for a period of time. You must make sure that the terms of the lease are acceptable, and that they do not in any way conflict with the terms of the loan you are granting.

A typical building lease will contain the following provisions:

1. *Date.* The date on which the lease was signed. This may or may not be the date the lease term commences.

2. *Lessor.* The party who currently owns the real estate and who is granting to someone else the right to use the premises.

3. *Lessee.* The party getting the right to use the premises.

4. *Premises.* The lease will include a description of the space that is being leased. This may be the entire building or a portion of the building.

5. *Term.* The length of time the lease is valid. There may be extension clauses granting continued occupancy at the option of the lessee when the original lease term expires.

6. *Rent.* The money that will be paid by the lessee to the lessor in exchange for the use of the real estate.

7. *Delayed Possession.* This clause is used when the real estate is to be built, and occupancy is to be delayed until construction is finished.

8. *Use.* Very often commercial leases have a clause specifying the use to which the property can be put.

9. *Maintenance, Repairs, and Alterations.* Such a clause spells out which party is responsible for maintaining the premises and making repairs to it. It also sets forth the procedure by which the lessee can make alterations in the property.

10. *Insurance.* This clause sets out the amounts of insurance which must be maintained by the parties to the lease. It will also state which party is responsible for the costs of insurance.

11. *Damage or Destruction.* You should look for a discussion of what happens in the event the property is partially damaged or entirely destroyed. Usually if the property can still be occupied, there is an abatement of rent on a pro rata basis depending on the percentage of area affected. If the property is totally destroyed, then the lease agreement may be cancelled.

12. *Real Property Taxes.* This clause identifies the responsibility for the payment of taxes, and who can fight the assessments made.

13. *Assignment and Subletting.* This clause will state the policy for allowing the lessee to assign its interest in the property to another lessee, or to sublet a portion of the space it is occupying. Usually permission is granted if the new lessee is as strong financially as the existing one. You should make sure that any attempt to assign or sublet requires lender approval.

14. *Defaults, Remedies.* Defaults are defined and the ways in which they can be dealt with are identified. If there are remedies for default, they are discussed.

15. *Condemnation.* Condemnation is the taking of all or part of a property, usually by the government for some public purpose. There should be a clause in the lease indicating what happens if such a taking occurs.

16. *Holding Over.* Holding over occurs when the term of the lease expires, but the lessee remains in occupancy of the subject property. If this is with the knowledge and consent of the landlord, then this clause will state the terms of the holding over, which are usually the same terms as the rest of the lease agreement.

17. *Subordination.* The lease should have a subordination clause, which states the agreement under which the lessee agrees to subordinate his lease interest to the interest of a lender making a mortgage loan.

Leases will contain other miscellaneous legal clauses. You should review them carefully to determine their impact on any loan contemplated. Further, if there are any questions, the lease should be reviewed by your legal counsel.

Provisions Particular to Ground Leases

A ground lease is a lease of land. The lessee then constructs and owns the building on the ground, at least for the term of the lease. Ground leases should be reviewed by legal counsel for their impact on the real estate loan.

Ground leases will contain the same kinds of clauses as building leases, with a few others to which special attention should be paid:

1. *Term.* You should make sure that the term of the ground lease runs beyond the term of the mortgage loan being granted. Otherwise, the borrower will lose the right to the property, and the income from it, before the loan is repaid. Most lenders like to make sure that the term of the loan is not more than five-eighths to two-thirds of the remaining term of the ground lease. For example, if the ground lease has a remaining term of 20 years, the loan term should be no more than 12.5 to 13.3 years.

2. *Subordination.* Whether or not the ground lease can be subordinated to the mortgage loan is important in determining loan amount and structure. If yes, then the fee owner can be foreclosed as well as the lessee in the event of a default on the loan, and the lender will take over both land and building. If not, then the lender is in effect making a second loan, junior to the interest of the ground owner. The lender must then make sure that in the event of a default, he can live with the terms of the ground lease should he foreclose on and take over the building.

3. *Right to Cure Defaults.* If the ground lease is not subordinated to the interest of the lender, then you must make sure that you have the right to cure defaults. A clause can be written into the ground lease stating that the owner will give the lender a right to step in and cure any default. You can then preserve the ground lease, and the right to use the property, while chasing the borrower on the building.

Why It's Important to Have Title Insurance

Title insurance protects both lender and borrower from defects in the title to the property. Title insurance is usually issued subject to certain exclusions, items of record that have, or will have, priority over the interest of any lender. Care must be exercised to determine the impact of those items that have a priority over the new loan.

A Preliminary Title Report should be ordered early in your analysis of a loan request. It shows those items that are recorded against the real estate, and it is extremely useful because it provides an opportunity to correct any problems with the title before the loan is closed.

Exceptions to title that might show up in a report include:

1. *Taxes.* Property taxes will usually show up as the first item in a preliminary title report. You do not need to be concerned with taxes in general, only with unpaid taxes. A borrower who doesn't pay his property taxes is cause for concern.

A clause identifying taxes assessed against the real estate might look like the following:

General and special property taxes for the fiscal year 1986–1987:

Total Amount	$5,000.00
First Installment	$2,500.00
Second Installment	$2,500.00
Parcel Number	25-4367-1

2. *Assessments.* Assessments can be levied for special taxes or for municipal services charged against the property. Not all properties will show such an item. The report may simply state:

"The lien of supplemental taxes, if any."

3. *Tax Liens.* Tax liens will show up on a preliminary title report. Liens may originate from nonpayment of property taxes, or federal and state income taxes. Unpaid business taxes, like state sales taxes, can also cause a lien to be filed against property owned by the taxpayer. Depending on the type of tax, such a lien may be a priority item; that is, take priority over even established liens. Tax liens should be cleared before the new loan is recorded.

4. *Easements.* Easements are created when a property owner grants the right of access to the subject property to someone else. The most common form of easement is one granted to utility companies for access to their equipment, lines, and meters located on the premises. Such an item might look like the following:

"An easement affecting the portion of said land and for the purposes stated herein, and incidental purposes:

In favor of:	Local water company
For:	Pipeline
Recorded:	In Book 2450, Page 998, Official Records
Affects:	That portion of Parcel 2 within a 10-foot-wide strip described more particularly as:"

This statement summarizes the actual recorded document. If there is concern as to the location of the easement, then the lender should have it plotted on a site map, or ask to see the entire document.

5. *Trust Deeds/Mortgages.* Existing liens recorded by lenders to secure loans will show up on the preliminary report. You must make sure that those liens that are reflected will be paid off, or that you are willing to have them prior to your lien. A preliminary title report might show:

"A Deed of Trust to secure an indebtedness in the amount shown below and any other obligations secured thereby, recorded February 1, 19___, as Instrument No. 80-1543982, of Official Records.

Amount:	$2,500,000.00
Dated:	December 23, 19___
Trustor:	Samuel H. Johnson
Trustee:	Title Insurance Company
Beneficiary:	1st National Bank"

6. *The Preliminary Report May or May Not Show Building Leases.* If they are recorded, they will show. If they are unrecorded, but the title company has become aware of their existence, then they will probably show as unrecorded leases. Whether or not to have these leases subordinated to the new loan is an underwriting consideration that should be addressed when the loan request is being analyzed.

7. *Covenants, Conditions, and Restrictions.* More commonly referred to as CC&Rs, these should show up on the preliminary report. Usually they are broad covenants as to what can be done with the real estate, and rarely have any significant impact on the lender. The document will be cited, but the whole document will have to be reviewed to determine what the CC&Rs cover.

Title policies can be issued with certain endorsements that are important to the lender. These give added protection for certain specific items related to the real estate.

For example, if new construction is contemplated, a foundation endorsement can be obtained that will satisfy the lender that the foundations, when complete, are within the property lines and do not encroach on any easements. You should consult a title company in your state to determine which endorsements are available.

When to Use an Indemnity Agreement

Indemnity Agreements are used with construction loans, where construction may have already begun, or will begin, prior to recordation of the lender's loan. In such a case there exists the possibility that a Mechanic's Lien may arise from work already begun that will be prior to the mortgage loan.

An Indemnity, offered by the borrower or general contractor to the title company, assures the title company that it will be held harmless in the event priority is lost due to a claim arising from the work begun prior to loan recording. This allows the title company to issue its policy of title insurance and the loan to close.

Using an Estoppel Letter to Certify Lease Agreement Status

An Estoppel Letter or Estoppel Certificate is a document that asks tenants to certify to the lender as to the status of a lease agreement with the owner. The tenant gives independent verification of the terms of the lease, and certifies that all the terms are still in effect and that no defaults have arisen. Use of an estoppel is a good way to discover problems with property management, since tenants, if they know financing is pending, will tend to complain to the lender about such problems.

Exhibit 9-1 is a sample of an Estoppel Certificate. The document should be completed as follows:

1. The name of the tenant completing the certification. A separate form should be used for each tenant from whom certification is requested.
2. The date of the lease.
3. The name of the Lessor.
4. The name of the Lessee.
5. The name of the Lender.
6. The name of the Borrower.
7. The date through which rent is paid on the lease, based on the last rental payment received/made.
8. The amount of any security deposit the lessee gave to the lessor when the lease began.
9. The address for notices which might be sent to the tenant.
10. The name and address for the lender, to which notice might be sent by the lessee.
11. The date on which the certificate is signed.
12. The name of the company executing the certificate.
13. The signature of an authorized representative from the tenant.

EXHIBIT 9-1

ESTOPPEL CERTIFICATE

The undersigned, _____ (1) _____ , tenant under that certain lease dated _____ (2) _____ from _____ (3) _____ , Lessor, to _____ (4) _____ , Lessee, certifies as hereinafter set forth to _____ (5) _____ , Lender. Whereas the Lender has agreed to extend construction/permanent loans to _____ (6) _____ (the "Borrower"), and that it is a condition of the Lender's obligation to make such loan that the tenant execute this Certificate, the tenant hereby certifies as follows:

1. A complete and correct copy of the Lease is attached to this Certificate.

2. The lease is unamended and in full force and effect, unless otherwise specified in writing and attached to this Certificate, and to the best knowledge of the undersigned there exists no default of the landlord under the Lease.

3. The last date to which rent has been paid under the Lease is _____ (7) _____ , and no other rent has been paid in advance by the undersigned.

4. The amount of the security deposit held by the landlord under the Lease is $_____ (8) _____ .

5. As of the date of this Certificate, the undersigned has no charge, lien, or claim of offset under the Lease or otherwise against rent or other charges due or to become due thereunder.

6. The address for notices to be sent to the undersigned is: _____ (9) _____
_____ .

The undersigned further agrees with the Lender that from and after the date hereof, the undersigned will not pay any rent under the Lease more than one month in advance of its due date, will not surrender or consent to the modification of any of the terms of the Lease nor to the termination thereof by the landlord, and will not seek to terminate the Lease by reason of any act or omission of the landlord until (i) the undersigned shall have given written notice of such act or omission to _____ (10) _____
_____

and (ii) until a reasonable period of time shall have elapsed following the giving of such notice, during which period the Lender shall have the right, but shall not be obligated, to remedy such act or omission.

The undersigned acknowledges that this Certificate is delivered in order to induce the Bank to make a loan upon the security of the premises demised under the Lease, that in making such loans the Bank will act in reliance upon the truth and accuracy of statements contained in this Certificate, and that without this Certificate the Bank would not make such a loan.

Dated: _____ (11) _____

_____ (12) _____
By: _____ (13) _____

By: _____

EXHIBIT 9-2

CHECKLIST

Is the real estate leased? ( ) Yes   ( ) No
    If Yes:
    ( ) Property lease(s) received.   Date _____ (1) _____
    ( ) Property lease(s) reviewed.   Date _____ (2) _____
    ( ) Estoppel Certificates required on: (3)
        ( ) All tenants
        ( ) Select tenants. Specify which tenants:

_____
_____ (4) _____
_____

Is the real estate subject to a ground lease? ( ) Yes ( ) No
    If Yes:
    ( ) Ground lease received. Date _____ (5) _____
    ( ) Ground lease reviewed. Date _____ (6) _____
( ) Preliminary Title Report received. Date _____ (7) _____
( ) Preliminary Title Report reviewed. Date _____ (8) _____
    The following items need to be cleared from title prior to loan closing:

_____
_____ (9) _____
_____

End Note

Understanding property rights is important in making sure that the borrower will be able to perform, and that no rights of other parties against the property can interfere with the lender's lien. Use the checklist in Exhibit 9-2 to make sure property rights are properly reviewed.
Fill in the checklist as follows:

1. Check the appropriate boxes and fill in the date that building leases were received.
2. Fill in the date that building leases were reviewed.
3. Indicate whether estoppel certificates are to be taken on all tenants or just certain key tenants.
4. Indicate which tenants should be asked to complete estoppel certificates.
5. Check the appropriate box and fill in the date that the Ground Lease was received.
6. Fill in the date the ground lease was reviewed.
7. Fill in the date the preliminary title report was received.
8. Fill in the date the preliminary title report was reviewed.
9. Fill in those items appearing on the preliminary title report that need to be cleared.

10

How to Document Property Ownership

The issue of property ownership is related to the issue of property rights. The latter determines who can use the real estate, while the former identifies ownership of the property. As lender you want to make sure that title is clear, not clouded by unclear documents. If you are financing a purchase, you want to make sure that the borrower gets clear title to the property.

Grant Deeds

A grand deed is used to transfer ownership of real estate. The document is recorded, giving legal notice that transfer has taken place.

You do not complete this document. That will be handled by the escrow people or attorneys handling the purchase transaction. You do want to make sure that the new owner is the party to whom the loan is being made.

Exhibit 10-1 is an example of a Grant Deed.

Documenting a Loan Involving a Land Sale Contract

Tax laws can sometimes make buying real estate on an installment basis attractive. This can be a way for someone lacking the cash down payment to acquire real estate.

A Land Sale Contract is the document used to purchase a property on installment. This document gives out the terms of the sale. Financing an installment sale is difficult because the title to the property usually doesn't pass to the buyer until the contract has been completed. We recommend consulting with legal counsel as to the ramifications and the proper way to document a loan on a Land Sale Contract.

EXHIBIT 10-1

GRANT DEED

When Recorded, Mail This Deed To:
Name: Atlas Packaging Company
Address: 1412 North First Street
City & State: Burbank, California 91545

GRANT DEED

The undersigned declares that the documentary transfer tax is
    $1,217.75, and is
(x) computed on the full value of the interest or property conveyed, or is
( ) computed on the full value less the value of liens or encumbrances remaining
    thereon at the time of sale. The land, tenements, or realty is located in
( ) Unincorporated area ( ) City of ___Burbank___

For a valuable consideration, receipt of which is hereby acknowledged,
Sam Jones and Fred Smith
hereby Grant(s) to
Atlas Packaging Company
the following described real property in the

county of Los Angeles, State of ___California___

As per attached Exhibit "A" which is by this reference made a part hereof.

Dated ___May 24, 19___

_____Sam Jones_____
_____Fred Smith_____

What You Can Learn from Escrow Instructions

For those states that use escrows as intermediaries in a purchase transaction, escrow instructions are used to document the purchase agreement between buyer and seller. When the various requirements and conditions detailed in the instructions have been met, the sale can close.

Lenders should review the escrow documents, along with the purchase agreement or other agreements between buyer and seller, to gain a complete understanding of the terms of the transaction. Make sure that the terms conveyed to you during the application process are correct. Escrow instructions are a good place to discover if there is any additional financing contemplated, either from another institution or from the seller. If so, the lender must decide how to react to such financing.

Note the conditions which must be met for the sale to close. Are these conditions acceptable to you? What is the real cash equity the buyer/borrower will put into the transaction?

Exhibit 10-2 shows sample escrow instructions. Note the following information:

1. The date of the escrow instructions.

2. The escrow number. This will be useful for future reference and dealings with the escrow company.

3. The page number. Note the total number of pages—for example, page 1 of 4—and make sure you see the entire set of instructions.

4. The name of the seller.

5. The name of the buyer.

6. Note which boxes are checked and the form of the cash down payment.

7. Notice which liens of record are to remain. Are these acceptable to you?

8. Are additional deeds of trust/mortgages to be obtained? Can the borrower service these loans?

9. The date by which additional funds must be provided, and the amount of such funds.

10. Any other funds and their source.

11. The total amount of the purchase price.

12. The type of title insurance policy to be obtained for the buyer.

13. The legal description of the property being transferred. Note whether this corresponds to the legal description of the property on which you've been asked to lend.

14. The name in which title to the property will vest. This should be the same as the name in which your loan documents will be drawn.

15. The fiscal year for which property taxes must be paid. Make sure that taxes are paid current by the seller.

16. Any other exceptions to title that will remain. The lender should make sure that he's satisfied with these exceptions.

17. Section III is reserved for the special contingencies and conditions of this particular transaction. You should read these carefully, understand them, and make sure that they correspond to your assumptions in granting the loan.

Making Use of Loan Escrow Instructions

Loan escrow instructions can be used by a lender to indicate the documentation needed and conditions that must be met before the loan is funded. Exhibit 10-3 shows a sample of such instructions. Fill it out with the following information:

1. The date of the instructions.

2. The name and address of the lending institution.

3. The loan number.

4. The name of the lending institution.

5. Deed of Trust or Mortgage, whichever is appropriate.

6. The amount of the loan.

7. The nature of the improvements.

8. The county and state in which the property is located.

9. The legal description of the property.

10. The name in which title will vest.

11. The required amount of the fire insurance policy.

EXHIBIT10-2

ESCROW INSTRUCTIONS

Date: _____ (1) _____

Escrow No: _____ (2) _____

Page No: _____ (3) _____

Section I

_____ (4) _____, Seller(s) hereunder will hand you a deed conveying the property described herein to vestee named below,

_____ (5) _____, Buyer(s) herein:

( ) hand(s) you upon opening of escrow	$_____ (6)_____
( ) and will cause to be handed your deposit	$_____
paid to broker	$_____
( ) and proceeds of new loan to be procured by buyer in the amount of:	$_____
( ) and the encumbrances of record will remain, having approximate unpaid balance(s) in favor of:	

1._____ (7) _____

2._____

( ) and will hand you deed(s) of trust/mortgages in priority shown securing note(s) in favor of:	$_____

1._____ (8) _____

2._____

	$_____
( ) having paid outside this escrow to seller	$_____
( ) and will hand you prior to _____ (9) _____	$_____
( ) _____ (10) _____	$_____
To Complete a Purchase Price of:	$_____ (11) _____

Section II

You are authorized to deliver and/or record all documents and disburse all funds when you will issue your current form of _____ (12) _____ policy of title insurance (and lender's policy as required by buyer's lender) with liability in the amount of the purchase price or amount of liability required by buyer's lender, whichever is greater, on the real property described as:

(13)

showing title vested in: (14)

Subject to:

( ) Real Property general and special taxes for the fiscal year _____ (15) _____ and subsequent years, including reassessments if any and including any special district levies or personal property taxes, payment for which are included therein and collected therewith, and improvement bond assessments, when applicable.

( ) Covenants, conditions, restrictions, rights of way, easements, and reservations of record.

( ) _____ (16) _____

EXHIBIT 10-2 (Cont'd.)

Section III
(17) 1

EXHIBIT 10-3

LENDER'S INSTRUCTIONS

Date: (1)
To: (2)

Loan Number   (3)

The undersigned Borrower(s) will deliver to _____ (4) _____ (hereinafter "Lender"), a Note, _____ (5) _____ executed by the Borrower for a loan in the amount of _____ (6) _____ in connection with _____ (7) _____ to be located in the County of_____ (8) _____, State of _____ (8) _____ and further described as follows: _____ _____ (9) _____

The Lender is authorized and instructed to cause the _____ (5) _____ to be recorded and to disburse loan proceeds in accordance with these instructions when it has procured, at the expense of the Borrower, an acceptable policy of title insurance with a liability limit at least equal to the loan amount and showing title in the above-described property vested in the following name:_____ (10) _____ and showing the _____ (5) _____to be a first lien against the above-described property, subject only to such exceptions as lender shall have approved.

Lender shall receive a fire insurance policy in the amount of _____ (11) _____ on the above-described property with lender's loss payable endorsement No. 438BFU attached naming lender as the first mortgagee and such other insurance and endorsements as the lender deems appropriate and as are identified below.

The Borrower agrees to pay on demand all costs, charges, and expenses paid or incurred by the lender in connection with the loan.

In the event the proceeds of the loan are not sufficient to enable the lender to comply with these instructions, the borrower will, upon demand, pay to the lender such additional funds as may be needed.

Following the recording of the _____ (5) _____, and from time to time thereafter, the lender is instructed to pay the following items of costs and charges from the proceeds of the loan and from other funds, if any are furnished by the borrower.

Costs and charges to be paid from loan proceeds:

(12)

The borrower will deliver to the lender the following listed documents and instruments, and warrants and represents to the lender that such documents and

EXHIBIT 10-3 (Cont'd.)

instruments will be in form and substance satisfactory to the lender, that they will be properly executed and supported by documentation showing that the persons executing them have the authority to do so. It is understood that the following list is not exclusive and other items may be required by lender in connection with the loan.

(13)

(   ) Permanent loan commitment
(   ) Insurance Policies, including:
    (   ) Fire Insurance
    (   ) Liability Insurance
    (   ) Workers Compensation Insurance
    (   ) ——————
    (   ) ——————
(   ) Title insurance policy with the following endorsements:
    (   )——————
    (   )——————
    (   )——————
    (   )——————
(   ) Promissory Note
(   ) Deed of Trust/Mortgage
(   ) Construction Loan Agreement
(   ) Construction Contract
(   ) Cost Breakdown
(   ) Building Permit
(   ) Approved Plans and Specifications
(   ) Payment and Performance Bond, or
    (   ) Waiver of Bond
(   ) Guaranty of construction by:
    (   ) ——————————————
    (   ) ——————————————
    (   ) ——————————————
(   ) Lease(s)
(   ) Estoppel Certificate(s)
(   ) Assignment of Lease(s)
(   ) Corporate Resolution to Borrow
(   ) By-Laws
(   ) Articles of Incorporation
(   ) Partnership Authorization to Borrow
(   ) Statement of Partnership
(   ) Partnership Agreement
(   ) Guaranty of note by:
    (   ) ——————————————
    (   ) ——————————————
    (   ) ——————————————
(   ) Financial Statements for the following:

EXHIBIT 10-3 (Cont'd.)

( ) _____ Dated:_____
( ) _____ Dated:_____
( ) _____ Dated: _____
( ) _____
( ) _____
( ) _____

 The failure of the Borrower to comply with the terms and provisions of these instructions shall be a default under the Loan documents including but not limited to the right to declare the loan immediately due and payable.

 The loan must be closed and the _____ (5) _____ recorded not later than _____ (14) _____ days from the date hereof. If the loan is not consummated on or before _____ (14) _____ days from the date hereof, all documents and instruments must be returned to the lender without further notice unless a written extension is signed by the lender. Failure to close the loan within the _____ (14) _____-day period may necessitate a renegotiation of the transaction and will require the execution of new documents.

 It is understood and agreed by the Borrower that the Lender shall not be obligated to disburse any proceeds of the loan, notwithstanding any language herein or in any other document or instrument executed in connection with the loan, if and so long as the making of such disbursement would cause the loan to be in violation of any law or regulation applicable to the lender, including but not limited to legal lending limits requirements.

_____ (15) _____

By: _____ (16) _____

By: _____

12. A detailed listing by type of the costs and charges to be borne by the borrower.

13. Check the appropriate boxes for the documents to be provided/signed by the borrower. Indicate where necessary which the additional documents are, who needs to provide certain documents, and other information needed.

14. The number of days granted to the borrower in which to comply with the lender's instructions.

15. The name of the borrower or borrowing entity.

16. The signature of the borrower or the authorized representatives of the borrowing entity.

Amendments to Escrow Instructions

Once the instructions are signed and delivered to the escrow or other third party acting as intermediary, they define the nature of the transaction and detail conditions required before escrow closes. After that date, changes must be in writing and approved by both parties to the transaction.

Such amendments are not unusual. The lender should be aware of any changes to

EXHIBIT 10-4

CHECKLIST

Transaction involves a: (1)
( ) Purchase
( ) Property already owned by the borrower.
If already owned, ownership document was received and reviewed: (2)
( ) Grant Deed Date: _____
( ) Land Sale Contract Date: _____
If purchase transaction, purchase documents were received and reviewed: (3)
( ) Purchase Agreement Date: _____
( ) Certified Escrow Instructions Date: _____
( ) Amendments to the purchase transaction: (4)
    ( ) Amendment No. ___ Date: _____
    ( ) Amendment No. ___ Date: _____
    ( ) Amendment No. ___ Date: _____
( ) Escrow Settlement Sheet Received and Reviewed: (5)
    Date: _____
Title to Vest in the Name of: (6)

_____

( ) Ownership documents correspond to vesting
( ) Loan documents correspond to vesting
Approved By: _____ (7) _____ Date: _____

the transaction, and prior to the close of the loan should require a certified copy of all instructions and amendments. The lender should review these to insure that the transaction has not been altered in a way that would affect the loan decision.

Using an Escrow Settlement Sheet to Document Funds Use

The escrow settlement sheet is issued by the escrow after the transaction has closed. It is a detailed statement of the source and use of funds, where funds were generated, and how they were used. Since it is available after the loan has closed, its interest to the real estate lender is more for file documentation than anything else. Obtain one just to satisfy yourself that funds went where they were supposed to go.

End Note

Documenting property ownership enables you to make sure that the loan is made to the party that owns the real estate. If the transaction involves a purchase, you can make sure that the terms are acceptable.

Use the checklist in Exhibit 10-4 to make sure that proper documentation is received and reviewed:

1. Indicate whether the transaction involves a property to be purchased or one that is already owned by the borrower.

2. If the property is already owned, check the ownership document reviewed and the date.

3. If the property is to be purchased with loan proceeds, indicate receipt and approval of the purchase documents.

4. Indicate whether there were any amendments to the purchase agreement/ escrow instructions.

5. Indicate whether an escrow settlement sheet was received and reviewed.

6. The name in which title is to vest. Indicate that ownership and loan documents have been checked to make sure that they correspond to the vesting.

7. The party approving these documents should sign and date the checklist.

11

How to Handle Miscellaneous Documentation Needs

Sometimes other documentation proves useful or necessary to commercial real estate transactions. This chapter will consider some of the more common forms that can be used to cover certain aspects of a loan situation. Every deal is a little different, so you may find other items are needed for individual loan transactions.

Using Letters of Credit

Letters of Credit (L/Cs) are used in real estate transactions instead of putting up cash. These L/Cs are given to the real estate lender by other financial institutions.

In construction lending borrowers may have to offer L/Cs to outside parties to guarantee performance of certain work, sometimes before the construction lender is prepared to release funds. As an example government agencies might ask for an L/C in return for issuing a permit for certain work, as evidence that funds are available to the borrower to do the work. The construction lender can issue a L/C that can be retired later when work is satisfactorily completed.

A L/C is an instrument drawn on a financial institution that guarantees payment of a sum of money in the event of a default as defined in the L/C. For example, say a borrower is planning to build an apartment building. The city requires certain improvements to the local street system in the vicinity of the project, and requires that the borrower put up a L/C in favor of the city to demonstrate that the funds are available to do the work.

Exhibit 11-1 shows what such a L/C might look like. If you are the issuing lender, make sure that you understand what constitutes a default. You must insure that sufficient funds are available under the loan for the work to be done, and make sure

EXHIBIT 11-1

LETTER OF CREDIT

Date: October 7, 19 _____

( ) Advised Preliminarily by ( ) To Advising Bank
    Cable of Today   (X) to Beneficiary
(X) Advised by Mail

IRREVOCABLE STANDBY LETTER OF CREDIT

_____ Advising Bank _____ Applicant _____
                                        Jones Construction Company
                                        4365 Main Street
                                        Carson, Alabama

_____ Beneficiary _____

City of Carson
c/o Building Department
5350 National Avenue
Carson, Alabama

_____ Amount _____
US$250,000.00 (Two Hundred Fifty and No/100 U.S. Dollars)

Expiration Date: October 1, 19 _____ at 12:00 p.m. Midnight

We hereby issue in your favor this irrevocable standby letter of credit which is available for payment by your drafts at sight drawn on American First National Bank, Carson, Alabama, accompanied by the following documents:
—Your signed statement, on your letterhead, signed by the appropriate authorized City representative, certifying that there has been a default under the terms of your agreement with the applicant.

---

that they are applied only to that work. That way, if the L/C is drawn, you will be able to cover it with funds already set aside in the loan for that purpose.

If you have required that a L/C be given to you as additional collateral, say to make sure that the borrowers have sufficient cash equity in the event additional funds are needed, then you will want to be satisfied about:

1. The financial strength of the issuing institution. You want to feel comfortable that the issuing entity will be there, with adequate liquidity, in the event you need to

call on the L/C. You should require that the L/C be issued by an organization of which you approve.

2. The expiration date of the L/C should be after the maturity date of your loan. Otherwise, the L/C could expire with your loan still in place.

3. The default language must be carefully written to give maximum protection in the event you must call on the L/C. Make sure that there is no room for the issuing entity to refuse to honor the L/C because of ambiguous or unclear language.

Three Kinds of Insurance You Must Have

Insurance is crucial to the real estate lender. The loan should not be closed and funded without proper documentation showing that the necessary coverages and amounts are in place. Failure to do so could expose the collateral for the loan to loss that cannot be replaced.

Lenders have different policies on whether insurance binders are sufficient evidence of insurance or whether the policy itself must be in hand. The problem with requiring policies is that insurance companies can be slow to issue them, sometimes taking months to finally put a policy into the lender's hands. The need to close loans on a timely basis makes reliance on binders necessary.

You should have certain kinds of insurance protection:

1. *Fire and Extended Coverage, or All-Risk Insurance.* This covers damage to the physical real estate from the named perils, usually excluding loss from things like war, civil strife, acts of rebellion, and acts of God. Other exclusions are perils of nature common to the area, like floods, earthquakes, tornadoes, and hurricanes. Coverage for these perils can usually be purchased at extra cost.

Most lenders require an amount of insurance equal to the loan amount. That may be onerous, though, in areas with high land values, or for buildings where the nature of the construction, say a lot of concrete and steel, means little chance of major destruction. Usually an amount sufficient to cover the replacement cost of the improvements is adequate.

2. *Liability Insurance.* This insurance covers losses from injury to people that occur on the real estate. As a rule $1 million should be the minimum required by the real estate lender.

3. *Workers' Compensation.* If the project involves new construction, worker's compensation insurance should be provided. This insurance protects both owner and lender from losses occurring as a result of injury to construction workers, and is usually carried by the general contractor.

Exhibit 11-2 shows a typical insurance binder listing coverages written for the property insured. A binder does not substitute for the actual policy. You should follow up to make sure the policy is received, and that the terms of the policy are consistent with the terms of the binder.

The fire insurance policy should include a loss payee endorsement, commonly called a 438BFU. In the event of a loss, the proceeds paid by the insurance company will be given to the lender instead of the policyholder. It will then be the lender's

EXHIBIT 11-2

INSURANCE BINDER

This binder is a temporary insurance contract subject to the conditions shown on the reverse of this form.

Name and Address of Agency:
Wilson, Slade & Company
P.O. Box 427
Denver, Colorado

Company:
First Nationwide Insurance

Effective: 12:01 a.m. 4-5-____
Expires: 12:01 a.m. 4-5-____

Name and Address of Insured:
American Construction Company
47 South Broadway
Denver, Colorado

Type and Location of Property	Coverage/Perils	Amt. of Insurance	Deductible
Building located at: 7249 Amber Drive Aurora, Colorado	All risk	$2,000,000	$25,000

Liability Insurance	Coverage/Forms	Limits of Liability Each Occur. Aggregate
( ) Schedule Form		Bodily Injury:
(X) Comprehensive Form		
(X) Premises/Operations		Property Damage:
(X) Products/Completed Operations		
(X) Contractual		
(X) Other (Specify below)		Bodily Injury &
(X) Med.Pay. $1,000 per $10,000 per		Property Damage
person accid		Combined:
( ) Personal Injury		$1,000,000 $1,000,000

( ) Workers' Compensation—Statutory Limits

Special Conditions/Other Coverages:

Name and Address of
(X) Mortgagee (X) Loss Payee ( ) Additional Insured
Colorado National Bank
Real Estate Loan Department
P.O. Box 549A
Denver, Colorado

_____
Signature of Authorized Representative

_____
Date

decision whether to rebuild, or apply the insurance proceeds to reduce or pay off the outstanding balance on the loan. Receipt of this endorsement should be a requirement of every loan.

The lender needs to be named as additional insured on all liability or workers' compensation insurance policies. This gives protection from the owner's insurance company in the event of a loss. Failure to obtain this protection puts the lender's insurance company at risk in the event of claims.

Ordering Tax Service

A tax service contract is usually provided by a title insurance company. This service advises the lender if real estate taxes are not paid. Unpaid taxes can jeopardize the loan by creating liens against the property that will eventually cause foreclosure by the state or local government.

Exhibit 11-3 shows a sample contract. It should be completed with the following information:

1. The date the order for tax service is placed.
2. The amount of the real estate loan.
3. The lender's loan number.
4. The name of the borrower.
5. The address of the property for which tax service is being ordered.
6. The city and state in which the subject property is located.
7. The former owner of the property, if any.
8. The number of the customer ordering the tax service, the lender's number. This number will be established for you by the title company from whom you order tax service.
9. The name of the lending institution.
10. The type of tax service contract being ordered. Contact your title company for the services available.
11. The address of the lending institution.
12. The term of the real estate loan.
13. The fee for the tax service contract. This cost is usually passed on to the borrower.
14. The name and address of the title company, escrow or other entity to whom the bill for the tax service should be sent.
15. The escrow or file number that will serve as reference for the entity to whom the bill will be sent.
16. The legal description of the subject property.
17. For each taxing entity, give the name of the district that collects taxes.
18. For each taxing entity, give the tax number that identifies the subject property.

End Note

There may be other miscellaneous documentation that can be used for a commercial real estate transaction. The items discussed in this chapter are regularly used. Use

EXHIBIT 11-3

TAX SERVICE CONTRACT

Order Date:	Loan Amount:
(1)	(2)

Loan Number:	(3)
Borrower Name:	(4)
Property Address:	(5)
City/State:	(6)

Former Owner:	(7)

Customer No:	(8)	Service ( ) Delinquency
Customer:	(9)	Type (10)
Address:	(11)	Term of Loan: (12)
		Contract Fee: (13)

Escrow or File No. (15)	Bill to: Address:	(14)

Complete Legal Description:

(16)

District	Collection District Name	Permanent Tax Number
County		
City, Town, or Borough	(17)	(18)
School		
Other		

the checklist in Exhibit 11-4 as a guide to special documentation needs:

1. The amount of fire insurance required.
2. The endorsements you are requiring be attached to the policy.
3. The name and address of the loss payee as it should appear on the insurance policy. This should be the name and address of the lending institution.

EXHIBIT 11-4

CHECKLIST

Insurance Requirements:

( ) Fire Insurance   Amount Required: _____ (1) _____
Endorsements: (2)
   ( ) Extended Coverage
   ( ) Malicious Mischief
   ( ) Vandalism
   ( ) Loss Payee—438BFU
     In Name of:

_____

_____ (3) _____

_____

   ( )Other Endorsements:
     ( ) _____
     ( ) _____
( ) Liability Insurance   Amount Required: _____ (4) _____
   ( ) Lender to be named as additional insured
( ) Workers' Compensation Insurance (5)
   ( ) Lender to be named as additional insured
   ( ) Carried by:
     ( ) Borrower
     ( ) General Contractor
( ) Course of Construction Insurance (6)
Loan to be closed upon receipt and approval of: (7)
   ( ) Binder   Date Received: _____
   ( ) Policy   Date Received: _____
Name and Address of Insurance Agent:

_____

_____ (8) _____

_____

( ) Tax Service Required (9)   ( ) Ordered Date: _____

4. Use this area to indicate whether liability insurance is required, and if so, how much.

5. Indicate whether workers' compensation insurance is needed, and who will provide the policy.

6. Check this box if course of construction insurance is needed instead of normal fire insurance. This kind of policy protects the property from hazards during the time it is being built. It can then be rolled into a normal fire insurance policy when construction is complete.

7. The loan officer should indicate preference as to condition of insurance documentation needed before the loan is allowed to close.

8. Space is provided to show the name and address of the borrower's insurance agent. This individual is usually the best contact for information and help regarding the borrower's coverages.

9. Indicate whether tax service is required. If so, show the date the service was ordered.

12

How to Document Loan Servicing

After the commercial real estate loan is funded, the monitoring and followup process begins. This is usually handled by a servicing area within the real estate loan department.

In a normal situation, servicing a loan involves collecting payments, following up to make sure taxes are paid, making sure insurance is kept in force, and periodically updating the borrower's financial statement. Sometimes, however, changes in the loan structure are needed after the loan is funded.

Granting Assumptions

Assumptions occur when a new borrower takes over the obligation of the original borrower. This usually results from a sale of the real estate that is the collateral for the loan. The lender needs to decide if it's appropriate to allow the new owner to assume the existing loan.

The right to have assumptions may be granted at the outset of the loan or accommodated on a case-by-case basis when the request is made. Assuming that the new buyer has the same relative financial strength as the current owner/borrower, the overall risk of the loan is probably unchanged.

Before granting an assumption, the lender should update the underwriting. The current condition of the property should be reviewed and property economics re-analyzed. The new borrower should be asked to provide thorough financial information, which should meet current credit standards.

Once the transaction is approved, the lender can issue an assumption agreement/ loan revision agreement and allow the new buyer/borrower to assume the loan.

When to Use the Deed of Reconveyance

When the loan is fully paid, the trust deed or mortgage recorded against the property should be released. This is accomplished by recording a deed of recon-

EXHIBIT 12-1

WHEN RECORDED MAIL TO:

(1)

FULL RECONVEYANCE

_____ (2) _____ , a _____ (3) _____ corporation, as _____ (4) _____ dated _____ (5) _____ , made by _____ (6) _____ , ____(7) ____ , and recorded as Instrument No. ____ (8) ____ on _____ (9) _____ , Book ____ (10) ____ , Page ____ of Official Records in the office of the County Recorder of _____ (11) _____ County, State of _____ (12) _____ describing land therein as:

(13)

having received from holder of the obligations thereunder a written request to reconvey, reciting that all sums secured by said _____ (14) _____ have been fully paid, and said _____ (14) and the note or notes secured thereby having been surrendered to said _____ (15) _____ for cancellation, does hereby reconvey without warranty, to the person or persons legally entitled thereto, the estate now held by it thereunder.

IN WITNESS WHEREOF, _____ (16) _____ , as _____ (17) _____ , has caused its corporate name and seal to be hereto affixed by its duly authorized officer.
Dated: _____ (18) _____

_____ (19) _____
By: _____ (20) _____
By: _____

veyance. Reconveyance language can sometimes be found at the end of the trust deed/mortgage instrument, and a signature here releases the lender's interest in the real estate. Alternatively, a separate form can be used.

Exhibit 12-1 is a reconveyance form, which should be completed as follows:

1. The name and address to which the recorded reconveyance should be returned.

2. The name of the corporation issuing the reconveyance. This will be the trustee if a trust deed was recorded, or the mortgagee if the document was a mortgage.

3. The state in which the company is incorporated.

4. Identifying language; for example; "As Trustee, under the Deed of Trust" or "As Mortgagee under the Mortgage."

5. The date of the recorded document.

6. The name of the borrower or borrowing entity.

7. The nature of the borrower, whether "mortgagor" or "trustor."

8. The number of the originally recorded document, whether trust deed or mortgage.

9. The date on which the document was recorded.

10. The book and page number of the official records in which the document is recorded.

11. The county in which the document is recorded.

12. The state in which the document is recorded.

13. The legal description of the subject property.

14. The nature of the instrument, either "trust deed," or "mortgage."

15. The party to which the note was returned, either "trustee" or "mortgagor."

16. The name of the party who is reconveying interest in the property.

17. The nature of the reconveying party, either "trustee" or "mortgagee."

18. The date of issuance for the reconveyance document.

19. The name of the entity issuing the reconveyance.

20. Signature(s) of the authorized representative(s) of the reconveying entity.

A reconveyance must be recorded to be effective. Therefore the document must be notarized.

Issuing a Partial Reconveyance

Depending on the nature of the collateral, you may get a request to release part of the property, perhaps in exchange for partial payment of the loan.

Exhibit 12-2 is a partial reconveyance, which should be completed in the following manner:

1. The name and address to which the recorded reconveyance should be returned.

2. The name of the corporation issuing the reconveyance. This will be the trustee if a trust deed was recorded, or the mortgagee if the document was a mortgage.

3 & 4. Identifying language; for example: "As Trustee, under the Deed of Trust" or "As Mortgagee under the Mortgage."

5. The name of the borrower or borrowing entity.

6. The nature of the borrower, whether "mortgagor" or "trustor."

7. The recording information, including instrument number, book page, and date of recording.

8. The county and state in which the document is recorded.

9. The type of document, "deed of trust," or "mortgage."

10. The holder of the security instrument, the "trustee," or the "mortgagee."

11. The legal description of the portion of the property being reconveyed.

12. The date of the reconveyance document.

13. The name of the company which is reconveying its interest in a portion of the real estate.

14. Authorized signature(s) from officers of the reconveying organization.

How to Deal with a Lis Pendens

There are times when a party engaged in a lawsuit wants to make sure that assets of the opposing party are frozen until such time as the court can hear the case. A lis pendens is a notice of pending action in court, and filing one creates a lien against a

EXHIBIT 12-2

WHEN RECORDED MAIL TO:

(1)

PARTIAL RECONVEYANCE

——————————— (2) ——————————— , as ———— (3) ———— under the ———— (4) ———— made by ——————— (5) ——————— , —— (6) —— , and recorded as ———— (7) ——————— , of Official Records in the office of the County Recorder of ———— (8) ——————— having been requested in writing by the holder of the obligations secured by said ———— (9) ———— , to reconvey a portion of the estate granted to said ———— (10)———— thereunder does hereby reconvey unto the person or persons legally entitled thereto, without warranty, all the estate, title, and interest acquired by said—— (10) —— under that ———— (9) ———— in and to that portion of the property described as fol-lows:

(11)

The remaining property described in said ———— (9) ———— shall continue to be held by said ———— (10) ———— under the terms thereof. As provided in said ———— (9) ———— this partial reconveyance is made without affecting the personal liablility of any person for payment of the indebtedness secured by said ———— (9) ———— .
Dated: ———— (12) ————

——————————— (13) ———————————
By: ——————— (14) ———————
By: ————————————————————

piece of real estate. It is like other liens in that its priority is determined by recording date.

Naturally if such a notice is recorded prior to the date of loan recording, you should exercise caution in going forward without first checking with legal counsel for an opinion.

Late Notices to Use with Past Due Borrowers

All loans do not always perform as intended. When payments are late, the servic-ing area follows by sending a late notice to the borrower. Such notice is very often the only action needed to prompt payment of the past due amount.

Exhibits 12-3 and 12-4 are late notices to use with past due borrowers. The first letter is friendly in tone, a helpful reminder. The second letter can be used when all

EXHIBIT 12-3

——— (1) ———

_____
——————— (2) ———————
_____

Re: _____ (3) _____
_____

Dear _____ :

    Our records show that your loan payments for _____ (4) _____ have not yet been received by us. The total amount owing as of this date is $ _____ (5) _____ . As is provided in the Promissory Note, we are assessing a late charge of $ _____ (6) _____ for each past due payment.

    We realize that there can be reasons for an oversight in the making of payments. We would appreciate receiving the total amount due at this time. Please call us at _____ (7) _____ to discuss this matter further.

Sincerely,

_____ (8) _____
By: _____ (9) _____

efforts to solicit payment have failed and adverse action is imminent. They can be completed as follows:

    1. The date of the notice.
    2. The name and address of the borrower to whom the notice is being addressed.
    3. Reference the loan for which payments are delinquent, including loan number, borrower's name, and property address.
    4. Identify the date for which payment or payments are delinquent. For example, "Payments due 10-1-__ and 11-1-__."
    5. The total amount owing as of the date of the letter.
    6. The amount of the late charge you are assessing for the past due payments.
    7. A phone number the borrower can use to contact someone within your organization to discuss past due payments.
    8. The name of the lending organization.
    9. The signature of the person writing the letter.

Fill out the letter in Exhibit 12-4 with the following information:

    1. The date of the letter.
    2. The name and address of the party to whom the letter is being addressed.
    3. A reference to the loan, including loan number, borrower's name, and property address.

4. The date of all payments due that have not yet been received.

5. The amount of payment that was due on the dates reflected.

6. The amount of any late charges being assessed for payments not yet made.

7. The total amount of the payment needed to clear the delinquency.

8. The date by which payment must be received by the lender in order to avoid further action.

9. The penalty rate of interest set under the terms of the note.

10. The name of the lending organization.

11. The signature of the party sending the letter.

Delinquency letters are a necessary part of the loan servicing process. They insure that the borrower is given adequate notice of delinquencies and pending actions the lender will take to cure the default. They also serve to bring in payments from those borrowers who simply need to be prodded a little in order to make the payment due.

EXHIBIT 12-4

——————— (1) ———————

——————— (2) ———————

Re:——————— (3) ———————

Dear ——————— :

Repeated attempts by phone and letter have been made to bring to your attention the serious delinquent staus of the referenced loan. To date we have had no response from you. As of the date of this letter, the following payments have not been received:

Date Due	Amount	Late Charge
——— (4) ———	——— (5) ———	——— (6) ———

We feel that we have no alternative but to take steps to protect the Bank's interests. Unless $ ——— (7) ——— is received in this office by ——————— (8) ——————— the Bank will exercise its right to accelerate all sums due under the Note. In addition from the date of such acceleration the interest rate applicable to the Note will increase to ——— (9) ——— %.

Sincerely,

——— (10) ———

By: ——— (11) ———

Request for Notice of Default

A request for notice is recorded against a property to inform other lenders that a new loan is being made. It would most usually be used by a junior lender, say one making a second loan. It requires that a noteholder who is filing a notice of default against the property give notice of that filing to the party who recorded the request for notice.

Exhibit 12-5 shows a Request for Notice of Default. Complete the document with the following:

1. The name and address of the party to whom the recorded notice should be sent.
2. Identify the nature of the document, whether "deed of trust" or "mortgage."
3. The instrument number of the recorded document.
4. The date on which the document was recorded.
5. The book and page number, or other reference, to locate the recorded document.
6. The county in which the document was recorded.
7. The state in which the document was recorded.
8. The legal description of the property.

EXHIBIT 12-5

WHEN RECORDED MAIL TO:

(1)

REQUEST FOR NOTICE

Request is hereby made that a copy of any Notice of Default and a copy of any Notice of Sale under that certain _____ (2) _____ recorded as Instrument No. _____ (3) _____ on _____ (4) _____, in _____ (5) _____ of Official Records of _____ (6) _____ County, State of _____ (7) _____, and describing land therein as:

(8)

Executed by _____ (9) _____, as _____ (10) _____, in which _____ (11) _____ is named as _____ (12) _____, be mailed to _____ (13) _____ at _____ (14) _____

Dated: _____ (15) _____
_____ (16) _____
By: _____ (17) _____
By: _____

9. The borrowing entity.

10. The nature of the borrower, whether "trustor" or "mortgagor."

11. The name of the lending institution.

12. The nature of the lender, whether "mortgagee" or "beneficiary."

13. The name of the party to whom notice should be mailed, usually the lending institution requesting the notice.

14. The address of the party to whom notice should be mailed.

15. The date of the request for notice.

16. The organization requesting notice.

17. The signature(s) of authorized representatives of the lending organization.

How to Handle Defaults

When late notices fail to prompt payment, the lender will need to pursue action against the borrower and the secured real estate. How and when to do this, and what documents to use, depends a great deal on the laws of the individual state. Eventually foreclosure and litigation may be necessary to protect your interests. You should seek the advice of your attorney when the loan deteriorates to that point.

End Note

Servicing is an important part of the real estate lending function. A lot of work is needed to properly follow commercial loans. Knowing how to react to delinquencies and how to follow up to insure collection of past due amounts, will maximize collections and minimize the need for more drastic action to protect your portfolio.

13

How to Document the Construction Loan: Putting It on the Books

Construction loans require specialized documentation. They are extremely time-consuming, both at the outset and during the course of the construction process. Extra staffing and training in the real estate department is a must.

Using Payment and Performance Bonds for Added Protection

Performance bonds insure the lender against default by the contractor in the performance of his contractual duties. Knowledge of and past history with the contractor will dictate whether a bond should be required as a condition of making the loan. If the contractor is well-known and has a long, successful track record, a performance bond may not be necessary.

Not all contractors are able to obtain bonds. Other contractors can obtain bonds, but are limited in the dollar amount or number of projects bonded at any one time. Bonding capacity results from investigation by the insurance company, and is indicative of the experience level and creditworthiness of the contractor.

Bonds generally consist of two parts. Payment bonds guarantee the payment of subcontractors by the general contractor. Performance bonds guarantee the performance of the general contractor under the terms of the construction contract.

Exhibit 13-1 is a sample Performance Bond. Exhibit 13-2 is the other part of the bond, the Payment Bond.

Eliminating the Bonding Requirement with a Bond Waiver Agreement

If you desire to waive the requirement for a payment and performance bond, take documentation from the owner committing him to the completion of the project in the

EXHIBIT 13-1

PERFORMANCE BOND

American Insurance Company
Madison, Wisconsin

KNOW ALL MEN BY THESE PRESENTS: that
Smith Construction Company
43 North 51st Street
Portland, Oregon
as Principal, hereinafter called Contractor, and American Insurance Company, a Delaware corporation, whose principal office is located at
5544 Lakefront Avenue
Madison, Wisconsin
as Surety, hereinafter called Surety, are held and firmly bound unto
Richard G. Clark & Company
982 First Street
Portland, Oregon
as Obligee, hereinafter called Owner, in the amount of
Twelve Million Five Hundred Thousand and No/100 Dollars ($12,500,000)
for the payment whereof Contractor and Surety bind themselves, their heirs, executors, administrators, successors, and assigns, jointly and severally, firmly by these presents.

WHEREAS,
Contractor has by written agreement dated March 1, __, entered into a contract with Owner for the construction of a three-story, wood frame and stucco office building to be built in Portland, Oregon, in accordance with Drawings and Specifications prepared by
Oregon Architectural Services, Inc.
which contract is by reference made a part hereof, and is hereinafter referred to as the Contract.

NOW, THEREFORE, the condition of this obligation is such that, if Contractor shall promptly and faithfully perform said Contract, then this obligation shall be null and void, otherwise it shall remain in full force and effect.

The Surety further agrees that any modifications, additions, or alterations that may be done under the terms of the Contract or in the Work to be done thereunder, or any extensions of the Contract, shall not in any way release the Surety, its heirs, executors, administrators, successors, and assigns from its liability hereunder, notice to the Surety of any such modifications, additions, or extensions being hereby expressly waived.

Whenever Contractor shall be, and declared by Owner to be in default under the Contract, the Owner having performed Owner's obligations thereunder, the Surety may promptly remedy the default, or shall promptly,

1) Complete the Contract in accordance with its terms and conditions, or

EXHIBIT 13-1 (CONT'D.)

2) Obtain a bid or bids for completing the Contract in accordance with its terms and conditions, and upon determination by Surety of the lowest responsible bidder, or, if the Owner elects, upon determination by the Owner and the Surety jointly of the lowest responsible bidder, arrange for a contract between such bidder and Owner and make available as work progresses (even though there should be a default or succession of defaults under the contract or contracts of completion arranged under this paragraph) sufficient funds to pay the cost of completion less the balance of the contract price; but not exceeding, including other costs and damages for which the Surety may be liable hereunder, the amount set forth in the first paragraph hereof. The term "balance of the contract price," as used in this paragraph, shall mean the total amount payable by the Owner to Contractor under the Contract and the amendments thereto, less the amount properly paid by Owner to Contractor.

Any suit under this bond must be instituted before the expiration of two (2) years from the date on which final payment under the Contract falls due.

No right of action shall accrue on this bond to or for the use of any person or corporation other than the Owner named herein or the heirs, executors, administrators, or successors of the Owner.

Signed and sealed this 15th day of May, 19 ___.

American Insurance Company
(Surety)

By: _____

event the contractor doesn't. Exhibit 13-3 is a Bond Waiver Agreement, which can be filled in as follows:

1. The date of the agreement.
2. The name and address of the lending institution to whom the agreement is given.
3. The loan number for the construction loan.
4. The name of the borrowing entity.
5. The dollar amount of the loan being granted.
6. The date by which construction will begin.
7. The date by which construction will be completed.
8. The name of the lending institution which will be making the loan and approving the plans.
9. The security instrument, a deed of trust or mortgage.
10. The date on which the agreement is signed.
11. The name of the borrowing entity.
12. Authorized signature(s) from the borrower.

EXHIBIT 13-2

PAYMENT BOND

American Insurance Company
Madison, Wisconsin

KNOW ALL MEN BY THESE PRESENTS: that

Smith Construction Company
43 North 51st Street
Portland, Oregon

as Principal, hereinafter called Contractor, and American Insurance Company, a Delaware corporation, and whose principal office is located at

5544 Lakefront Avenue
Madison, Wisconsin

as Surety, hereinafter called Surety, are held and firmly bound unto

Richard G. Clark & Company
982 First Street
Portland, Oregon

as Obligee, hereinafter called Owner, in the amount of

Twelve Million Five Hundred Thousand and No/100 Dollars ($12,500,000)

for the payment whereof Contractor and Surety bind themselves, their heirs, executors, administrators, successors, and assigns, jointly and severally, firmly by these presents.

WHEREAS,

Contractor has by written agreement dated March 1, 19__, entered into a contract with Owner for the construction of a three-story, wood frame and stucco office building to be built in Portland, Oregon, in accordance with Drawings and Specifications prepared by

Oregon Architectural Services, Inc.

which contract is by reference made a part hereof, and is hereinafter referred to as the Contract.

NOW, THEREFORE, the condition of this obligation is such that, if Principal shall promptly make payment to all claimants as hereinafter defined, for all labor and material used or reasonably required for use in the performance of the Contract, then this obligation shall be void, otherwise it shall remain in full force and effect, subject, however, to the following conditions.

1. A claimant is defined as one having a direct contract with the Principal or with a Subcontractor of the Principal for labor, material, or both, used or reasonably required for use in the performance of the Contract, labor and material being construed to include that part of water, gas, power, light, heat oil, gasoline, telephone service, or rental of equipment directly applicable to the Contract.

2. The above-named Principal and Surety hereby jointly and severally agree with the Owner that every claimant as herein defined, who has not been paid in full before the expiration of a period of ninety (90) days after the date on which the last of such claimant's work or labor was done or performed, or materials were furnished by such claimant, may sue on this bond for the use of such claimant, prosecute the suit

EXHIBIT 13-2 (CONT'D.)

to final judgment for such sum or sums as may be justly due claimant, and have execution thereon. The Owner shall not be liable for the payment of any costs or expense of any such suit.

3. No suit or action shall be commenced hereunder by any claimant:

a. Unless claimant, other than one having a direct contract with the Principal, shall have given written notice to any two of the following:
the Owner, the Principal, or the Surety above-named within sixty (60) days after the completion of the construction stating with substantial accuracy the amount claimed and the name of the party to whom the materials were furnished, or for whom the work or labor was done or performed. Such notice shall be served by mailing the same by registered mail or certified mail, postage prepaid, in an envelope addressed to the Principal, Owner, or Surety, at any place where an office is regularly maintained for the transaction of business, or served in any manner in which legal process may be served in the state in which the aforesaid project is located, save that such service need not be made by a public officer.

b. After the expiration of one (1) year following the date on which Principal ceased work on said Contract, it being understood, however, that if any limitation embodied in this bond is prohibited by any law controlling the construction hereof, such limitation shall be deemed to be amended so as to be equal to the minimum period of limitation permitted by such law.

c. Other than in a state court of competent jurisdiction in and for the county or other political subdivision of the state in which the Project, or any part thereof, is situated, or in the United States District Court for the district in which the Project, or any part thereof, is situated, and not elsewhere.

4. The amount of this bond shall be reduced by and to the extent of any payment or payments made in good faith hereunder, inclusive of the payment by Surety of mechanics' liens which may be filed of record against said improvement, whether or not claim for the amount of such lien be presented under and against this bond.

Signed and sealed this 15th day of May, 19__.

American Insurance Company
(Surety)

By: _____

The Importance of Obtaining a Building Permit

Issuance of a building permit is necessary before construction can begin. This document should be in the lender's hands before funds are disbursed. Cities have different requirements that must be met before the permit is issued. Some cities issue a grading permit, requiring that grading and other site work be completed before a full building permit is granted.

If grading is to be done first before the full permit is given, then you should only disburse funds for grading.

EXHIBIT 13-3

BOND WAIVER AGREEMENT

———————— (1)————————

————————— (2) —————————

Re: Loan No.———————— (3) ————

Gentlemen:

The above-referenced loan is being made to ———————— (4) ————————
("Borrower"), to be evidenced by a Promissory Note in the amount of
$———— (5) ————. We request that you consent to the construction proceeding
without the benefit of a payment and performance bond, and in consideration of such
consent, agree as follows:

1. That construction of said improvements shall be commenced on or before———————— (6) ————————, shall thereafter be diligently prosecuted,
and shall be fully completed on or before ———————— (7)————————.

2. That said improvements shall be constructed and completed in strict accordance with plans and specifications acceptable to ————————
(8) ————————.

3. Should the contractor fail to commence or complete the building within the
time and in the manner herein provided, we hereby agree that we will commence and
complete the same at our own cost and expense.

4. That we will protect and indemnify you against any loss sustained by you and
by reason of your having waived a payment and performance bond.

5. In the event that any liens should be filed against this property in connection
with the erection of the improvements, or any attachments, or executions, be filed
against building funds being held by you, we will pay on your demand, the amount
necessary for the release of such liens, attachments, or executions in order that the
building may be completed.

6. That the obligations and agreements herein contained shall in no event
be construed as altering, amending, diminishing, or affecting in any manner
whatsoever the covenants, obligations, and agreements contained in the
———— (9)————executed by us, securing the loan herein mentioned.

This agreement shall be binding upon our heirs, successors, and assigns.

Executed this ———— (10) ———— day of ————, 19——.

———————— (11) ————————
By:———————— (12) ————————

EXHIBIT 13-4

Conclusions:

The existing fill should not be used for support of the foundation systems. Consideration could be given to a construction plan where the footings are extended through the fill and seated in the underlying native soils. A better approach, we conclude, would be to remove and recompact the fill under the buildings.

Pay Close Attention to the Soils Report

The soils report is written by a licensed geologist. It is an assessment of the adequacy of the soil on site to support the planned construction. A soils report should be a requirement for commercial real estate loans. Pay attention to the recommendation section of the report, and make sure that those recommendations are incorporated into the architect's plans. Problems with the soil should be adequately explained.

A major problem for lenders is the possible presence of contaminants in the soil. This is especially true of sites previously used by a potential polluter. Examples include former agricultural land, where certain fertilizers may have contaminated the soil, or gas station properties, where underground tanks may have leaked contaminants.

Note the comments in Exhibit 13-4, which might be included in a soils report.

Observe Survey Findings

A survey may be performed to insure that the buildings are being or have been built within the boundaries of the site, and that there are no encroachments onto easements. Whether you require a survey will depend on the size and complexity of the project, and where on the site the buildings will be located.

Pay attention to the findings of the survey and any comments made. For example, the survey might indicate:

"This survey does not include any location or research for underground utilities or other utilities or other facilities, if any, other than shown," or

"No structures were located by field survey which are more than five (5) feet from the property lines, except as shown."

Any comments made that might adversely impact the proposed loan should be reviewed closely. Additional clarification from the surveyor may be required.

Surveyor's Certificate

The surveyor's certificate attests to the work performed by the surveyor. It should be provided along with the survey. Exhibit 13-5 is a sample certificate.

EXHIBIT 13-5

SURVEYOR'S CERTIFICATE

The undersigned hereby certifies to Ajax Development Company and First Title Insurance Company as of the date hereof, that this survey correctly shows, on the basis of field survey and in accordance with the minimum standard detail requirements for land surveys jointly established and adopted by ALTA and ACSM: (1) a fixed and determinable position and location of the land described hereon (including the position of the point of beginning); (2) the location of all buildings, structures, and other improvements situated on the land; and (3) all driveways or other cuts in the curbs along any street on which the land abuts. Except as shown on said print or survey, there are no visible easements or rights of way affecting the land or other easements or rights of way of which the undersigned has been advised or which are of record nor, except as shown, are there any building restrictions or setback lines, party walls, encroachments, or overhangs of any improvements on any easements, rights of way, or adjacent land on the described land. The print of survey reflects boundary lines of the described land which "close" by engineering calculations.

_____

Surveyor

Assigning the Construction Contract

The construction loan depends a great deal on the construction contract. As was discussed in Chapter 4 the contract identifies the responsibilities of owner and contractor in the construction process. A construction lender will want the right to assume the contract in the event of a default by the owner.

An assignment of the construction contract gives the lender the right to take over the owner's responsibilities under the contract and complete the project. Exhibit 13-6 is an Assignment. Complete it with the following information:

1. The name of the borrowing entity. This should be the owner under the construction contract, and the party who is granting the assignment to the lender.
2. The name of the lending institution.
3. The date of the construction contract.
4. The name of the general contractor under the contract.
5. A general description of the property to be built; for example, "A two-story garden retail building of approximately 25,000 square feet."
6. The nature of the security instrument, whether "deed of trust" or "mortgage."
7. The amount of the loan.
8. The date the Assignment is executed.
9. The name of the assigning party, which should be the borrowing entity.
10. The signature(s) of the authorized representative(s) of the borrowing entity.

EXHIBIT 13-6

ASSIGNMENT OF CONSTRUCTION CONTRACT

FOR VALUE RECEIVED, the undersigned _____
_____ (1) _____ ("Borrower"), hereby assigns, transfers, and sets over unto _____ (2) _____ ("Lender") all of its rights, title, and interest in and to that certain construction contract dated _____ (3) _____

entered into by and between _____
_____ (4) _____
("Contractor") for the construction of the improvements generally described as _____ (5) _____
_____ .

Said improvements are to be constructed on real property legally described in that certain _____ (6) _____ of even date herewith which secures that certain Promissory Note of even date herewith made by Borrower in favor of Lender in the amount of $ _____ (7) _____ . This assignment is made as additional collateral to secure the construction loan evidenced by said note.

IN WITNESS WHEREOF, Borrower has executed this Assignment of Construction Contract this _____ (8) _____ day of _____ , 19 ___ .

_____ (9) _____
By: _____ (10) _____
By: _____

Contractor's Consent to Assignment of Construction Contract

The contractor should be asked to acknowledge and approve the assignment of the construction contract to the real estate lender as additional collateral for the loan being made. The consent to assignment form should be used along with the assignment, and attached to it as Page 2. That way similar information doesn't have to be repeated. Exhibit 13-7 shows the consent form, which can be completed as follows:

1. The date the document is executed.
2. The name of the entity signing the document, which should be the general contractor.
3. The signature of an authorized representative from the general contractor.

Architect's Assignment of Plans and Specifications

An assignment of the plans and specifications by the architect can also be obtained. That way the lender has the right to use them to complete the project in the event of a default.

EXHIBIT 13-7

CONSENT TO ASSIGNMENT

The undersigned Contractor hereby consents to said assignment and in consideration of Bank's making the construction loan to Borrower described on Page one agrees with Bank as follows:

1. In the event of default by Borrower under any of the construction loan documents, Contractor, at Bank's request, shall continue performance on Bank's behalf under the Construction Contract in accordance with terms thereof, provided that Contractor shall be reimbursed in accordance with the contract for all work, labor, and materials rendered in Bank's behalf.

2. Contractor shall not without Bank's written consent perform work pursuant to any change order which will result in an increase in the contract price by more than the change order amount specified in the Construction Loan Agreement between Bank and Borrower of even date herewith which Contractor has signed.

3. That the disbursement schedule as outlined in said Construction Loan Agreement shall control the disbursement of loan funds and payment to Contractor, notwithstanding any conflicting provisions contained in the Construction Contract.

Contractor hereby represents and warrants to Bank that it is duly licensed to conduct business in the jurisdiction where such construction work is to be performed.

This Consent to Assignment of Construction Contract is made as of this _____ (1) _____ day of _____ , 19____ .

_____ (2) _____
By: _____ (3) _____
By: _____

Exhibit 13-8 is an Assignment form that can be used for this purpose. Complete it with the following:

1. The name of the borrowing entity, the party who is assigning over interest in the architect's agreement, plans, and specifications.
2. The name of the lending institution.
3. The dollar amount of the loan being granted.
4. The state in which the loan is granted.
5. The date of the Architect's Agreement between the owner and the architect.
6. The name of the architect.
7. A description of the project which the architect will draw.
8. The city, county, and state in which the project is located.
9. The date of execution of the assignment.
10. The name of the borrowing entity.
11. The signature(s) of the authorized representative(s) of the borrowing entity.

EXHIBIT 13-8

ASSIGNMENT OF ARCHITECT'S AGREEMENT AND OF ARCHITECT'S PLANS AND SPECIFICATIONS

FOR VALUABLE CONSIDERATION, the receipt and sufficiency of which are hereby acknowledged, _____ _____ (1) _____ ("Borrower") as additional security for the obligations incurred and to be incurred pursuant to a Construction Loan Agreement of even date herewith between Borrower and _____ _____ (2) _____ ("Lender") relating to a Promissory Note in the amount of $ _____ (3) _____ between Lender and Borrower, hereby assigns and transfers to Lender, its successors and assigns, and hereby creates in favor of Lender a security interest under the Uniform Commercial Code of the State of _____ (4) _____ in and to all of Borrower's rights in and to (i) that certain Agreement Between Owner and Architect ("Architect's Agreement") dated _____ (5) _____ between Borrower as Owner and _____ (6) _____ ("Architect") as Architect for the construction of _____ (7) _____ and all facilities and appurtenances related thereto on certain real property ("Property") located in _____ (8) _____ and (ii) the original plans ("Plans"), plus revisions heretofore or hereafter made, and the specifications ("Specifications") therefor, all-inclusive, all of which were prepared by Architect pursuant to the Architect's Agreement, a true and correct copy of which plans and specifications has been deposited with and is held by Lender.

Borrower and Architect, by executing the Consent to this Assignment attached hereto, agree that Lender does not assume any of Borrower's obligations or duties concerning the Plans, including, but not limited to, the obligations to pay for the preparation of the Plans, until and unless Lender shall exercise its rights hereunder.

Borrower hereby irrevocably constitutes and appoints Lender as its attorney-in-fact to demand, receive, and enforce Borrower's rights with respect to the Plans, to give appropriate receipts, releases, and satisfactions for and on behalf of Borrower, and to do any and all acts in the name of Borrower or in the name of Lender with the same force and effect as Borrower could do if the Assignment had not been made.

Borrower hereby represents and warrants to Lender that no previous assignment of its interest in the Plans and Specifications has been made, and Borrower agrees not to assign, sell, pledge, transfer, mortgage, or otherwise encumber its interest in the plans so long as this Assignment is in effect.

This Assignment shall be binding upon and inure to the benefit of the heirs, legal representatives, assigns, or successors in interest of the Borrower and Lender.

IN WITNESS WHEREOF, Borrower has caused this Assignment to be executed as of _____ (9) _____ .

_____ (10) _____

By: _____ (11) _____

By: _____

EXHIBIT 13-9

ARCHITECT'S CONSENT

The undersigned, as Architect, hereby consents to the assignment of the Architect's Agreement and the Plans and the Specifications, and further agrees as follows:

1. In the event of any default by Borrower under the Construction Loan Agreement referred to above or any document or instrument contemplated thereby, the undersigned shall at Lender's request continue performance on Lender's behalf under the Architect's Agreement in accordance with the terms and provisions thereof without additional cost to the Lender other than the making of payments to the undersigned in accordance with the Architect's Agreement for all services performed subsequent to such event of default. Lender shall also be entitled to use the Plans and Specifications and all additions, modifications, or extensions thereof pertaining to the construction of the improvements contemplated by the Architect's Assignment, without extra cost to Lender other than as provided in the preceding sentence.

2. The undersigned hereby certifies that (i) the Property is zoned and generally planned so as to permit the construction, ownership, and operation of the improvements contemplated by the Plans and Specifications, (ii) upon payment of customary fees, there is or there will be available to the Property all utility services intended to be connected to or used in connection with the construction contemplated by the Architect's Agreement, including, without limitation, water, electric, telephone, gas, sewer, and sanitation disposal facilities, and (iii) the Plans and Specifications are in compliance with all covenants, conditions, and restrictions affecting the Property and with all requirements and restrictions of all governmental authorities having jurisdiction, including, without limitation, all applicable zoning, environmental, building, fire, health, and safety legislation, ordinances, rules, and regulations.

3. The undersigned covenants and agrees that it will not claim any default under the Architect's Agreement without giving at least fifteen (15) days' prior written notice to Lender, said notice to provide Lender with a reasonable opportunity to cure the default. Nothing herein shall require Lender to cure said default, but only gives it the option to do so.

Dated: _____ (1) _____

_____ (2) _____
By: _____ (3) _____
By: _____

Architect's Consent to Assignment

The architect should also sign a consent form approving and acknowledging the assignment of his contract, plans, and specifications to the lender. Exhibit 13-9 is such an assignment. It can be attached to the Assignment as Page 2. Fill in the following information:

1. The date the document is executed.
2. The name of the architectural entity, the party executing the document.
3. The signature(s) of the authorized representative(s) of the architect.

Borrower's Disbursement Schedule

A disbursement schedule is a detailed summary of the disbursements to be made under the construction loan, and the purpose for which the funds will be used. A schedule can be included as part of the Construction Loan Agreement.

However, a separate statement can be prepared for signature by the borrower. Exhibit 13-10 can be used for this purpose. Complete it with the following information:

1. The dollar amount of funds to be disbursed at loan recording.
2. The purpose for which these funds will be disbursed; for example, "Representing land draw" or "Loan fee" or "Title, legal, documentation, and miscellaneous fees."
3. The dollar amount of funds to be disbursed during the course of construction.
4. The purpose for which funds will be disbursed; for example, "Direct building cost for construction, to be disbursed monthly to the contractor" or "Interest Reserve."
5. The date on which the borrower signs the document.
6. The name of the borrowing entity.
7. The authorized signature(s) of the borrower.
8. The date on which the contractor acknowledges receipt of the disbursement schedule.
9. The name of the general contractor.
10. The signature(s) of the contractor's authorized representative(s).

Documenting Agreement to Complete with a Completion Agreement

A completion agreement is provided by the contractor, and in signing it the contractor agrees to complete construction and guarantees that completion. Agreements vary widely, and many contractors are reluctant to sign one that is too broad. While they are willing to be bound by the terms of their contract with the owner, they do not want to guarantee performance not included in the contract.

Exhibit 13-11 is a Completion Agreement for use with contractors. Fill it in with the following information:

1. The name of the lending institution.
2. The name of the borrowing entity.
3. A description of the property to be built.
4. A legal description of the property.
5. The date of execution of the completion agreement.
6. The name of the entity executing the document, the general contractor.
7. The signature(s) of the authorized representative(s) of the general contractor.

EXHIBIT 13-10

DISBURSEMENT SCHEDULE

I. The following funds will be disbursed at loan recording:

$ _____ _____

$ _____ _____

$ _____ (1) _____ _____ (2) _____

$ _____ _____

$ _____ _____

II. The following disbursements are to be made monthly during the course of construction:

$ _____ _____

$ _____ _____

$ _____ _____

$ _____ _____

$ _____ (3) _____ _____ (4) _____

$ _____ _____

$ _____ _____

$ _____ _____

$ _____ _____

$ _____ _____

The disbursement schedule above is hereby approved and accepted.

Date: _____ (5) _____

_____ (6) _____

By: _____ (7) _____

By: _____

The undersigned general contractor acknowledges receipt of a copy of this disbursement schedule.

Date: _____ (8) _____

_____ (9) _____

By: _____ (10) _____

By: _____

EXHIBIT13-11

COMPLETION AGREEMENT

To: _____ (1)_____ ("Lender")

WHEREAS, _____ (2) _____ ("Borrower") has applied to Lender for a certain real estate loan to finance the construction of _____ (3) _____

_____

on property legally described as _____

_____ (4) _____ .

_____

WHEREAS, as a condition to the making of the loan, Lender requires that undersigned execute this completion agreement and Guaranty ("Agreement"),

NOW THEREFORE, undersigned in consideration of Lender's making the Loan to Borrower, unconditionally and independently of any liability of Borrower, guarantees and agrees with Lender as follows:

1. All works of improvement shall be constructed and completed in accordance with all applicable laws and regulations, the construction contract, and the plans and specifications, relating to such works of improvement, free and clear of mechanic's or materialmen's liens and stop notice claims, and all costs of such works of improvement shall be paid.

2. If the improvements and construction are not so completed, undersigned shall, at Lender's request, immediately proceed to so complete and shall pay or bond around any mechanic's or materialmen's liens and stop notice claims that may come into existence.

3. Undersigned authorizes Lender, without notice or demand and without affecting any liability hereunder, from time to time to: (a) renew, compromise, extend, accelerate, or to otherwise change the time for payment of, or to otherwise change the terms of the loan, or any part thereof, including increase or decrease of the rate of interest thereon or increase the amount of the Loan, (b) waive any terms of the loan or security, (c) take and hold security for the payment of this Agreement or the indebtedness guaranteed, and exchange, enforce, waive, subordinate, and release any such security, (d) apply such security and direct the order or manner of sale thereof as Lender, in its discretion may determine, and (e) release or substitute any one or more of any endorser or guarantor.

4. Undersigned agrees to pay a reasonable attorney's fee and all other costs and expenses which may be incurred by Lender in the enforcement of this Agreement.

5. If undersigned fails to perform as herein provided, Lender may, at its option, proceed to so perform on behalf of Undersigned, and Undersigned shall, upon demand, pay to Lender all sums expended by Lender in such performance on behalf of Undersigned plus interest at the rate of ten percent (10%) per annum.

IN WITNESS WHEREOF, the Undersigned has executed this Agreement this _____ (5) _____ day of _____ , 19 ___ .

_____ (6) _____

By: _____ (7) _____

By: _____

EXHIBIT 13-12

CHECKLIST

Payment/Performance Bond Required ( ) Yes ( ) No (1)
   If Yes:
   Name of Bonding Company: _____ (2) _____
   Amount of Bond: _____ (3) _____
   Date Bond Received: _____ (4) _____
   If No:
   ( ) Bond Waiver Agreement Required (5)
( ) Building Permit (6)
   ( ) Received   Date: _____
Construction ( ) has ( ) has not begun (7)
   If construction has begun: (8)
   ( ) Indemnity Agreement received Date: _____
   The following documentation is required if checked: (9)
( ) Soils Report
   Date Received: _____
( ) Survey
   Date Received: _____
( ) Assignment of Construction Contract
   Date Received: _____
  ( ) Consent to Assignment of Construction Contract
   Date Received: _____
( ) Assignment of Architect's Agreement/Plans and Specifications
   Date Received: _____
  ( ) Consent to Assignment
   Date Received: _____
( ) Separate Disbursement Schedule
   Date Received
( ) Completion Agreement Required From:
_____ (10) _____

End Note

The construction loan process is unique because of the voluminous documentation required to properly record a loan. Not only is there a borrowing entity to document, but a contractor and architect as well.

Use the checklist in Exhibit 13-12 as a guide in putting together the construction loan documentation needed. The form can be completed with the following:

1. Indicate whether a bond is required.
2. The name of the company providing the bond.

3. The amount of the bond required, usually the amount of the construction contract.

4. The date the bond was received.

5. If no bond is required, indicate whether a bond waiver agreement will be obtained.

6. Indicate your requirement for a building permit, and follow up with the date the permit is received.

7. Indicate whether construction has begun on-site.

8. If construction has begun, indicate the date on which an acceptable indemnity agreement was received.

9. Check those documents that are required, and follow up with the dates the documents are received.

10. Show the names of those parties from whom a completion guaranty will be required.

14

Construction Loans, Part II: How to Control the Loan During the Building Process

Once the construction loan is booked, controlling it during the building process is crucial to the success of the loan. There is on-going documentation that you can obtain and review during this period in order to feel comfortable with job progress. That documentation is the subject of this final chapter.

Obtaining a Notice to Proceed with Construction to Substantiate the Borrower's Intent to Begin

Notice to Proceed is given by the owner to the contractor. It is notification that financing is in place and that construction work can begin. Document your file with this Notice in order to substantiate your borrower's willingness to proceed.

Exhibit 14-1 is a sample Notice. Complete it as follows:

1. The date of the letter.
2. The name and address of the contractor to whom the letter is addressed.
3. Reference should be made to the subject project.
4. The date of the construction contract.
5. The name of the lending institution.
6. The signature of the owner.

When to Use a Builder's Control Service

Not every lender does enough construction lending to be able to keep a disbursement group with the real estate loan department. Yet control of loan funds is necessary

EXHIBIT 14-1

NOTICE TO PROCEED WITH CONSTRUCTION

_____ (1) _____

_____
_____ (2) _____
_____

RE: _____ (3) _____
_____

Dear Sirs,

In accordance with our construction contract dated _____ (4) _____ , for the construction of the above-referenced project, please accept this letter as authorization to proceed with construction as soon as the necessary permits have been obtained. Our loan has been funded by _____ (5) _____ and you may draw against it as soon as work is begun.

Sincerely,

_____ (6) _____

for the success of a construction loan. It may be appropriate to turn this control over to a builder's control service.

A control service is an outside company that separately contracts with your owner/borrower to handle and control the loan disbursements. Further, they will inspect the job and authorize payment requests made by the contractor.

You should consider using a builder's control service on larger jobs, which are more complex and require closer monitoring. Also use them on any job where the contractor is unknown, or where there are concerns about the ability of the owner and contractor to carry the job through to completion.

Preparing Set-Aside Letters to Confirm Availability of Funds

There are times when the construction lender is asked to give written confirmation that loan funds are available for certain construction purposes. The party making the request wants to insure that funds will be there for the work they will do, and requests that the lender specifically "set aside" these funds only for that specific work. The document used for this purpose is called a set-aside letter.

Exhibit 14-2 (page 239) is an example of a Set-Aside Letter. Fill it in with the following information.

1. The date of the letter.
2. The party to whom the letter is addressed.
3. A reference identifying the project for which the funds will be set aside.
4. The name of the borrower.

5. A complete description of the address of the project or its legal description.

6. The type of account to be established; for example, "An off-site improvement account."

7. The dollar amount of loan proceeds to be set aside for this work.

8. A description of the work for which the funds will be used.

9. The name of the party requesting the set-aside letter.

10. The name of the lending institution.

11. The signature of the authorized representative of the lender.

12. The name of the borrowing entity.

13. The signature of the borrower or borrower's authorized representative.

Approving the Application for Payment

The application for payment is used by the contractor to communicate to the owner and the lender the amount of payment he is requesting for the work completed during the pay period. The form should be completed and submitted at least monthly during the course of construction.

The contractor should sign attesting to the accuracy of the completion percentages used. The architect should also be required to sign, if possible. He should attest to the percentage completion figure, and indicate that the work is being performed in accordance with his plans. Before the payment application reaches the lender, the owner/borrower should approve the request.

Once the form is received by the lender, the work can be inspected and a determination of job progress made. With the lender's approval of the request, funds can be drawn from the construction loan to pay the contractor.

Exhibit 14-3 is an Application and Certificate for Payment provided by the American Institute of Architects. It is one of the best forms available for presenting the pay request in an understandable manner. The lender should look for the following information on the certificate:

1. The name of the owner, your borrower.

2. The name of the project, if applicable.

3. The number of the pay request; for example, a "1" signifying that the request is the first one.

4. The pay period; for example, "Month ending 3/31/__."

5. The name of the contractor who is submitting the pay request.

6. The name of the architect, if he is approving the pay request.

7. The project number for reference.

8. A description of the project.

9. The date of the construction contract.

10. If there are change orders to the work, the number of the change order(s) on which payment is being requested for the pay period; for example, "Change Order No. 3."

11. The date the change order was approved by the owner.

12. The amount of the change order, whether positive or negative. If there are more than one, then they should be totalled in the space provided.

13. The total amount of the original contract.

14. The total amount of all change orders to date.

15. The new contract amount—the sum of the original amount and the change orders.

16. The total amount of the job completed to the date of the pay request, along with any materials stored on the site.

17. Retainage is the amount to be held back from the contractor until completion of the job. This is discussed more fully in Chapter 4. Fill in retainage on completed work.

18. Total earned is computed by subtracting total retention from the total completed and stored figure.

19. The amount paid on previous applications for payment.

20. Current payment due is computed by subtracting previous payments from total earned.

21. Balance to finish is computed by subtracting the amount earned from the total contract sum (including change orders).

22. The application should be signed and dated by an authorized representative of the contractor.

23. The form can be notarized attesting to the contractor's signature.

24. The form can be signed and dated by the architect.

Information you can get in summary form from a review of the certificate includes total change orders approved, the amount of the job completed, how much retention has been held, and the amount of the job yet to be completed.

Proper Use of Continuation Sheets

Continuation sheets are used for a line-item by line-item analysis of progress on the job. Adding up all the line items by columns gives the totals that are summarized on the certification page.

Exhibit 14-4 is a Continuation Sheet. It should be completed with the following information:

1. The number of the pay request.

2. The date of the pay request.

3. The period covered in the pay request.

4. The project number, if applicable.

5. The item number for the particular line item, if one is assigned by the contractor.

6. A description of the line item; for example, "Concrete" or "Rough Plumbing."

7. The scheduled value is the original budget for the particular line item.

8. The dollar amount of work completed for the line item as reflected on previous pay requests.

9. The dollar amount of work completed for the particular line item, for which payment is being requested.

10. Materials stored on-site for which credit will be given in the pay request.

11. The total completed and stored on-site.

12. The percent completion for the line item is computed by dividing the dollar amount completed by the original scheduled value, or budget, for that item.

EXHIBIT 14-2

SET-ASIDE LETTER

_____ (1) _____

_____
_____ (2) _____
_____

RE: _____ (3) _____
_____

Gentlemen:

We have committed to construction financing for _____
(4) _____ for the above-referenced project more fully described as
_____ (5) _____ .
This letter is written subject to the borrower meeting all of the terms of that
commitment and the funding of the loan.

Upon recording and funding of said loan, we agree to establish
an _____ (6) _____ account in the sum of not less
than _____ (7) _____ . Withdrawal of funds from this account will be on authorization of the principal and in keeping with the terms of our Construction Loan
Agreement.

It is agreed that the funds in said account will be used only for the purpose
of _____ (8) _____ .

In the event that the principal fails to complete and/or pay for the work
described in the preceding paragraph, all funds remaining in said account shall be
immediately available to _____ (9) _____ to complete and pay
for the cost of said improvements.

This is an irrevocable commitment of funds, subject to loan funding, which is
not subject to recall.

_____ (10) _____
By: _____ (11) _____

Agreed and accepted:

_____ (12) _____
By: _____ (13) _____

13. The balance to finish is computed by subtracting the total completed to date
from the original scheduled value.

14. Retainage can be computed for each line item.

15. After all of the line items are shown on the continuation sheets, each column
can be totalled.

Detailing line items in this manner facilitates a review to determine the accuracy
of the pay request.

EXHIBIT 14-3

AIA copyrighted material has been reproduced with the permission of The American Institute of Architects under permission number 87149. Further reproduction is prohibited.

Because AIA Documents are revised from time to time, users should ascertain from the AIA the current edition of the Document reproduced herein.

This Document is intended for use as a "consumable" (consumables are further defined by Senate Report 94-473 on the Copyright Act of 1976).

Copies of the current edition of this AIA Document may be purchased from The American Institute of Architects or its local distributors.

APPLICATION AND CERTIFICATE FOR PAYMENT AIA DOCUMENT G702 (Instructions on reverse side) PAGE ONE OF ____ PAGES

TO (OWNER): (1)

PROJECT: (2)

APPLICATION NO: (3)

Distribution to:
☐ OWNER
☐ ARCHITECT
☐ CONTRACTOR

PERIOD TO: (4)

FROM (CONTRACTOR): (5)

VIA (ARCHITECT): (6)

ARCHITECT'S PROJECT NO: (7)

CONTRACT FOR: (8)

CONTRACT DATE: (9)

CONTRACTOR'S APPLICATION FOR PAYMENT

Application is made for Payment, as shown below, in connection with the Contract. Continuation Sheet, AIA Document G703, is attached.

CHANGE ORDER SUMMARY	ADDITIONS	DEDUCTIONS
Change Orders approved in previous months by Owner TOTAL		
Approved this Month		
Number (10)	Date Approved (11)	
TOTALS	(12)	
Net change by Change Orders		

1. ORIGINAL CONTRACT SUM .... $ _____ (13)
2. Net change by Change Orders .... $ _____ (14)
3. CONTRACT SUM TO DATE (Line 1 ± 2) .... $ _____ (15)
4. TOTAL COMPLETED & STORED TO DATE .... $ _____ (16)
   (Column G on G703)
5. RETAINAGE:
   a. _____ % of Completed Work $ _____ (17)
      (Column D + E on G703)
   b. _____ % of Stored Material $ _____
      (Column F on G703)
   Total Retainage (Line 5a + 5b or
   Total in Column I of G703) .... $ _____ (17)
6. TOTAL EARNED LESS RETAINAGE .... $ _____ (18)
   (Line 4 less Line 5 Total)
7. LESS PREVIOUS CERTIFICATES FOR
   PAYMENT (Line 6 from prior Certificate) .... $ _____ (19)
8. CURRENT PAYMENT DUE .... $ _____ (20)
9. BALANCE TO FINISH, PLUS RETAINAGE .... $ _____ (21)
   (Line 3 less Line 6)

The undersigned Contractor certifies that to the best of the Contractor's knowledge, information and belief the Work covered by this Application for Payment has been completed in accordance with the Contract Documents, that all amounts have been paid by the Contractor for Work for which previous Certificates for Payment were issued and payments received from the Owner, and that current payment shown herein is now due.

CONTRACTOR:

By: _____ Date: _____ (22)

State of:
Subscribed and sworn to before me this _____ day of _____ , 19 ____
Notary Public:
My Commission expires: (23)

County of:

ARCHITECT'S CERTIFICATE FOR PAYMENT

AMOUNT CERTIFIED .... $ _____
(Attach explanation if amount certified differs from the amount applied for.)
ARCHITECT: (24)

In accordance with the Contract Documents, based on on-site observations and the data comprising the above application, the Architect certifies to the Owner that to the best of the Architect's knowledge, information and belief the Work has progressed as indicated, the quality of the Work is in accordance with the Contract Documents, and the Contractor is entitled to payment of the AMOUNT CERTIFIED.

By: _____ Date: _____

This Certificate is not negotiable. The AMOUNT CERTIFIED is payable only to the Contractor named herein. Issuance, payment and acceptance of payment are without prejudice to any rights of the Owner or Contractor under this Contract.

AIA DOCUMENT G702 • APPLICATION AND CERTIFICATE FOR PAYMENT • MAY 1983 EDITION • AIA ® • © 1983

Courtesy of the American Institute of Architects.

EXHIBIT 14-4

CONTINUATION SHEET

AIA DOCUMENT G703 (Instructions on reverse side) PAGE OF PAGES

AIA Document G702, APPLICATION AND CERTIFICATE FOR PAYMENT, containing
Contractor's signed Certification is attached.
In tabulations below, amounts are stated to the nearest dollar.
Use Column I on Contracts where variable retainage for line items may apply.

APPLICATION NUMBER: (1)
APPLICATION DATE: (2)
PERIOD TO: (3)
ARCHITECT'S PROJECT NO: (4)

A	B	C	D	E	F	G	H	I
			WORK COMPLETED		MATERIALS			
ITEM NO.	DESCRIPTION OF WORK	SCHEDULED VALUE	FROM PREVIOUS APPLICATION (D + E)	THIS PERIOD	PRESENTLY STORED (NOT IN D OR E)	TOTAL COMPLETED AND STORED TO DATE (D+E+F)	% (G ÷ C)	BALANCE TO FINISH (C − G)	RETAINAGE
(5)	(6)	(7)	(8)	(9)	(10)	(11)	(12)	(13)	(14)
			(15)						

SAMPLE

1. AIA copyrighted material has been reproduced with the permission of The American Institute of Architects under permission number 87149. Further reproduction is prohibited.

2. Because AIA Documents are revised from time to time, users should ascertain from the AIA the current edition of the Document reproduced herein.

3. Copies of the current edition of this AIA Document may be purchased from The American Institute of Architects or its local distributors.

4. This Document is intended for use as a "consumable" (consumables are further defined by Senate Report 94-473 on the Copyright Act of 1976). This Document is not intended to be used as "model language" (language taken from an existing document and incorporated, without attribution, into a newly-created document). Rather, it is a standard form which is intended to be modified by appending separate amendment sheets and/or filling in provided blank spaces.

G703-1983

Courtesy of the American Institute of Architects.

EXHIBIT 14-5

CERTIFICATION

Pursuant to the terms of our construction contract dated _____ (1) _____ ,
the Contractor certifies that the work covered by our Invoice
No. ____ (2) ____ dated _____ (3) _____ has been performed in accordance with
our agreements and payment has not been received.

_____ (4) _____
By: _____ (5) _____

Whether any backup is taken with the draw request to substantiate individual line items will depend on your level of comfort with the borrower and the contractor. You might want to see invoices, or cancelled checks from prior pay requests, before approving the current one.

Preparing a More Specific Certification

The pay request discussed above already includes a Certification from the Contractor. You might want one to be more specific, however, by referencing the contract. Exhibit 14-5 shows one that can be used:

1. The date of the construction contract.
2. The contractor's invoice number for the particular draw request.
3. The date of the pay request.
4. The name of the contractor.
5. The signature of the authorized representative for the contractor.

What to Look for in Change Orders

Contracts rarely include all of the items necessary to complete the project. Unforeseen circumstances can add to the original cost. When extras occur, they need to be documented, then approved by the owner. They should also be approved by the lender, who will probably be asked to make funds available to cover the extra cost.

Exhibit 14-6 is a Change Order form. The lender should look for the following information:

1. The number of the particular change order.
2. The name of the contractor on the job.
3. The contractor's job number for reference.
4. The contractor's mailing address.
5. The date of the change order.
6. The name of the project under construction.
7. The address of the project.

EXHIBIT 14-6

CHANGE ORDER

Change Order ———————— (1) ————
No.
Contractor: ———————— (2) ———— Job No. ———— (3) ——
Address: ———————— (4) ———— Date: ——— (5) ————

———————————

Project Name: ———————— (6) ————
Address: ———————— (7) ————

———————————

The undersigned owner hereby approves the following changes to the scope of the work outlined in the construction contract dated ————————————————
(8) ———————— :

Item (9)	Description (10)	Amount (11)
————————	————————	————————

———————————————————————

Approved and Authorized
———————— (12) ————————
By: ———— (13) ————————
Date: ———— (14) ————————
Accepted by:
———————— (15) ————————
———————— (16) ————————
Date: ———— (17) ————————

8. The date of the construction contract.

9. The item for which a change is needed; for example, "Concrete."

10. A description of the work that necessitates the change; for example, "Price increase effective 4-1-__."

11. The dollar amount of the change. More than one change can be reflected on the same form as long as there is a clear identification of each one. Show the total dollar amount for the change order.

The rest of the form should be completed with:

12. The name of the owner/borrower.

13. The signature of the owner.

14. The date the owner signed the change order.

15. The name of the general contractor issuing and accepting the change order and the responsibility to do the extra work.

16. The signature of the contractor or his representative.

17. The date the contractor signed the change order.

How to Properly Use Credit Memos

A Credit Memo is the reverse of a Change Order. It deletes work to be performed under the contract and credits the owner with the cost of the work that will not be performed. You should determine whether the deleted work still needs to be performed, and, if so, who will do it.

A form identical to the Change Order form can be used for credit memos, with some minor changes to identify it as a Credit Memo instead of a Change Order. Exhibit 14-7 shows the amended form. Completion of the form is very similar to that for the Change Order:

1. The number of the particular credit memo.

2. The name of the contractor on the job.

3. The contractor's job number for reference.

4. The contractor's mailing address.

5. The date of the credit.

6. The name of the project under construction.

7. The address of the project.

8. The date of the construction contract.

9. The item for which a credit is needed; for example, "Concrete."

10. A description of the work that necessitates the credit; for example, "Deletion of two walls at the rear of the building."

11. The dollar amount of the credit. More than one credit can be reflected on the same form as long as there is a clear identification of each one. Show the total dollar amount for the credit memo. Before signing the contractor should certify whether the work deleted will need to be performed.

12. The name of the contractor.

13. The signature of the contractor or his representative.

14. The date the contractor approved the credit.

15. The owner should also certify whether the work deleted will need to be completed at a later date. If the work is needed, he should indicate who will do it.

16. The name of the owner.

17. The signature of the owner.

18. The date the owner approved the credit.

Guarding Against Excessive Backcharges

Backcharges probably cause more disputes on construction jobs than anything else. They arise when the work of a subcontractor is not acceptable to the general contractor. The work is corrected by someone else at additional cost, and the cost is

EXHIBIT 14-7

CREDIT MEMO

Credit Memo ——————— (1) ——————
No.
Contractor: ——————— (2) —————— Job No. ———— (3) ————
Address: ——————— (4) —————— Date: ——— (5) ——————

Project Name: ——————— (6) ——————
Address: ——————— (7) ——————

The undersigned owner hereby approves the following deletions to the scope of the work outlined in the construction contract dated
——————— (8) ——————— :

Item (9)	Description (10)	Amount (11)

The contractor hereby certifies that the deleted work ( ) is ( ) is not needed.
Approved and Authorized:

——————— (12) ——————
By: ——————— (13) ——————
Date: ——————— (14) ——————
The owner acknowledges that the deleted work ( ) is ( ) is not needed. If needed, the work will be performed by ——————————————————————
——————— (15) ——————————————

Accepted by:

——————— (16) ——————
——————— (17) ——————
Date: ——————— (18) ——————

deducted from the money owed to the original subcontractor. The document used to do this is called a backcharge.

Since this matter is between the general contractor and the subcontractor, you do not need to become directly involved with it. A problem can arise when the sub-contractor who received a lower payment disagrees with the backcharge. He will then probably lien the job. Too many of these liens may indicate a job that is out of control, and should prompt a review by the construction lender.

Using the Release of Lien to Certify Contractors' Payment

As a job progresses and payments are made to the general contractor and his subcontractors, those parties should release their right to lien for nonpayment at least to the extent that they have already been partially paid. A Conditional Release of Lien should be submitted with the pay request. This form releases a contractor's right to lien, conditioned on receipt of payment.

An Unconditional Release should be provided after the payment has been received. That way, throughout the project, the lender will be assured that payments are being made to subcontractors and vendors, and the prospect of liens will be increasingly limited.

Exhibit 14-8 is a Conditional Release form; that is, conditioned on receipt of proper payment. It should be completed with the following information:

1. The date of the conditional release.
2. The project name on which the work was performed.
3. The address of the project.
4. The name of the general contractor for whom the subcontractor worked. If the release is being provided by the general contractor, this space can be left blank.
5. The mailing address of the general contractor.

EXHIBIT 14-8

CONDITIONAL RELEASE OF LIEN

Date: _____ (1) _____
Project Name: _____ (2) _____
Address: _____ (3) _____

Contractor: _____ (4) _____
Address: _____ (5) _____

The undersigned does hereby release all mechanic's lien, stop notice, equitable lien, and labor and material bond rights against the above-described project. This release is for the benefit of, and may be relied upon by the owner, the prime contractor, the construction lender, and the principal and surety on any labor and material bond.

This release is CONDITIONAL, and shall be effective only upon payment to the under-signed in the sum of $ _____ (6) _____ . If payment is made by check, this release is effective only when the check is paid by the bank upon which it is drawn.

_____ (7) _____
By: _____ (8) _____

6. The amount of the payment due, and the portion of work which will be released from lien when the payment is received.

7. The name of the contractor issuing the release.

8. The signature of the contractor issuing the release.

Once payment is received the contractor should sign an Unconditional Waiver of Lien Rights. This form is shown in Exhibit 14-9. Complete it with the following information:

1. The date of the unconditional release.

2. The project name on which the work was performed.

3. The address of the project.

4. The name of the general contractor for whom the subcontractor worked. If the release is being provided by the general contractor, this space can be left blank.

5. The mailing address of the general contractor.

6. The amount of the payment and the portion of the contract for which lien rights are being waived.

7. A description of the work provided, for which payment is being received.

EXHIBIT 14-9

UNCONDITIONAL WAIVER

Date: _____ (1) _____

Project Name: _____ (2) _____

Address: _____ (3) _____

_____

Contractor: _____ (4) _____

Address: _____ (5) _____

_____

For and in consideration of the receipt of $ _____ (6) _____ in payment of the following labor and/or materials furnished: _____ (7) _____ the receipt and sufficiency of which is hereby acknowledged, the undersigned does hereby waive, release, and relinquish any and all claims, demands, and rights of lien to the extent of the amount shown hereon for all work, labor, materials, machinery, or other goods, equipment, or services done, performed, or furnished for the construction located at the site described above.

The undersigned further warrants and represents that any and all valid labor and/or material and equipment bills, now due and payable, on the property herein-above described on behalf of the undersigned, have been paid in full to the date of this waiver, or will be paid from these funds.

IN WITNESS WHEREFOR, the signatory has caused these presents to be duly executed this_____ (8) _____ day of _____ , 19 __ .

_____ (9) _____

By: _____ (10) _____

8. The date on which the lien waiver is being executed.
9. The name of the contractor giving the waiver of lien.
10. The signature of the contractor giving the waiver of lien.

Handling a Mechanic's Lien

When a contractor on a job has not been paid for the work performed, the law provides rights to file liens against the property. Lien laws vary from state to state, especially as to the timing required for filing liens, and the steps to be followed.

As construction lender you should be concerned about liens if they occur too frequently, or if there are too many of them. The nature of the construction industry leads to disputes and liens. As long as these are resolved and the liens removed, you do not need to be overly concerned.

Exhibit 14-10 shows a Mechanic's Lien form that might be used by a subcontractor to file a lien against a property. You should note the following information:

1. To whom and where the form is to be returned when recorded. In order to be valid, a mechanic's lien must be recorded against the property on which the work was performed.
2. The name of the contractor claiming a lien for lack of payment.
3. The city in which the subject property is located.
4. The county in which the subject property is located.
5. The state in which the subject property is located.

EXHIBIT 14-10

MECHANIC'S LIEN

WHEN RECORDED MAIL TO:
      (1)

The undersigned, _____ (2) _____ ,
Claimant, claims a mechanic's lien upon the real property located in the City of
_____ (3) _____ , County of _____ (4) ___ , State of
_____ (5) _____ , more particularly described as: _____ (6) _____
_____ .
The sum of $ _____ (7) _____ is due claimant, together with interest thereon at the rate of _____ (8) ___ per annum from _____ (9) _____ , is due claimant for the following work and material furnished by claimant: _____
_____(10) _____
Claimant furnished the work and materials at the request of, or under contract with, _____ (11) _____ . The owners or reputed owners of the property are _____ (12) _____ .

                                   _____ (13) _____
                              By: _____ (14) _____

6. A description of the subject property against which the lien is filed, either the street address or the legal description.

7. The amount of the lien.

8. The penalty rate of interest which the contractor is assessing on the unpaid sum.

9. The date from which the contractor is assessing interest on the unpaid sum.

10. A description of the work that was performed and for which payment was not received.

11. The party with whom the contractor had his contract. This may be the owner, the general contractor, or someone else connected with the project.

12. The name of the party or parties believed to be the owners of the property.

13. The name of the contractor filing the lien.

14. The signature of the contractor or his representative.

Obtaining a Release of a Mechanic's Lien

When payment is received for a lien that is already recorded against the property, the contractor who filed the lien must record a release.

Exhibit 14-11 is a Release of Lien form, which should be completed in the following manner:

1. The name and address of the party to whom the recorded release should be returned.

2. The name of the party who claimed and recorded the mechanic's lien.

EXHIBIT 14-11

RELEASE OF MECHANIC'S LIEN

WHEN RECORDED RETURN TO:

    (1)

KNOW ALL MEN BY THESE PRESENTS:

That the Mechanic's Lien claimed by _____ (2) _____ against _____ (3) _____ upon the property described as _____ (4) _____

is hereby released, the claim thereunder having been fully paid and satisfied, and that certain Notice of Mechanic's Lien recorded as Instrument No. _____ (5) ___ on _____ in Book _____ , Page _____ of Official Records of _____ County, State of _____ is hereby satisfied and discharged.

Dated: _____ (6)_____

                        _____ (7) _____

                      By: _____ (8) _____

3. The name of the party against whom the lien was recorded, probably the owner and the general contractor.

4. A description of the subject property on which the lien was filed.

5. Recording information as to the date and location of the recorded document.

6. The date of the release of lien.

7. The name of the party releasing the lien, which should be the same as the name of the party who filed the mechanic's lien.

8. The signature of the contractor releasing the lien.

Using a Release of Mechanic's Lien Bond to Support a Release of Lien

When a lien is filed against a property, it creates a cloud on the title that may affect funding of the permanent loan. If an honest dispute exists between the subcontractor who filed the lien and the general contractor, the latter may not wish to pay the disputed amount. Other steps must be taken to clear title to the owner's property.

One way this can be accomplished is by the filing of a bond, written by the contractor's insurance company, which protects the title company from any loss arising from the dispute. The title company can issue their policy of title insurance without the lien showing. This bond protects the owner and lender from further problems regardless of the outcome of the dispute. The bonding company agrees to pay the claim if the contractor is held liable and does not pay it.

Exhibit 14-12 is an example of a Release of Mechanic's Lien Bond. Have the contractor obtain one to clear the owner's property of liens and allow you to fund the permanent loan.

1. The name of the general contractor.

2. The name of the insurance company issuing the bond.

3. The state in which the bonding company is operating.

4. The name of the property owner.

5. The amount of the bond.

6. The name of the subcontractor who filed the mechanic's lien.

7. The mechanic's lien number.

8. The amount of the lien.

9. The date on which the lien was recorded.

10. The county and state in which the lien was recorded.

11. The recording information identifying the location of the recorded lien.

12. A description of the project on which the lien was filed, including the legal description or property address.

13. The date of the release bond.

14. The name of the general contractor.

15. The signature of the general contractor or his authorized representative.

16. The name of the insurance company.

17. An authorized signature from the insurance company.

What to Do if You Receive a Stop Notice

When a subcontractor files a lien against the property, he establishes a right to collect if the property is in some way liquidated. Without a sale or foreclosure,

EXHIBIT 14-12

RELEASE OF MECHANIC'S LIEN BOND

KNOW ALL MEN BY THESE PRESENTS:

That we, _____ (1) _____, as Principal, and _____ (2) _____, a _____ (3) _____ corporation, duly qualified as Surety, are held and firmly bound unto _____ (4) _____ as Obligee, in the sum of _____ (5) _____ lawful money of the United States of America, for which payment well and truly to be made, we bind ourselves, our heirs, executors, administrators, successors, and assigns, jointly and severally, firmly by these presents.

THE CONDITION OF THIS OBLIGATION IS SUCH THAT:

Whereas, _____ (6) _____, is the claimant under that certain Mechanic's Lien No. _____ (7) _____, in the amount of _____ (8) _____ which was recorded on or about _____ (9) _____ in the Official Records of _____ (10) _____ as Instrument No. _____, Book No. ____ (11) ____, Page No. covering: _____ (12) _____ _____;

Whereas, the Principal disputes the correctness or validity of such claim of Mechanic's Lien and desires to free all the above-described real property from the effect of such claim of lien.

Now, therefore, if the said Principal shall pay or cause to be paid in full or otherwise discharged, the claim of the above claimant, then this obligation shall be void, otherwise to remain in full force and effect.

Signed, Sealed, and Dated this ____ (13) ____ day of _____, 19 ____ .

_____ (14) _____
By: _____ (15) _____
_____ (16) _____
By: _____ (17) _____

however, he may have to wait to collect. By use of a Stop Notice, he can require that the construction lender hold the funds due him from the general contractor's payments until such time as the dispute is resolved.

The Stop Notice must generally be accompanied by a bond in order to be effective. If you receive such a Notice, check with your legal counsel to make sure that it is in proper form. If so, you must hold money aside from your construction funds.

Exhibit 14-13 is a Stop Notice form. It should be filled in with the following information:

1. The name and address of the lending institution.

2. The name, address, and telephone number of the subcontractor filing the stop notice.

3. A description of the work that was done by the subcontractor.

EXHIBIT 14-13

STOP NOTICE

To: _____

_____ (1) _____

_____

You are hereby notified that the undersigned, whose address and telephone number are: _____ (2) _____ , has furnished labor, services, equipment, or materials of the following general description: _____ (3) _____ for the building, structure, or other work of improvement described as: _____ (4) _____ .

The undersigned furnished the labor, services, equipment, or materials at the request of, or under contract with: _____ (5) _____ .

The total value of the labor, services, equipment, or materials agreed to be furnished by the undersigned was $ _____ (6) _____ , and the value of the labor, services, equipment, or materials actually furnished as of the date of this Notice is $ _____ (7) _____ . The sum of $ _____ (8) _____ has been paid to the undersigned therefor.

The amount of $ _____ (9) _____ , together with interest thereon at the rate of ____ (10) ____ %, from _____ (11) _____ , is due and unpaid to the undersigned for the furnishing of the labor, services, equipment, or materials described above.

You are hereby notified to withhold, from the prime contractor or construction fund, money or other funds in an amount sufficient to answer the claim stated hereinabove, plus any other costs provided by law to be withheld.

_____ (12) _____

By: _____ (13) _____

I am the claimant or claimant's representative who executed the foregoing Stop Notice; I have read said Stop Notice and know the contents thereof; the same is true of my own knowledge.

I declare under penalty of perjury that the foregoing is true and correct.

Executed on _____ (14) _____ at _____ (15) _____

_____ (16) _____

4. A description of the property or project on which the work was done.

5. The party with whom the subcontractor had his contract, usually the general contractor.

6. The total dollar amount of the subcontractor's contract.

7. The dollar amount of the work actually done by the subcontractor.

8. The dollar amount of payments received by the subcontractor for the work performed.

9. The dollar amount currently due to the subcontractor, including any interest.

10. The rate of interest charged by the subcontractor on unpaid sums.

11. The date from which interest is accrued.

EXHIBIT 14-14

STOP NOTICE BOND

KNOW ALL MEN BY THESE PRESENTS, that _____ (1) _____ , as Principal, and _____ (2) _____ , a _____ (3) _____ corporation, as Surety, are held and firmly bound to _____ (4) _____ as Obligee, in the sum of _____ (5) _____ , lawful money of the United States of America, to be paid to the said _____ (6) _____ for which payment well and truly to be made, we bind ourselves, our heirs, executors, administrators, successors, and assigns, jointly and severally, firmly by these presents.

The condition of the above obligation is such that whereas the Principal has furnished labor and/or materials to _____ (7) _____ , hereinafter called Defendent, in connection with the construction of certain building improvements located at _____ (8) _____

_____ ;

Whereas, the said Principal has filed, or is about to file, or is filing concurrently with this bond a verified claim covering said labor and/or materials and has requested or is by said verified claim now about to request, the Obligee, who is holding building funds, to withhold said funds, and in connection with said Principal is required to file a bond in the sum of _____ (9) _____ , being _____ (10) _____ times the amount of said claim.

Now, therefore, the condition of the above obligation is such that if the Defendant recovers judgment in an action brought on said verified claim or on the lien filed by the Principal, the Principal will pay costs as provided and all damages that said Obligee or person holding such funds may sustain by reason of the equitable garnishment effected by the claim or by reason of the withholding of said funds by the Obligee, not exceeding the sum specified in this undertaking, then this obligation shall be null and void, otherwise to remain in full force and effect.

IN WITNESS WHEREOF, the seal and signature of the said Principal is hereto affixed and the corporate seal and name of the said Surety is hereto affixed and attested by its duly authorized Attorney in Fact at _____ (11) _____ this ___ (12) ___ day of _____ , 19 ___ .

_____ (13) _____
By: _____ (14) _____

_____ (15) _____
By: _____ (16) _____

12. The name of the subcontractor filing the stop notice.
13. The signature of the subcontractor or his legal representative.
14. The date on which the stop notice is filed.
15. The place at which the stop notice was executed.
16. The signature of the subcontractor or his legal representative.

Proper Completion of the Stop Notice Bond

Exhibit 14-14 shows a Stop Notice Bond, which must accompany the Stop Notice. It should be completed as follows:

1. The name of the general contractor.
2. The name of the insurance company which is issuing the bond.
3. The state in which the insurance company is incorporated.
4. The name and address of the lender to whom the stop notice has been sent.
5. The dollar amount of the bond.
6. The name of the property owner, your borrower.
7. The name of the owner of the property, your borrower.
8. The address of the subject property.
9. The dollar amount of the bond being issued.
10. The size of the bond required, usually stated as so many times the amount of the claim by the subcontractor.
11. The city and state in which the bond is issued.
12. The date of the bond.
13. The name of the general contractor.
14. The signature of the general contractor or his representative.
15. The name of the insurance company issuing the bond.
16. The signature of the authorized representative of the insurance company.

Obtaining a Release of Stop Notice

If payment is made later, after the dispute is resolved, you should require that the subcontractor file a Release of Stop Notice. Exhibit 14-15 shows a Release of Stop Notice form, which should be completed as follows:

1. The name and address of the construction lender.
2. A reference as to the project name and address against which the claim was filed.
3. The dollar amount of the stop notice.
4. The name of the lending institution.
5. The date the release is signed.
6. The city and state in which the release is signed.
7. The name of the subcontractor issuing the release of stop notice.
8. The signature of the authorized representative of the subcontractor.

How to Record a Notice of Completion

When the job is substantially complete, a Notice of Completion should be recorded. The Notice is formal notification to all subcontractors and vendors that the job is complete. Liens must be filed within the time frame specified by the laws of the individual state.

Your disbursement people should be aware of last items to be resolved in order to turn the project over to the owner. You will want to take steps to get the loan ready for delivery to the permanent lender.

EXHIBIT 14-15

RELEASE OF STOP NOTICE

To: _____

_____ (1) _____

_____

Re: _____

_____ (2) _____

     The undersigned hereby withdraws the stop notice in the amount of $ _____ (3) _____ for labor, services, equipment, and/or material furnished in connection with the above contract. The undersigned also hereby releases _____ (4) _____ , its subdivisions and agents, from any further duty to withhold money or bonds in response to the stop notice, and waives any right of action against them that might accrue thereunder.

Dated: _____ (5) _____ at _____ (6) _____ .

_____ (7) _____

By: _____ (8) _____

Exhibit 14-16 is a Notice of Completion form. It should be filled in as follows:

1. The name and address of the party to whom the recorded Notice should be returned.

2. The name of the party filing the notice, which should be the property owner.

3. The address of the party filing the notice of completion.

4. The way in which title to the property is held; for example, "In Fee" or "Fee Simple."

5. The names and addresses, if any, of other owners holding title to the real estate.

6. The names and addresses, if any, of predecessors in title if the property was purchased by the current owner after the construction began.

7. The date on which construction work was finished.

8. The name of the general contractor who built the project.

9. The city in which the project is located.

10. The county in which the project is located.

11. The state in which the project is located.

12. A legal description of the subject property.

13. The street address of the property, if it is known.

14. The date the document is executed.

15. The signature of the owner, or other party filing the Notice of Completion.

Obtain a Certificate of Occupancy Before Making Final Payment

    A Certificate of Occupany is issued by the local city or county government. It signifies that all work is complete, that necessary permits have been issued, that the work is acceptable and the property is ready for occupancy. It marks the end of the

EXHIBIT 14-16

RECORDING REQUESTED BY

AND WHEN RECORDED MAIL TO

Name

Street
Address   (1)

City &
State

———————————————— SPACE ABOVE THIS LINE FOR RECORDER'S USE ————————.

INDIVIDUAL FORM

Notice of Completion

TO 1927 CA (3-75)   Before execution, refer to title company requirements stated on reverse side.   A. P. N._____

Notice is hereby given that:

1. The undersigned is owner of the interest or estate stated below in the property hereinafter described. (2)
2. The full name of the undersigned is _____ (3)
3. The full address of the undersigned is _____ (3)
4. The nature of the title of the undersigned is: In fee. _____ (4)
   (If other than fee, strike "In fee" and insert, for example, "purchaser under contract of purchase," or "lessee".)
5. The full names and full addresses of all persons, if any, who hold title with the undersigned as joint tenants or as tenants in common are:

   NAMES   ADDRESSES

   (5)

6. The names of the predecessors in interest of the undersigned, if the property was transferred subsequent to the commencement of the work of improvement herein referred to:

   NAMES   ADDRESSES

   (6)

   (If no transfer made, insert "none".)

7. A work of improvement on the property hereinafter described was completed on _____ (7)
8. The name of the contractor, if any, for such work of improvement was _____ (8)

   (If no contractor for work of improvement as a whole, insert "none".)

9. The property on which said work of improvement was completed is in the City of _____ (9)
   _____(10)_____, County of _____, State of (11) , and is described as follows:

   (12)

10. The street address of said property is _____ (13)
    (If no street address has been officially assigned, insert "none".)

Dated: _____(14)_____

Signature of owner named in paragraph 2 _____(15)_____
(Also sign verification below at X)

STATE OF CALIFORNIA, } SS.
COUNTY OF_____ }

_____

The undersigned, being duly sworn, says: That __he is the owner of the aforesaid interest or estate in the property described in the foregoing notice; that __he has read the same, and knows the contents thereof, and that the facts stated therein are true.

SUBSCRIBED AND SWORN TO before me

Signature of owner named in paragraph 2 X _____(15)_____

on _____

Signature_____

Notary Public in and for said State

Title Order No._____
Escrow or Loan No._____

**SEE REVERSE SIDE FOR
TITLE COMPANY REQUIREMENTS AS TO NOTICE OF COMPLETION**

(This area for official notarial seal)

EXHIBIT 14-17

CHECKLIST

( ) Notice to Proceed with Construction
    Issued: _____ (1) _____
( ) Disbursement Control by: _____ (2) _____
    If outside control service:
    ( ) Contract Received and Reviewed
        Date: _____ (3) _____
        Acceptable with the following changes:

        _____
        _____ (4) _____
        _____

( ) Set Aside-Letters Issued to:

Name	Date	Amount
_____ (5) _____	_____ (6) _____	_____ (7) _____

( ) Payment Requests: (8)
    ( ) Monthly ( ) Twice Monthly ( ) Other: _____
    Payment requests to be signed by: (9)
    ( ) Contractor ( ) Owner ( ) Architect ( ) Lender
    ( ) Other: _____
( ) Change orders to be approved by: (10)
    ( ) Contractor ( ) Owner ( ) Architect ( ) Lender
    ( ) Other: _____
    ( ) Change orders in excess of $ _____ (11) _____
        require the prior consent of the lender before the work is begun.
( ) Notice of Completion (12)
    ( ) Recorded. Date: _____
( ) Certificate of Occupancy (13)
    ( ) Issued. Date: _____

construction process, and is usually the last document needed before the construction loan can be paid off by the permanent lender.

When this document can be obtained depends on the municipality. Some will issue it when the basic construction is complete. Others want all tenant improvement work to be finished first. You should hold final payment to the contractor until the certificate is issued. That way you are sure that the building meets with the approval of the local governing agencies.

End Note

The construction process is more difficult because of the amount of work necessary to follow the loan from beginning to end. Proper documentation will insure a successful loan. Close monitoring during the construction process is essential.

Use the checklist in Exhibit 14-17 to help control the construction process. Complete it with the following information:

1. The date that the owner notified the contractor to proceed with the construction.

2. The name of the party who will control the disbursements, either your organization or an outside control service.

3. If disbursements are to be controlled by an outside service, indicate the date that the contract was received and reviewed.

4. The changes, if any, required in the disbursement control contract to be acceptable to you.

5. The name of all parties to whom set-aside letters are sent.

6. The date of the set-aside letter.

7. The amount committed to be set aside.

8. The frequency of pay requests.

9. The parties who will sign the pay requests.

10. The parties who must approve change orders.

11. You should establish a dollar limit beyond which change orders must be approved by you first before any work is begun.

12. The date on which the Notice of Completion was recorded.

13. The date on which the Certificate of Occupancy was received.

Index